Social Science
in Court

Social Science in Court
Mobilizing Experts in the School Desegregation Cases

Mark A. Chesler,
Joseph Sanders, and
Debra S. Kalmuss

The University of Wisconsin Press

Published 1988

The University of Wisconsin Press
114 North Murray Street
Madison, Wisconsin 53715

The University of Wisconsin Press, Ltd.
1 Gower Street
London WC1E 6HA, England

First printing

Printed in the United States of America

Library of Congress Cataloging-in-Publication Data
Chesler, Mark A.
  Social science in court: mobilizing experts in the school desegregation
cases/Mark A. Chesler, Joseph A. Sanders, and Debra S. Kalmuss.
304 pp.   cm.
  Bibliography: pp. 257–274.
  Includes index.
  ISBN 0-299-11620-4   ISBN 0-299-11624-7 (pbk.)
  1. Discrimination in education—Law and legislation—United
States—Trial practice.   2. Segregation in education—Law and
legislation—United States—Trial practice.   3. Evidence,
Expert—United States.   4. Social scientists—Legal status, laws,
etc.—United States.   5. Trial practice—United States.   I. Sanders,
Joseph A., 1944–   . II. Kalmuss, Debra S., 1953–   .   III. Title.
KF8925.D5C48   1988   88-6088
344.73'0798—dc 19   CIP
[347.304798]

Dedication

This book is dedicated to our children, Deborah and Naomi Chesler, Jonathan and Gabriel Kalmuss-Katz, and Robert, Thomas, and Elizabeth Sanders, and to all the children of the United States. Each deserves a quality education.

Contents

Tables and Figures

‹

Figures

Acknowledgments

We acknowledge the assistance of several groups of people in the conduct and completion of this work. First, thanks go to colleagues at the National Institute of Education, who responded to our suggestion that such a work was both desirable and feasible. Fritz Edelstein, Ray Rist and Mary von Euler approved and monitored Grant #78-0073. Our findings do not necessarily reflect the positions or policies of the Institute or any of the individuals within it. This grant was administered by the Center for Research on Social Organization at the University of Michigan. The Center provided a home and support for the investigators during the data collections phase of the work. Joseph Sanders received support during the writing of this book from the University of Houston Law Foundation. We were assisted in the research effort by two talented law students, Pamela House and Betty Rankin-Widgeon. Sheila Wilder also provided very competent secretarial assistance. At the University of Wisconsin Press, Gordon Lester-Massman and Rama Ramaswami willingly shared their expertise and enthusiasm for this project, and several reviewers graciously corrected errors and tried to improve the final versions of this manuscript.

Our special appreciation goes to the many social scientists, educators, attorneys and judges who agreed to participate in this study. These informants shared their time, and often their intimate experiences and perspectives, in the effort to enhance our understanding of the role and use of expert witnesses in the school desegregation cases. We hope these colleagues find themselves depicted appropriately in these pages.

The story of school desegregation is not complete. In the years to come, social movement organizations, old and new, will almost certainly continue to try to marshall resources with which to make and remake policy. There are, and will continue to be, many debates about the correct diagnoses of, and strategies for altering, racial isolation and inequality in education systems and communities. Likewise, there will continue to be conflicts about the proper role of law, of litigants and litigation, and of judges and the entire judiciary, in resolving these complex public disputes. And disagreement will continue to focus on the proper roles and functions of applied social science in resolving social problems in general, and in being of use to courtroom adversaries in particular. We hope that this volume helps frame these disagreements and debates more effectively, and that it alerts new generations of practicing attorneys and applied scholars to some of the costs and gains of various options in the settlement of public conflicts.

Social Science
in Court

1 Introduction

In the spring of 1954 the United States Supreme Court issued one of the most important opinions of this century, *Brown v. Board of Education of Topeka*, 347 U.S. 483. In 1979 black lawyers in Topeka, including the son and grandson of a lawyer in the original litigation, alleging a twenty-five-year failure of the Topeka school system to obey the mandate of *Brown*, again asked the Federal District Court to desegregate the Topeka schools (see Wolters 1984). Called *"Brown III"* by the parties, it was an attempt by the plaintiffs to instill new life into a quiescent social movement.[1]

The school desegregation effort dramatically altered the racial composition of American public school buildings. In 1954 less than one black child in a thousand attended a school with white children in the eleven southern states of the Confederacy. By 1973 86% of all black public school students in the Old South attended schools with white students, with the major changes occurring between 1965 and 1972. In 1968 64% of black students in the United States went to schools with enrollments of between 90 and 100% black, and by 1972 this percentage dropped to 39%. In 1980, it was 33%. Despite these figures, black school children are not fully integrated into the public school system; in 1980, 63% of all black public school children attended predominantly minority schools. (See Bullock 1984; Farley 1984; Orfield 1983). Yet, even though the movement did not achieve the goal of fully desegregated

---

1. Topeka, however, is not the only current or recent case. There are also recent or active cases in San Jose, Kansas City, and Yonkers, and in many cities desegregation plans remain in force. On the decline of the black civil rights movement in general, see McAdam (1983).

school systems, it did end the status of black children as an isolated minority, walled off from the rest of society.

This book is about the school desegregation movement when it played an important role in both local and national politics. Unlike most social movements, however, the movement was at its heart legal, not political. The effort of the National Association for the Advancement of Colored People (NAACP) and other groups to racially desegregate American schools was conducted primarily in the federal courts. In the decade between 1937 and 1946 there were approximately seven appellate cases involving school segregation. In the decade of *Brown* (1947–1957), there were twenty-one. Between 1957 and 1966 there was a dramatic growth to 151 cases, but the full dimension of the movement's litigation initiative could not be seen until the following decade when there were approximately 1,500 cases. The high volume of cases continued for another five years; between 1977 and 1981 there were 644 appellate cases. The decade of highest appellate caseload is also the decade of greatest school desegregation (Tyack and Benavot 1985).

As these caseloads suggest, the litigation effort consumed a substantial proportion of the resources of the organizations which led the movement. Litigation may be less costly than many other social change strategies, but it is still expensive. To take a case from initial complaint to Supreme Court review requires tens of thousands of dollars, and financial considerations frequently affected the pace and direction of the desegregation effort. Money, however, is not the only resource which must be mobilized. A movement which relies upon constitutional litigation to produce social change must mobilize a set of unique resources. It must first mobilize attorneys to try and appeal the cases, and they in turn must develop a set of legal arguments which will allow them to win a lawsuit. Then, the movement must mobilize evidence to support the legal arguments.

Our focus in this book is upon the mobilization of a key evidentiary resource in the school desegregation cases, social science evidence and the expert witnesses needed to present it in court. We focus more on the mobilization of experts than on desegregation per se, and concentrate upon the problems social scientists and lawyers experienced as they provided social scientific testimony in the school desegregation cases. Our database consists primarily of personal interviews conducted with lawyers and social scientists in a sample of seventeen desegregation cases[2] in litigation after 1970; all but one in the federal

2. The cities in our sample were Atlanta, Austin, Baton Rouge, Charlotte, Columbus,

courts. The cases were selected with a view to geographic diversity and diversity in the scientific and legal issues involved. We interviewed sixty-seven scientists who appeared as expert witnesses in these and other cases, sixty-nine lawyers who tried these cases for various plaintiff and defense groups, and ten trial judges who presided in the cases. The interviews present a rich picture of courtroom life, of scholars' and attorneys' strategies, and of the problems in courtroom interaction encountered by various parties. In addition to personal interviews, we have examined several thousand pages of courtroom testimony and records of meetings, conferences, and other published materials.

The interviews must be understood in the context of the mobilization efforts of the social movement organizations and their opponents, the traditions of the academic system, and the unique and changing nature of the school desegregation effort. These three factors produce different types of problems for lawyers, experts, and judges. For lawyers, using experts poses problems of tactical choices: how social science resources might best be used to win the lawsuit. The tactical decisions attorneys have to make in these cases include (*a*) the choice of legal theories most likely to win the case and produce the desired remedy; (*b*) balancing short-term and long-term goals, including how to persuade a particular trial judge versus the judges on higher appellate courts; (*c*) deciding whether the use of social science evidence will advance their litigation goals, and if so the best way to use experts to achieve these goals; and (*d*) the degree of control they wish to maintain as they seek to use semi-independent expert witnesses to achieve their objectives in the trial.

For experts, the problems often occur in the form of difficult choices concerning their appropriate role, each choice having some desirable and some undesirable features. Many of the experts' problems are rooted in differences between the environment and procedures of the academy and those of the courtroom. Experts have to make choices about adopting (*a*) a neutral versus a partisan value frame when electing to testify, interpreting evidence, and presenting evidence in court; (*b*) a teacher versus an advocate role when testifying in court; and (*c*) an academic role as the creator of knowledge versus a witness role as the applier of knowledge to specific problems or situations. How experts resolve these choices affects their decision to testify, their stance in court, and their long-term perspectives on the role of applied social science in the courtroom.

Corpus Christi, Dayton, Denver, Detroit, Indianapolis, Kalamazoo, Los Angeles, Minneapolis, Montgomery, Omaha, Richmond, and St. Louis.

Our data from judges is less complete. They do indicate that here, as in other situations where experts are used, judges often confront the twin problems of acquiring the information needed to make a decision and of choosing among uncertain options and outcomes. Specifically, the judges dealt with the problems of deciding (a) how to assure themselves of relatively unbiased evidence given the state of social science information and adversary court procedures and (b) whether and how to create effective remedies for school systems, rather than simply finding violations and leaving the remedy plan to the school district.

Throughout the book we examine the relationships among lawyers' tactics, experts' choices, and judges' decisions. We ground these interactions and relationships in the context of social science, legal institutions, and the school desegregation controversy.

The Organization of the Book

The book is divided into three parts: (1) The background of the desegregation movement and the choice to pursue desegregation through the courts, including a history of the legal arguments and social science evidence presented in court; (2) the processes and problems that lawyers and social scientists encountered in gathering and using social science resources in seventeen school desegregation cases; and (3) the consequences of using social scientists and social science for their disciplines, for the cases, and for the desegregation effort more generally.

The background. In the first section of this book we discuss the social movement organizations (especially the NAACP and the Legal Defense Fund, or LDF) involved in the school desegregation effort, their choice of litigation as a primary strategy, and their decision to enlist social science in the development of this strategy. The litigation strategy requires, as does any other, that particular sets of resources be developed. Beyond the ordinary tangible resources of money, personnel, facilities, and equipment, and intangibles such as publicity and good will, the litigation strategy requires other, special resources. The movement must develop legal resources: attorneys and legal arguments which turn objectives into a claim of right. It must also develop ideas and information which can shape that right and the remedy to which plaintiffs are entitled if the courts conclude that the right has been breached. We indicate how, in the search for a winning argument, the parties tried to generate and mobilize a coherent and persuasive body of empirical data and theory that could help guide and shape legal theory, and how this caused them to turn frequently to social scientists.

Mobilizing and using social science in court. In the 1950s and 1960s social science was often involved in liberal critiques of the status quo, and in the attempt to apply findings and more broadly-based theories to help solve perceived societal problems and conflicts. Applied social science threatens to violate the twin scientific norms of autonomy and neutrality. Those who become involved in applied work, including those who act as expert witnesses in controversial litigation, confront a set of problems when they engage in this type of work. Throughout part 2 we indicate how acting as an expert witness in a controversial area such as school desegregation creates these problems for experts. We also indicate how they, and the attorneys who employ them, deal with these problems, and we juxtapose the expert's resolution of these problems and the lawyer's tactical decisions.

Chapter 4 discusses the preparation of expert witnesses and chapter 5 presents an ideal type of what it is to be a "good witness." Using the interview data, we examine whether lawyers and experts differ in their perception of a good witness.

The adversary norms of the courtroom differ markedly from the detached, disinterested style of science. Chapter 6 examines the *normative discrepancies* and *role conflicts* that were anticipated and experienced by experts when testifying. Chapter 7 examines expert-lawyer interaction during the most adversarial and stressful part of trial—cross-examination. This discussion provides concrete examples of what it is to be a good witness (and a bad witness), and indicates how even a scientist committed to a neutral, teacher role can be caught up in the adversary interactions of the courtroom.

Effect upon the actors, their disciplines, and the courts. Part 3 begins in chapter 8 with an examination of the effect of witnessing on professional and personal conflicts experienced by the experts and how various experts dealt with these conflicts. Lawyers were also affected by their experiences, and many acquired new perspectives on the use of social science evidence when it is presented by party witnesses. Both lawyers and social scientists saw how their personal roles and the structure of the courtroom might be altered to make better use of social science testimony and simultaneously reduce conflict for witnesses. In chapter 9 we discuss how this experience affects lawyers' and social scientists' judgments as to the advisability of adopting the expert panel as an alternative to party witnessing.

In chapter 10 we consider the impact of social science evidence on the school desegregation cases themselves. We review the effects of the expert testimony on some judges' understanding of the causes and effects of school segregation, on the frame of reference from which one should interpret school board and other governmental decisions, and on the scope of the remedy ordered by the courts. In conclusion, chapter 11 presents a broad discussion of the limits of a nationally organized litigation strategy as a method of local institutional reform.

In appendix A we provide a fuller discussion of (*a*) the selection of the sample of cases and respondents; (*b*) the content of the questionnaires used with experts, lawyers, and judges; (*c*) the interview process; and (*d*) our coding and data analysis procedures.

2 The Early Mobilization of Resources

The story of school desegregation in the United States begins with the formation of the National Association for the Advancement of Colored People (NAACP). The organization was founded in 1909 by W.E.B. DuBois and other blacks, in coalition with white liberals. From the beginning, its membership consisted primarily of middle-class, educated blacks. The NAACP represented people who had much to gain from racial advances, but also something to lose from strategies that alienated moderate or liberal sections of the white community.

DuBois and other black leaders of the NAACP belonged to the mainstream of the American democratic and meritocratic heritage, which believes that education is a path to individual achievement and group mobility. Indeed, the upward mobility that blacks did achieve in the nineteenth and early twentieth centuries was tied to education. In southern public education, two key barriers, the apartheid of Jim Crow (Woodward 1957) and the lack of education, came together to lock large parts of the black population into low-skill occupations. The lack of education helped keep them "a discrete and insular minority," as noted by Justice Stone in *United States v. Carolene Products Co.*, 304 U.S. 114 at 152 (1938). Because segregation laws were a critical barrier to black equality, it is not surprising that the NAACP devoted a large proportion of its energy to attacking a dual school system which rarely kept the formal promise of separate but equal.

Choice of Litigation as a Social Change Strategy

Social movement organizations like the NAACP must mobilize some resources with which to operate. Freeman (1983, 193), building on Zald and McCarthy (1979), suggests that there are three major suppliers of resources. The first is the beneficiary constituency; in the 1930s and

1940s the beneficiary constituency of the NAACP was a poor and poorly organized group.[1] The second is a conscience constituency which may include white supporters and which believes in the objectives of the movement, but does not directly benefit from its gains. The third provider of resources are what Freeman (1983, 197) calls nonconstituency institutions, which include the legal system and its ability to enlist the power of the state on the side of the movement.

Attacking the dual school system offered several strategic advantages to the NAACP. Because segregated schools raised constitutional questions concerning the denial of equal protection, a challenge could take place primarily through the courts.[2] If litigation is successful, it enlists the state on the side of the movement, thus swelling the resources of the movement (Dahl 1961; Zemans 1984). Successful litigation thus legitimates the movement's agenda, making it less partisan and more a matter of right, embedded in core national values. This in turn may generate greater public support, both in goodwill and in new contributions, especially from a conscience constituency. In addition, the coercive power of the state may be brought to bear on reluctant or recalcitrant parties.[3]

For many decades there was no other way to enlist state power. The executive and legislative branches of government were not accessible or responsive to minority civil rights at either the national or the local level. Bland (1973) refers to the reluctance of the Roosevelt administration to risk challenges to the Southern wing of the Democratic party, because it was dependent upon their support for other programs of national importance, and Wasby, D'Amato, and Metrallier (1977) call attention to the silence of the newly elected Eisenhower Administration in the early 1950s.

1. We have, of course, begged the point of exactly who should be included in the category of beneficiary. At the broadest level it is all American blacks. But as later events in the 1960s showed, a substantial proportion of blacks rejected the goals of the NAACP (McAdam 1983; Stoper 1983). A narrower definition of the beneficiary constituency would be middle- and lower-middle-class blacks most able to benefit from increased educational opportunity.

2. Other strategies were later used in the effort to desegregate schools—pickets, demonstrations, and, ultimately, legislative efforts through the 1964 Civil Rights Act (codified in 42 U.S.C.§ 2000c *et seq.*) and the 1965 Aid to Elementary and Secondary Education Act (Pub. L. No. 89–10, 79 Stat. 27; Pub. L. No. 90–247, 81 Stat. 783). But the main effort, at least for the decade before and after *Brown,* involved litigation.

3. For example, although President Eisenhower was not a strong supporter of the *Brown v. Board of Education* opinion, he would not ignore Governor Orval Faubus's challenge to the Supreme Court's authority in the desegregation of Little Rock schools. When confronted with outright refusal, the plaintiffs had federal troops as well as national policy on their side.

The courts were also an especially attractive arena because the NAACP could pursue change there without a massive mobilization of its beneficiary constituency. More than other governmental institutions, courts decide issues on the basis of constitutional right rather than on public opinion. Organizing large numbers of poor and rural black families would have been an expensive and time-consuming process, whereas litigation required "finding" only a few families for each case. Thus, the NAACP acquired several of the characteristics of what McCarthy and Zald (1973, 1977) call a "funded social movement organization," with a professional full-time staff not dependent upon mass membership for financial support. A significant percentage of contributions for such organizations may come from outside or conscience constituency groups (see Oreshall 1973, 217).[4]

For example, the majority of funds for the school desegregation programs of the NAACP and the LDF in the 1960s and 1970s came either from court-awarded attorneys' fees in victorious cases or from contributions from a few national foundations, especially the Ford, Carnegie, and Rockefeller Foundations (Orfield 1978a, 380–86).

Still another advantage of litigation is that it forces a response from one's opponents, even when they will not or cannot respond or negotiate directly (Kalodner and Fishman 1978; Mnookin and Kornhauser 1979). From their study of superintendents and board members in a sample of interracial school districts in the early 1970s, Zeigler and Boss (1974) concluded that

> school governors apparently do not recognize such [racial] difficulties as being problems, a fact that undoubtedly upsets the black citizen. Rather, school governors appear to recognize racial problems only where major issues or crises have evolved. (332)

The threat of a desegregation lawsuit is a crisis for a school board. Although a few school districts took steps to develop comprehensive desegregation plans without court action (Evanston, Berkeley), most, in the absence of litigation, engaged in delay or denied culpability for local segregation, often creating citizen committees to "study the problem." Others engaged in token responses by creating freedom of choice or open enrollment plans which resulted in minimal desegregation and placed the burden of change and extended transportation on minority

---

4. There are important ways in which the NAACP does not fit the full model of a "funded social movement organization." The organization is federal in structure, with the principal organizing unit being the local chapter. The national organization and its staff could never disregard the interests of local chapters. This caused the organization to litigate some cases it might otherwise have avoided.

students. Still others counterattacked by attacking protest leaders and mobilizing antidesegregation groups in the community.[5]

Balanced against the advantages of a litigation strategy are several limitations. First, prodesegregation opinions are not guaranteed. The long shadows of *Plessy v. Ferguson,* 163 U.S. 537 (1896), itself a piece of planned litigation (see Lofgren 1987), and *Cumming v. County Board of Education,* 175 U.S. 528 (1899), remind plaintiff groups of the danger of an adverse opinion (see Wasby 1984, 131–132).

Still another limitation is that a litigation strategy is piecework. When one of our attorney informants was asked why the school board he represented continued to oppose the "law of the land" as announced in *Brown v. Board of Education,* he replied, "*Brown* is not the law of the land, it is the law of the case." Victory in one case or one locale does not guarantee victory in another. Winning in the South does not guarantee winning in the North, and winning in a central city does not guarantee winning a metropolitan suit. New cases always carry the potential for undermining old precedents, and in every case one must be concerned not only about the present outcome but the result of the court's reasoning for future cases.

Even when prodesegregation decisions are made, there are barriers to implementation and change at the local level. The courts must eventually turn to the school board and the school administration for the operation of the school system. As Nystrand and Staub (1978) note,

> judicial participation in education matters has been essentially a conservative process that endeavors to support state and local school officials insofar as their actions are consistent with constitutional guarantees. (27)

5. Many reports of these community challenges and school system responses exist; some are publicly accessible and others are in the files of civil rights organizations and governmental agencies. Scholarly and popular literature of early southern efforts is available in Aiken and Demerath (1967); Anderson (1966); Blaustein and Fergeson (1962); Carmichael and James (1957); Killian and Grigg (1964); Moreland (1963); *School Desegregation in Ten Communities* (1973); and United States Commission on Civil Rights (USCCR). Moreover, we have analyzed case study materials on northern and southern cities from several later sources, including the USCCR's rich series of reports called *Fulfilling the Letter and Spirit of the Law* (1976) and the many separate documents backing up this report (Rothenberg and Chesler 1980). Other such data are available in scholarly anthologies such as those by the National Opinion Research Center (1973), Kalodner and Fishman (1978), Mack (1968), Rist (1979), and Willie and Greenblatt (1981). Books have been written on the desegregation experience in specific cities such as Boston (Taylor 1986), Charlotte (Schwartz 1986), Nashville (Pride and Woodward 1985), St. Louis (Monti 1985), and Wilmington (Raffel 1980).

An angry, frustrated, and hostile school board which has recently lost in court is not the ideal enforcement agent for a desegregation plan. This situation is exacerbated when a school board hostile to desegregation comes to power either as a cause (Dayton, Detroit) or as a consequence (Los Angeles) of litigation, sometimes after recall elections in which more moderate school board members were removed. In addition to such political resistance, the type of enforcement required in a desegregation case, involving complex, long-term, and discretionary building- and classroom-level changes in ongoing practices, make successful change less likely (Handler 1978, 22). These realities have led several critics of "institutional litigation" to argue that courts are not competent or effective agents for this kind of social change (Glazer 1975; Horowitz 1977).[6]

The risks of the litigation strategy are increased in the school desegregation area because the leaders of the national social movement organizations never had complete control over local chapters and events. The decentralized structure of the NAACP meant that sometimes it was difficult to find willing plaintiffs (Handler 1978, 109) and that at other times local organizations put pressure on the national organization to proceed with a case which otherwise might not have been chosen for litigation (Hahn 1973, 393). In several cases there was less than a clear consensus among the several national organizations about the proper course of action (Orfield 1978a; Wasby 1986).

The movement's options were altered as it developed certain sources of popular and financial support within the black and white constituencies. For instance, white liberal support was not interested in funding a radicalizing grass-roots movement (Feagin 1980). This fact, and the resulting potential conflicts between beneficiary and conscience constituencies, caused some critics to argue that the NAACP attorneys could not "serve two masters," their wealthy white or black financial supporters and poor southern blacks (Bell 1976; 1980a).

However, in the years preceding 1954 the consensus within the NAACP was that there was no alternative strategy which offered any better chance of success than litigation. McAdam (1983, 299) lists three factors crucial to the development of a movement: its organizational strength, the structure of political opportunities, and the response of other groups to the challenge posed by the movement (Eisenger 1973).

---

6. Others argue that courts have become more proficient at formulating and enforcing judgments requiring various types of institutional reform (Cavanaugh and Sarat 1980; Chayes 1976; Clune 1984; Rebell and Block 1982).

It is difficult to challenge the NAACP's assessment that political opportunities existing in the late 1940s and early 1950s did not present superior alternatives to litigation, such as political organization in southern communities to improve schools. If segregated schools were the right target, litigation was the most viable strategy of attack.

The Mobilization of Legal Resources

The NAACP became more actively interested in planned litigation when it received a grant in 1929 from the American Fund for Public Service (The Garland Fund) (Kluger 1975, 132; Tushnet 1987).[7] The grant was given with the understanding that it would facilitate a legal assault to assure equality in the separate schools in the seven states which most flagrantly discriminated against blacks in the allocation of funds for public education. In 1930 the NAACP hired Nathan Margold to draft the outline of this legal effort to attack inequality in public instruction.[8]

In 1935 Charles H. Houston was hired as a full-time staff attorney. He prosecuted the first of the school cases, *Missouri ex. rel. Gaines v. Canada*, 305 U.S. 337 (1938) (McNeil 1983; Tushnet 1987). In 1939 the NAACP Legal Defense and Educational Fund, or LDF as it came to be known, was created. The LDF was to devote its efforts "exclusively to education and legal defense" (Hahn 1973, 394). Because it was a separate organization not involved in political activities, contributions to it were deductible.[9] The LDF became the NAACP's civil rights litigation

---

7. The Garland Fund was named after Charles Garland, a young man who rejected his father's and grandfather's estates on principle and gave $1,300,000 to support liberal and radical causes. One hundred thousand dollars was targeted for the NAACP. The Garland fund was the beginning of support from foundations representing a conscience constituency.

8. Even then, a number of people opposed this approach. Roger Baldwin of the ACLU and Ralph Bunche favored political action which involved "the union of white and black workers against their common exploiters" (Kluger 1975, 133). Later, in a remarkable issue of the *Journal of Negro Education* (1935), the debate continued with DuBois and Bunche arguing that the courts and the constitution offered no real hope for changing existing educational arrangements. DuBois also argued in the same journal article that blacks would be better served by education in separate schools where they were "treated like human beings" rather than by the abuse they would face in integrated schools. On the other side, Howard Long, then assistant superintendent in charge of research for the Washington, D. C., schools, argued a position that would be repeated by Kenneth Clark and others nearly twenty years later—that the consequence of state-mandated segregated education is that "ability is left undeveloped" (Kluger 1975, 171). Tushnet (1987) has recently completed a history of the early years of the school desegregation movement. For the papers of the NAACP school desegregation effort, see Meier and Rudwick (n. d.).

9. A new organization was needed because of the NAACP's political activity in

arm, and until 1957 the two organizations were closely intertwined (Vose 1959; Wasby 1984, 98). In 1940 Thurgood Marshall became chief counsel for the NAACP and special counsel for the LDF. He presided over a small staff of attorneys (led by Robert Carter) involved in the litigation leading up to and including *Brown* (Kluger 1975).

Litigation as a strategy required the NAACP-LDF to mobilize a special set of legal resources. These included people willing to go to court, attorneys with knowledge of and ability in constitutional litigation, a legal theory which would cause courts to grant the relief sought, facts to support the application of that theory in a specific situation, witnesses to present those facts, and enough money to support all of these people in their efforts and to pay the costs of litigation.[10] Simply put, the plaintiffs needed an argument to justify the conclusion that schools segregated by state action were unconstitutionally configured, and the facts necessary to prove that a given school was so segregated.

Development of the Legal Argument

The beginning point for all legal theories concerning school desegregation law is the Equal Protection Clause of the Fourteenth Amendment. In part it reads:

---

strengthening antilynching laws, which led the Internal Revenue Service to rule that contributions were not tax deductible (Wasby 1984; Zangrando 1980).

10. Because the expenses and expertise needed to mount serious constitutional attacks were too great for each local group, desegregation opponents soon realized that if local plaintiff groups could be cut off from the support and legal resources of national groups, the desegregation movement would be substantially demobilized. During the late fifties, opponents made two noteworthy attacks on the NAACP's organization, both focusing on the relationship between the NAACP or LDF organization and staff and the members of the black constituency on whose behalf litigation was undertaken. In the first type of attack, several southern states filed suits in state courts alleging that the NAACP had failed to register as a "foreign" or "out-of-state" corporation, and seeking to have it enjoined from conducting business in the state (Hahn 1973, 397). In Alabama the state attorney general went a step further and sought disclosure of NAACP membership and mailing lists as a means of assessing the organization's relationship with Alabama residents. The Supreme Court consistently overturned state court decisions holding the NAACPs in contempt for refusing to comply with these statutes. The Court found that these laws had a chilling effect on freedom of speech and association (*NAACP v. Alabama*, 357 U.S. 449 (1958)). A second thrust, with the same goal of demobilizing the desegregation movement by cutting the links between local beneficiaries and the resources of the national organization, focused on charges of barratry, arguing that poor and uneducated black clients were unknowingly manipulated by NAACP attorneys into being plaintiffs. In *NAACP v. Button*, 371 U.S. 415 (1963), the Supreme Court held that the NAACP's efforts to achieve school desegregation should not be judged by the same standards which might be used to judge attorney-client relations in a purely private lawsuit.

> Section 1 . . . nor shall any state deprive any person of life, liberty, or property, without due process of law; *nor deny any person within its jurisdiction the equal protection of the laws*. . . .

In *Plessy v. Ferguson*, 163 U.S. 537 (1896), the Court had adopted an interpretation of the Equal Protection Clause which permitted legislation segregating blacks from whites, creating separate but equal facilities in the language of the time. In the majority opinion Justice Brown stated,

> Laws permitting, and even requiring, [racial] separation in places where they are liable to be brought into contact do not necessarily imply the inferiority of either race to the other. . . . We consider the underlying fallacy of the plaintiff's argument to consist in the assumption that the enforced separation of the two races stamps the colored race with a badge of inferiority. If this be so, it is not by reason of anything found in the act, but solely because the colored race chooses to put that construction upon it. (163 U.S. 537, 544, 551)

Fortunately for the development of the NAACP's legal theory, the promise of equality was rarely kept, and thus the attack could and did begin on the "equal" part of separate but equal. The first successful efforts of the NAACP involved the very conservative step of asking the courts to fulfill the promise of *Plessy*, to provide equal facilities to blacks and whites in graduate and professional schools.[11] After the victory in 1938 in the *Canada* case, the attack upon unequal schools was slowed by the Second World War.

The assault was renewed in two cases decided together in 1950. In *Sweatt v. Painter*, 339 U.S. 629 (1950), and *McLaurin v. Oklahoma State Regents*, 339 U.S. 637, the Supreme Court dealt with the subterfuges and half-measures that Texas[12] and Oklahoma[13] had devised to avoid either

---

11. Peterson (1935) identified 113 cases between 1865 and 1935 which addressed the status of black separate schools. Of 44 cases challenging segregation in states where schools were segregated as a matter of law, all failed. Peterson notes that when cases claimed that pupils suffered a disadvantage because of the inequality of separate schools, the plaintiffs did win 33% of the suits. And all efforts challenging separate taxation for black and white schools succeeded (see Tyack and Benavot 1985, 366–367).

12. In the Texas case the state legislature created a "law school" out of three basement rooms in the State Capitol, staffed by three part-time faculty—this in substitution of and purportedly as an equal alternative to admission to the University of Texas Law School.

13. In the Oklahoma case the defendant was admitted to the Ph.D. program in education, but on a "segregated basis." As reported in the opinion, McLaurin, a 68-year-old black man, was required "[t]o sit apart at a designated desk in an anteroom adjoining

allowing blacks and whites to attend school together or providing fully equal facilities for black students. The Court honored neither sham, but did not strike down the separate-but-equal doctrine itself, even though it had been urged to do so by the NAACP, by the federal government, and by an *amicus* brief submitted by a group of law professors mobilized for this task by Thurgood Marshall and Yale law professor Thomas Emerson (see Entin 1986; Kluger 1975, 275).[14] *Plessy* survived. In *Sweatt*, the plaintiffs presented some expert evidence on the effects of segregation on the psychological well-being of blacks from Robert Redfield, chairman of the Department of Anthropology at the University of Chicago. The Court seemed to encourage the development of the plaintiffs' factual arguments in subsequent cases by implying that the plaintiffs might be well served by coordinating and presenting "contemporary knowledge" on the effects of racial segregation.[15] With this encouragement they would introduce a good deal more in *Brown* and its companion cases. Constructing this evidence helped the NAACP and ultimately the Court to move beyond a separate-but-equal interpretation of the Fourteenth Amendment.

The Development of Social Science Evidence Supporting the Legal Theory

When the NAACP decided to move past the efforts in *Sweatt* and *McLaurin*, toward a direct attack on *Plessy*, Marshall, Carter, and Jack Greenberg (later to become head of the LDF)[16] recruited and examined

---

the classroom, to sit at a designated desk on the mezzanine floor of the library, but not to use the desks of the regular reading room; and to sit at a designated table, and to eat at a different time from the other students in the school cafeteria" (339 U.S. at 640).

14. The primary thrust of the brief, written by Emerson and his colleagues John Frank and David Haber, and signed by 187 law professors, was that racial classifications were unreasonable per se. In the language of today's constitutional law, race is a suspect classification.

15. In *McLaurin* the court said the restrictions placed on the plaintiff (his physical isolation and ostracism) "handicapped [him] in his pursuit of effective graduate education" (339 U.S. at 641). And in *Sweatt* the Court said that it was not necessary in this case to "reach petitioner's contention that Plessy v. Ferguson should be re-examined in light of contemporary knowledge respecting the purposes of the Fourteenth Amendment and the effects of racial segregation" (339 U.S. at 636). Such language suggests that in some future case this evidence might be appropriate.

16. Carter and Greenberg were among the handful of attorneys who planned and executed the litigation effort. During the next twenty-five years, Marshall, Carter, and Greenberg were joined by James Nabrit, Thomas Atkins, Louis Lucas, Paul Dimond, Norman Chachkin, Nathaniel Jones, William Taylor, Peter Flannery, and Julius Chambers. At various times these individuals worked in a number of organizations at the heart

social science experts in the cases in South Carolina, Kansas, Delaware, and Virginia.[17] This turned out to be a fundamental decision, and began an alliance between plaintiff groups and social scientists which would continue for thirty years. The plaintiffs' view, the courts' view, and the nation's view of segregation and of what constituted desegregation was influenced by this decision.[18]

Of all the experts who appeared in the early cases the most central was Kenneth Clark, a professor at City University of New York. Professor Clark reports the beginning of his involvement in the school desegregation cases as follows:[19]

---

of the desegregation effort, including the NAACP, the LDF, the U. S. Department of Justice, the Lawyer's Committee for Civil Rights Under Law, and the Harvard Center for Law and Education (itself associated with the Legal Services Corporation). Members of the group taught, did legal research, tried cases, and wrote articles and books. Many moved on to other jobs, Robert Carter as a Federal District Court Judge in New York, Nathaniel Jones to the Eighth Circuit Court of Appeals, Peter Flannery to a law practice in Boston, and Thurgood Marshall to the Supreme Court. Others remained active in civil rights litigation.

17. *Briggs v. Elliott*, 98 F. Supp. 529 (E.D.S.C. 1951), 103 F. Supp. 920 (E.D.S.C. 1952); *Brown v. Board of Education*, 98 F. Supp. 797 (Kan. 1951); *Gebhart v. Belton*, 87 A.2d 862, *aff'd* 91 A.2d 137 (1952): *Davis v. School Board of Prince Edward County*, 103 F. Supp. 337 (E.D. Va. 1952).

18. The great majority of those recruited were psychologists or social psychologists. This was hardly surprising, because liberal academics had, since the 1930s, been refuting and undermining earlier social science writings which had been used to justify racial segregation. There were at least two fundamental tenets of early Social Darwinism that provided support for segregation. The first was that intelligence was to a very great extent a matter of heredity, and, as newly developed intelligence tests showed, blacks were "less intelligent" than whites (see McDougall 1909). The second was that society was governed by a group of "folkways" which were ingrained habits, the social parallel to individual drives and needs. Like needs, they were imperative and invariable. Racial attitudes are such folkways, and racial separation is a folkway of the human race. According to Sumner's (1906) famous dictum, "law-ways cannot change folkways," and so it was argued that the state and the legal system were powerless against segregation. Anthropologists and social psychologists began to attack the intelligence argument from many perspectives. Cooley (1902) and Mead (1934) argued that one's self-estimation derives substantially from the influence of others, and Boas (1911) argued that culture, not racial inheritance, shaped an individual's mental and social abilities. Otto Klineberg (1934), later to testify in the *Brown* cases, conducted studies on intelligence which indicated that improvement in social and educational environment enhanced test scores. And Dollard (1937) and Myrdal (1944) looked for the causes of Jim Crow not in some instinctive folkway but in the social and economic advantages accruing to whites from such an arrangement. As to Sumner's dictum, the school desegregation cases themselves would put it to the test (see Loh 1984, 57).

19. These passages are based upon notes from a presentation Professor Clark made at the September 1979 meeting of the Society for the Psychological Study of Social Issues, held in New York City.

In February of 1951, Robert Carter, an assistant to Thurgood Marshall, at the Legal Defense and Education Fund, approached Clark with an offer that Clark said later "would change my life." Carter said they wanted to make a challenge to the legal doctrine involved in *Plessy*. They did not want any longer to argue merely that separate educational facilities were unequal, but that the concept of separate educational facilities itself led to inequality. The lawyers' task was to demonstrate subtle or psychological damage to black youngsters from segregation. Was it possible for psychologists to show such damage or harm?

When Clark asked Carter why he had approached him, Carter replied that he had first approached Otto Klineberg, who had worked with the NAACP before, and then Gordon Allport. Klineberg had informed Carter of Clark's work with the Mid-Century Conference on Youth, at which Clark presented materials on "Prejudice's Effects on the Personality of Minority Youth." Clark shared that report with Carter and said if that kind of material helped, then maybe he could help.

To understand the importance of Clark's work for the plaintiffs' legal theory as well as for their factual argument, one must recall the Court's comment in *Plessy* that if blacks feel that enforced separation of the races stamps them with a badge of inferiority, this is not because of anything found in the act, but solely because "the colored race choose to put that construction upon it" (163 U.S. 537 at 551 (1896)). Clark's testimony was intended to show that the intellectual and psychological harm to black children was real, not the imagining of the plaintiffs in lawsuits (see Clark and Clark 1947; Clark 1953). Moreover, he argued that segregation created a vicious circle in which white prejudice suppressed black achievement, in turn increasing white prejudice (Longshore 1982, 41; Stephan 1978). He was joined by a number of other social psychologists of varying degrees of prominence, a group which collectively acted as pioneers in applied and activist social psychology.[20]

20. Most were involved in the founding of the Society for the Psychological Study of Social Issues. The society's journal, the *Journal of Social Issues*, printed several reports dealing with problems of race relations and social change. The scientists involved included: (1) in the Clarendon, South Carolina case: Kenneth Clark, David Krech, Helen Traeger, and waiting in the wings but not called, Robert Redfield and Theodore Newcomb; (2) in the Topeka, Kansas case: Louise Holt, Horace English, Wilbur Brookover, John Kane, Bettie Belk; (3) in the Prince Edward County, Virginia case: Merril Brewster Smith, Isadore Chein, Kenneth Clark, Horace English, Alfred M. Lee, Mamie Clark; (4) in the Delaware case: Otto Klineberg, George Lane, Kenneth Morland, Frederick Parker, Jerome Bruner, Kenneth Clark and Frederick Werthham.

Only in the Virginia case did the defendants attempt to rebut the plaintiff's expert testimony with their own experts. They presented William Kelly, a child psychiatrist, and John Nelson Buck, a clinical psychologist, neither of whom was an academic. As their star witness they had Henry Garrett, past president of the American Psychological Association and at that time chairman of the Psychology Department at Columbia (Kluger 1975, 482, 501).[21]

Upon appeal of the *Brown* cases to the Supreme Court, the plaintiff witnesses prepared a collective brief that went beyond the "harm" argument that most had made as witnesses on the stand. The brief argued that the end of segregation could break the circle of harm-prejudice-harm and produce a positive circle wherein contact with blacks would improve white racial attitudes, in turn benefiting black self-esteem and achievement, and ultimately improving white racial attitudes (Topeka Social Science Brief 1953). This latter argument has generally been called the "contact hypothesis" (Allport 1954; Amir 1976). [22]

The central argument of the brief may be summarized as follows: (1) existing differences among racial groups are explained by environmental factors; (2) a key environmental difference between white and black children is the imposition of state mandated segregated schools, a factor more potent than individual prejudice or low social status; (3) minority children learn inferiority from official segregation, suffering a loss of personal dignity, a depression of educational aspiration, and an impairment of academic ability; and (4) under the proper circumstances, desegregation will lead to more favorable attitudes, improved race relations, and academic gains for minorities.

An excerpt provides a flavor of the argument:

> On the basis of this general fund of knowledge, it seems likely that feelings of inferiority and doubts about personal worth are attrib-

21. Clark had been a graduate student of both Garrett and Otto Klineberg at Columbia. Before the Virginia trial, Clark reports, he and Isadore Chein met several times with Garrett trying to convince him that he was in error and that he should not testify (Clark 1979).

22. The social science signers to this brief were Floyd H. Allport, Gordon Allport, Charlotte Babcock, Viola W. Bernard, Jerome S. Bruner, Hadley Cantril, Isadore Chein, Kenneth B. Clark, Mamie P. Clark, Stuart W. Cook, Bingham Dai, Allison Davis, Else Frenkel-Brunswik, Noel P. Gist, Daniel Katz, Otto Klineberg, David Krech, Alfred McClung Lee, R. M. McIver, Robert K. Merton, Gardner Murphy, Theodore M. Newcomb, Robert Redfield, Ira DeA. Reid, Arnold M. Rose, Gerhart Saenger, R. Nevitt Stanford, S. Stanfield Sargent, M. Brewster Smith, Samuel A. Stouffer, Wellman Warner, and Robin M. Williams.

utable to living in an underprivileged environment only insofar as the latter is itself perceived as an indicator of low social status and as a symbol of inferiority. In other words, one of the important determinants in producing such feelings is the awareness of social status difference. While there are many other factors that serve as reminders of the differences in social status, there can be little doubt that the fact of enforced segregation is a major factor.

This seems to be true for the following reasons among others: (1) because enforced segregation results from the decision of the majority group without the consent of the segregated and is commonly so perceived: and (2) because historically segregation patterns in the United States were developed on the assumption of the inferiority of the segregated.

In addition, enforced segregation gives official recognition as sanction to these other factors of the social complex, and thereby enhances the effects of the latter in creating the awareness of social status differences and feelings of inferiority. The child who, for example, is compelled to attend a segregated school may be able to cope with ordinary expressions of prejudice by regarding the prejudiced person as evil or misguided: but he cannot readily cope with symbols of authority, the full force of this authority of the State— the school or the school board, in this instance—in the same manner. Given both the ordinary expression of prejudice and the school's policy of segregation, the former takes on greater force and seemingly becomes an official expression of the later. (Topeka Social Science Brief 1953, 432–433)

The social science brief was an important part of the plaintiff's argument that separate but equal is a vacuous concept in a situation where one of the two groups is a distinct, insular minority held as slaves less than a hundred years before. Yet, the appendix and the entire body of testimony presented by the social scientists might have passed from public view with scant notice had the Supreme Court not included the famous footnote eleven in its opinion. Whatever else the *Brown* opinion said, it had to deal with *Plessy v. Ferguson* in some way, and with the separate-but-equal argument that it stood for. Chief Justice Warren did so in the following language:

Whatever may have been the extent of psychological knowledge at the time of Plessy v. Ferguson, this finding [that state mandated segregation has a tendency to retard the educational and mental development of black children] is amply supported by modern au-

thority [footnote 11]. Any language in Plessy v. Ferguson contrary
to this finding is rejected. (347 U.S. 483, 494 (1953))

Footnote eleven was a list of seven works by contemporary social scientists, cited in the NAACP brief.[23] According to both Warren and his
clerk, Earl Pollock, the footnote was merely an afterthought. As Warren
said, "It was only a note, after all" (Kluger 1975, 706). But it was more
than that. Opponents of the opinion could attack it as turning over "the
making of law to social science opinion and the writers of books on
psychology" (Wilkinson 1979, 33). Even some supporters of the decision reacted negatively to this intrusion of social science evidence.

One argument against social science involvement was that what was
at stake in school desegregation was a constitutional guarantee, a moral
principle that should not rest on public opinion polls, attitude studies,
or something as ephemeral as the current fads and fashions of social
science (Weschler 1959).

> In the months since the utterance of the Brown and Bolling opin-
> ions, the impression has grown that the outcome, either entirely
> or in part major, was caused by the testimony and opinions of the
> scientists, and a genuine danger has arisen that even lawyers and
> judges may begin to entertain this belief. The word "danger" is
> used advisedly, because I would not have the constitutional rights
> of Negroes—or of other Americans—rest on any such flimsy foun-
> dation as some of the scientific demonstrations in these records.
> (Cahn 1955, 157–158)

A second critique focused on the technical, jargon-laden, and often
tendentious nature of social science evidence. Cahn charged that the
social science was nothing more than common sense and added nothing new to judicial knowledge:

> For at least 20 years, hardly any cultivated person has questioned
> that segregation is cruel to Negro school children. The cruelty is
> obvious and evident. Fortunately, it is so very obvious that the Jus-
> tices of the Supreme Court could see it and act on it even after
> reading the labored attempts by plaintiffs' experts to demonstrate
> it "scientifically". When scientists set out to prove a fact that most

23. Heading the list was Clark's address to the Mid Century White House Conference
on Children and Youth in 1950, the work which had attracted the NAACP to Clark in the
beginning. Another citation was to Deutscher and Chein's relatively unsystematic survey
of social scientists as to whether they felt that segregation was harmful. The note ended
with a general reference to Myrdal's (1944) An American Dilemma.

of mankind acknowledges, they may provide a rather bizarre spectacle. (1955, 159)

A third line of critique to the social science evidence in Brown came from social scientists themselves, and it reflects some of the problems facing all applied scholars (see chap. 4, pp. 64–67). Some scholars disagreed with the substantive findings or methods of the studies used in these cases. For instance, the opinion surveys of scientists were challenged as representing nothing very valid (based on problems of sampling, question clarity and specificity, etc.). The specific work most frequently attacked was Clark's doll studies, with scholars arguing that black children's choice of a doll of a different color from themselves was not adequate or conclusive evidence of psychological harm.

Scholars argued that to demonstrate harm required standardized and conventional measures of dysfunction or maladjustment.[24] Earlier work by Kenneth and Mamie Clark opened the doll studies to a second critique. In a larger study comparing 134 black children in the segregated schools of Pine Bluff, Arkansas, with 119 black children in the desegregated schools of Springfield, Massachusetts, the Clarks found that 29% of the Arkansas children said that the white doll looked like them, whereas 39% of the children in Massachusetts said that the white doll looked like them. Critics argued that even if harm was demonstrated, it was not clear how school segregation, apart from other forms of segregation and discrimination in society, could be identified as the cause. Based on the Arkansas-Massachusetts data, van den Haag (1960) went so far as to argue that "the only thing that Professor Clark has proved is that if there is damage, it is not due to school segregation" (77).[25]

24. The results obtained in this area appear to be affected by experimental procedure (Banks 1976) and by the developmental stage of the children-subjects (Katz 1976; Porter and Washington 1979). The most complete early replication of Clark's work is probably that of Porter (1971).

25. Such an interpretation is not unlike DuBois's original concern about the abuse that black children would face in integrated schools. Clark's response, as reported by Kluger (1975), was, "But I believe, and I so argued at the time, that what the findings show is that the black children of the South were more adjusted to the feeling that they were not as good as whites and, because they felt defeated at an early age, did not bother using the device of denial. But that's not health. Adjusting to a pathology is not health. The way the Northern kids were fighting it can be seen as a better sign. The little Southern children would point to the black doll and say, 'Oh, yeah, that's me there—that's a nigger—I'm a nigger,' and they said it almost cheerfully. In the Northern cities, the question clearly threw the kids into a much more emotional state and often they'd point to the white doll" (356).

Other scientists argued that desegregation could only worsen existing inequalities and cause further harm.[26]

A further critique of social science involvement in these cases came from a more traditional, academic wing of the social science community. Various leaders of the profession argued that involving social science in public policy making threatened the neutrality of science itself. These critiques extended well beyond the specific issue of school desegregation, or even of litigation as a strategy.[27]

These general controversies about the nature and use of social science evidence have continued throughout the school desegregation cases.[28] However, just as the critiques continued, so did the presentation of scientific testimony in court.

Twenty-Five Years of Social Science Testimony

Twenty-five years after *Brown*, an ex-NAACP attorney, William Taylor, head of the Center for National Policy Review at Catholic University, requested a group of social scientists to once again submit a brief to the Supreme Court, this time as an appendix to the Columbus and Dayton cases (Columbus Social Science Brief 1979). The central arguments of the Columbus brief bear small resemblance to those in *Brown*. The appendix argued the following:[29] (1) residential segregation was widespread and attributable "in important measure to actions of public officials, including school boards"; (2) school segregation and residential segregation were interdependent; and (3) in several ways school segregation had maintained or increased residential segregation, both immediately by causing people to migrate in certain patterns and in the

---

26. This line of argument basically attacked the contact hypothesis underlying the optimism of the *Brown* appendix. According to that hypothesis, social contacts in school can reduce prejudice and other harms of segregation if the contact is among equals. The critics argued, for a variety of reasons, that contacts would not be among equals and therefore would not necessarily reduce white prejudice or lessen psychological harm and academic inequality. It is difficult to attribute admirable motives or values to those advancing this line of argument, but their implicit predictions about the "benefits" of physical desegregation were probably more realistic than those of plaintiff experts (see Stephan 1978). Of course, part of the problem is that the social structure of contacts did remain the same, and suggestions made in the brief to alter these structures were not included in court orders or in later implementation efforts.

27. See Clark (1959/60) for a response to many of these critiques.

28. See our discussion in chapter 4 and the later exchange between Gerard (1983) and Cook (1984), which partly involves what the 1954 social science statement really said.

29. For a discussion of the circumstances of its creation see Orfield (1980).

longer run by maintaining prejudicial attitudes which reduced toler-
ance for integrated neighborhoods.[30]

An excerpt from this appendix illustrates the argument:

> Residential segregation between white and black Americans and
> other racial and ethnic minorities prevails in all large cities in the
> United States. This segregation is attributable in important mea-
> sure to the actions of public officials, including school authorities.
>
> Education is a pervasive governmentally organized activity that
> reaches into every community. The institutionalization of racially
> discriminatory practices throughout the public school system is a
> substantial cause as well as effect of society's other racial practices.
> Society's major institution for socializing the young, aside from the
> family, is the public school system. Most children are greatly influ-
> enced by their school experiences, not simply in formal academic
> learning but in developing a sense of self and knowledge and feel-
> ings about social life and behavior.
>
> The actions of school officials are part of a set of discriminatory
> actions by government agencies and other institutions. This web of
> institutional discriminations is the basic cause of school and resi-
> dential segregation. Economic factors and personal choice are often
> considered as additional causes. (Columbus Social Science Brief
> 1979, 3a, 7a, 13a)

Not only are the arguments quite different, so are the authors and
signers. Of the thirty-two signers of the *Brown* brief, twenty were clearly
identifiable as psychologists or social psychologists, and nine were sociologists or anthropologists. Of the thirty-eight signers of the Columbus brief, nineteen are identifiable primarily as sociologists, three as
political scientists, and two as educational scientists; only six are clearly
psychologists or social psychologists.[31] These disciplinary differences
are also reflected in the contents of the brief. The first is composed of

---

30. Research in this area has continued since the brief was written. It tends to confirm
the relationship between segregated schools and segregated neighborhoods in large cities. See Pearce, Crain, and Farley (n.d.) and Pearce (1985).

31. The following is a list of the signers of the Penick Brief Appendix: Andrew Billingsley,
James E. Blackwell, Ernst Borinski, Everett Cataldo, Kenneth B. Clark, Paul Courant,
Robert L. Crain, Robert A. Dentler, G. Franklin Edwards, Edgar G. Epps, Reynolds Far-
ley, Joe R. Feagin, John Hope Franklin, Eli Ginsberg, Robert L. Green, Charles Grigg,
Amos Hawley, Joyce Ladner, James W. Loewen, Cora B. Marrett, James M. McPartland,
Dorothy K. Newman, Gary Orfield, Diana Pearce, Thomas F. Pettigrew, Ray C. Rist,
Christine H. Rossell, Juliet Saltman, Julian Samora, M. Brewster Smith, Michael J. Stolee,
D. Garth Taylor.

arguments concerning the effects of segregation and desegregation on the psychological and cognitive well-being of school children. The second speaks of such matters only in passing. It is, primarily, a document concerning the effects of social and demographic patterns on institutional arrangements in society. The differences in the two documents reflect a change over twenty-five years in the scientific issues, databases, and methods presented in court. The differences flow from changes during that time in the legal arguments and theory that undergirded these cases.

3 The Development of New Legal Theory and Social Science Evidence

Two Models of School Desegregation Law

With its opinion in *Brown*, the Supreme Court completed the process of rejecting the pseudoformalism of *Plessy*, which pretended that the history of American race relations was of no moment in determining the purpose and effect of segregative legislation (see Lempert and Sanders 1986, 417–419). Given this history (and influenced perhaps by the social science evidence purporting to show the effects of segregation), the Court concluded that such statutes produce institutions which are "inherently unequal." In retrospect, deciding the *Brown* case was deceptively easy. The state, by its use of Jim Crow statutes, admitted intentional segregation, After *Brown*, the plaintiff's counsel had, by showing segregative purpose, shown discriminatory purpose, barred by the Equal Protection Clause of the Fourteenth Amendment. As the years went by, however, admissions and obvious evidence of segregative purpose disappeared, as did the early hope that striking down the segregation statutes would end segregation. New legal theories would need to be developed, theories that would provide new justifications for the imposition of judicial authority.

Twenty years after *Brown*, Chayes (1976) differentiated issues of public policy from ordinary litigation. *Public law* and *private law* models of litigation are ideal types which provide templates against which we can examine the development of school desegregation law.[1]

---

1. Although we have adopted Chayes's (1976) labels and his basic distinction between public law and private law models, we have emphasized certain aspects of the two models which seem most salient in the school cases. As we indicate, the public law model routinely takes a more structural view of society, whereas the private law model takes a more

The private law model best describes most ordinary litigation. In it, the lawsuit is a self-contained episode, initiated and controlled by the parties. The private law model of litigation generally adopts a view of disputes in which individuals and their actions play the central role. Thus, in the case of school desegregation, this model looks for the causes of racial inequality in personal prejudice and more or less intentional discrimination on the part of individuals. The social science evidence in *Brown* began to erode this view, arguing that the use of state authority to establish and maintain segregation added to the impact of prejudice and intentional discrimination, uniformly victimizing an entire class of citizens.

Chayes observed that cases dealing with public issues, especially those cases involving institutional reform, presented a different set of characteristics. The party structure is not necessarily bilateral, and even unrepresented groups' claims intrude on the courtroom process; the cases may go on for years, returning to court several times; remedy is forward-looking and legislative in character; and the judges play a more active role in the litigation of the suit. This public law model of litigation "is not a dispute between individuals about rights, but a grievance about the operation of public policy" (1976, 1302). From this perspective, school segregation is caused by and embedded in the operation of institutions throughout our society. Thus, the "acting party" in segregated schools is not an individual as much as it is a network of forces.[2] This orientation is evident in the social science appendix to the Columbus brief, and is captured in the notion of a "web of institutional discrimination."

When these different models are applied to the legal issues surrounding school segregation they should be understood at four levels: (*a*) attributing responsibility, (*b*) determining the matters in dispute, (*c*) deciding the proper remedy, and (*d*) selecting an appropriate procedure.

Responsibility. In adjudicating equal protection cases, like other dis-

---

individual view, and the former forces the judge to attempt to settle conflict within a complex and ongoing relationship rather than to decide a specific legal issue (see Lempert and Sanders 1986).

2. Of course, this view recognizes that individuals still carry out the specific acts which produce segregated schools, but it sees these acts as the normal, and, in a sense, proper, actions of people in particular institutional roles. Lest this idea be reified by abstraction, consider the critical example of school board members who assign students according to a nearest-school assignment plan.

putes, a primary consideration is what it is to be responsible. A responsibility standard which focuses upon conscious intentions adopts a more individualistic, private law perspective. Organizations cannot have intentions, except through the individuals who staff them (Coleman 1974). As it relates to school systems, the private law model will look to members of the senior administration and the school board. It will examine their intention to segregate and will determine whether they have acted unconstitutionally. A public law understanding, on the other hand, will look to the workings of the entire school system.

Matters in dispute. An individual model of the matter in dispute is influenced by the nature of the responsibility rule. It asks whether there have been specific school board incidents of wrongdoing, in order to assess the responsibility of the board for those incidents. In Fiss's (1979) terms, this model (which he calls the "dispute resolution model") examines the purpose and impact of particular decisions within the control of the school board. From the public law perspective, the matter in dispute is not an incident, or even a set of discrete incidents. Rather, it is the relationship of the school system to segregation and to "the conditions of social life and the role that large scale organizations play in determining those conditions" (18). The structural perspective of the public law model looks to the wider set of social conditions within which the school system operates, including such matters as community housing patterns and zoning decisions.

Remedy. In constructing a remedy, the private law model concerns itself with reestablishing the rights of the individual. The public law model, on the other hand, looks also to organizations and groups. From this perspective, one objective of a remedy is to alter the status of a group which finds itself in a position of "walled-off inferiority" (Black 1960).

Within the private law model, part of the purpose of the Equal Protection Clause is the creation of equal opportunity among citizens. With regard to public education, this involves equal educational opportunity, both academically and psychologically. Private law is concerned with questions of "micro justice" (Brinkman et al. 1980). The scope of the remedy should be determined by the scope of the intentional wrongdoing by school officials which has denied equal protection to individual minority students.[3]

---

3. From this perspective, the importance of the *Brown* opinion was not that it was adjudicated within the context of a public law model. On the contrary, we argue that it was

A public law understanding, however, focuses upon a second virtue, that of the interracial community of equals. The objective is not solely to provide juridical equality among individual citizens, but to bring black Americans into the mainstream of society. The equality implied by this public law model is more than equality of opportunity for individuals; it is equality in school outcomes and environmental conditions among groups (Fiss 1976). The model is concerned with questions of "macro justice." The appropriateness of a remedy is measured by its ability to produce certain distributional properties among entire populations (e.g., racial balance and greater equality of academic success).

Procedure. Private law and public law models differ procedurally as well as substantively. In fact, adopting a substantive view of the case causes the parties to adopt different views of appropriate procedures. Traditional adjudication within a private law model involves procedures designed to maintain tight control over the evidence which is introduced into the case. Evidence is appropriate only if it speaks to the narrow legal issues which are relevant within a private law model. The objective of the procedure is to come up with legally relevant material sufficient to allow the judge to determine (by a preponderance of the evidence) which party is legally in the right. Within a private law model the judge adopts a traditionally passive role, allowing the parties to present their case, and then reaching a decision in camera.

In a public law model, the range of the matters in dispute is much wider, and the remedy reaches well beyond the restoration of the situation which would have existed without intentional school-board wrongdoing. Procedures should allow a wide range of issues to enter into the determination of the case. The objective is to reach a general settlement of the aspects of the parties' relationship which are in conflict. The judge's role within a public law model is more active. It includes assisting, indeed pushing, the parties toward a wide-ranging settlement of their conflict, rather than imposing the winner's solution on the loser of the case. Figure 3.1 summarizes the two models.

The two models are, as we have noted, ideal types. Actual cases present a more complex picture. The usefulness of the models is that they allow us to see more easily how the legal theory underlying school desegregation law changed over time.

---

litigated from a private law perspective. *Brown*'s importance was the Court's unwillingness to accept the pseudoformalistic neutrality of the separate-but-equal doctrine.

Figure 3.1. Two Models of the School Desegregation Cases

Issues	Private Law	Public Law
Responsibility	Concerned with individual acts	Concerned with institutional behavior
	Concerned with the intentions and purposes of individuals	Less concerned with intentions, more with institutional arrangements and outcomes
Matters in Dispute	Focuses upon specific incidents that produce inequality	Focuses upon social conditions that produce inequality
	Adopts a narrow focus of legal relevance: the purpose and impact of school board decisions	Adopts a wide frame of legal relevance: the conditions within which the school system operates
Remedy	Adopts an ahistorical perspective: treating people as juridicial equals	Adopts a structural perspective: considering the substantive inequalities between blacks and whites in the United States
	Focuses upon the treatment of individuals as equals and the restoration of individual rights (micro justice)	Focuses upon building equality and community between groups (macro justice)
Procedure	Judge plays a passive role	Judge plays an active role in constructing a remedy
	Procedure is more legalistic and more adversarial (Issue Decision)	Procedure is less legalistic and less adversarial (Relationship Settlement)

From *Brown* to *Swann*: Toward a Public Law Model of Remedy

In the years after *Brown*, the plaintiffs (the NAACP and the LDF) came to urge a public law model more and more explicitly upon the courts. Partly in response, the defendants came to sharpen their commitment to a private law model. The executive branch of the government seemed to waver back and forth between these two perspectives, its position determined by the current administration. The Supreme Court, too, wavered, but in a peculiar way. It maintained many elements of a private law model of responsibility, trod an uncertain path concerning the matter in dispute, but with few exceptions approved remedies which are best understood as public law attempts to alter the structural relationship among racial groups. A brief survey of the key cases from Topeka to Columbus will demonstrate how judicial decisions were influenced by precedent from early opinions, changes in legal theory, and social science evidence.

In 1963–64, ten years after *Brown*, only 1.2% of the black students in southern districts were attending desegregated schools (Weinberg 1977). The key issue for plaintiffs was not whether there was harm from segregation, nor whether there were gains from desegregation, but whether they could persuade the courts to reject "freedom of choice" and compel substantial desegregation.[4] For the first decade and more after *Brown*, most school desegregation law was remedy law. Concluding that lower courts would best be able to assess each local situation, the Supreme Court remanded the *Brown* cases to the district courts with the directive that they should use their general equity powers to "take such proceedings and enter such orders and decrees consistent with this opinion as are necessary and proper to admit to public schools on a racially nondiscriminatory basis with all deliberate speed the parties to these cases" (*Brown v. Board of Education II*, 349 U.S. 294, 301 (1955)).[5]

4. Most obviously, these plans tended to disregard (or purposely ignore) the intimidation which kept some black families from exercising this choice (see *Green v. County School Bd. of New Kent County*, 391 U.S. 430 at 434 n. 5 (1968); USCCR 1967). More subtly, the plans typically did not attempt to alter the educational program within formerly white schools. Equality was defined as equality of opportunity with little or no consideration given to helping black children overcome years of inferior schooling. Not only did this approach impede the achievement of educational equality, but it acted as a deterrent to black parents when they considered overcoming the community barriers to sending their children to the "white school."

5. The gradualist language of "deliberate speed," and the implicit willingness of the Court to consider the sensibilities of white southerners in the process of constructing a remedy, have been among the most discussed aspects of the decision (see Carter 1968; Kluger 1975; Orfield 1978b; Wilkinson 1979). The NAACP did not push for plans which would require immediate segregation, even though the social science brief in *Brown I* (reflecting the views of Kenneth Clark) clearly implied that a gradualist approach would not be as effective, and would lead to greater rather than less resistance.

> Much depends, however, on the circumstances under which members of previously segregated groups first come into contact with others in unsegregated situations. Available evidence suggests, first, that there is less likelihood of unfriendly relations when the change is simultaneously introduced into all units of a social institution to which it is applicable (e.g., to all of the schools in a school system or all of the shops in a given factory). When factories introduced Negroes in only some shops but not in others the prejudiced workers tended to classify the desegregated shop as inferior

In further describing considerations which the district courts might entertain, the Court noted that they might consider

> problems related to administration, arising from the physical con-
> ditions of the school plant, the school transportation system, per-
> sonnel, revision of school districts and attendance areas into
> compact units to achieve a system of determining admission to the
> public schools on a nonracial basis. . . . (349 U.S. at 300)

This passage, in using phrases such as "nonracial" and "compact units," suggests what was almost certainly the dominant expectation of plaintiffs, defendants, and other parties at the time: that the long-run objective of desegregation was a neighborhood school system.[6] Affirmative duties to reorganize the school system are nowhere suggested. The remedy is that of a private law model.[7]

It has been argued that by allowing southern districts considerable time to create desegregation plans, and by using the equity language to allow districts to consider the practicalities of the situation (i.e., administrative problems and white resistance), the court made a serious error (see Carter 1968). Until the late 1960s it seemed that this assess-

---

"Negro work". Such objections were not raised when complete integration was introduced.

The available evidence also suggests the importance of consistent and firm enforcement of the new policy by those in authority. It indicates also the importance of such factors as: the absence of competition for a limited number of facilities or benefits; the possibility of contacts which permit individuals to learn about one another as individuals; and the possibility of equivalence of positions and functions among all of the participants within the unsegregated situation. The conditions generally can be satisfied in a number of situations, as in the armed forces, public housing developments, and public schools (Topeka Social Science Brief 1953, 437–438).

Wasby, D'Amato, and Metrallier (1977) note, in this regard, that "if Brown I has been criticized for containing too much social science, Brown II has been criticized for not containing enough—for the Court's failure to recognize the effect of a weak statement on those who would resist the ruling" (125).

6. The court cites with favor the efforts already under way in Kansas and Washington, D.C., which, when completed, would lead to a single school system (349 U.S. at 299; Kluger 1975,725 ff.; see also *Brown v. Board of Education I*, 347 U.S. 483, 495 n. 13).

7. All of this is of course only implicit in *Brown II*. The Court does not specifically address the issue of affirmative duty. Circuit Judge John Parker made this position explicit. In his opinion in Briggs v. Elliott on remand from the Supreme Court after *Brown II*, he stated that "[t]he Constitution, in other words, does not require integration. . . . It merely forbids the use of governmental power to enforce segregation" (*Briggs v. Elliott*, 132 F. Supp. 776, 777 (E.D.S.C. 1955)).

ment was correct (see Peltason 1974). But from the longer view one might argue that by providing southern districts the leeway of "deliberate speed," the Court gave the plaintiffs and the courts time to come to a more developed view of the remedy necessary in school cases. It did so, in part, by giving southern school boards time to hang themselves. By first resisting and then adopting complicated pupil assignment laws, and finally by hiding behind formally nondiscriminatory freedom-of-choice plans, the southern school boards pushed the courts (especially the Supreme Court and the Fifth Circuit Court of Appeals) to an orientation which demanded that whatever else a plan might do, it must desegregate school buildings.[8] The courts and the plaintiffs did not suddenly look toward a new model for remedies. As Justice Tom Clark noted, federal remedial power grew in small increments "like Topsy" (Wilkinson 1979, 101). As the judiciary increasingly began to demand results, it implicitly moved toward a results-oriented, public law view of the remedy necessary in these cases.

During this period, the social movement organizations were very active in the effort to add legislative and executive support for school desegregation litigation. In the early 1960s the civil rights movement was more and more frequently in the national media, bringing national attention and concern to protest activity and to acts of repression taking place in response.[9] In Washington, officials of the United States Civil

---

8. At the same time the courts were expanding what was required by way of desegregation. In *Griffin v. Prince Edward County* the Court held that a school board could not close the public schools and support private schools. It said that the lower courts could in fact order the county supervisors to levy taxes to provide public schools (377 U.S. 216 (1967)). Several other schemes to use state funds to support private schools were struck down (see *Poindexter v. Louisiana Financial Commission,* 275 F. Supp. 833 (E.D. La. 1967), *aff'd per curiam,* 389 U.S. 215 (1968)). Earlier, the Court had struck down transfer procedures which allowed minority to majority transfers (*Goss v. Board of Education,* 373 U.S. 683 (1963)). In both the *Griffin* case and in *Bradley v. School Board of Richmond,* 382 U.S. 193 (1965), the Court said that the time for deliberate speed had run its course. And in *Rogers v. Paul,* 382 U.S. 198 (1965), the Court held that faculty desegregation was part of the relief required by the *Brown* decision.

9. In one of the very few efforts to do more than speculate as to the effect of social movement organizations' efforts to influence Congress, Burstein (1985, 95) concludes that Congress does not directly respond to movement activity and protest. His analysis of civil rights employment statutes indicates that the primary determinant of congressional action was a change in public opinion. However, the civil rights movement affected Congress in two ways. It caused Congress to monitor public opinion more closely, strengthening the link between opinion and legislative action. And the movement provoked violent response that increased the salience of the issue for the public, which then joined in the demand for congressional action.

Rights Commission and the Leadership Conference on Civil Rights (a confederation of national civil rights groups) pressured the Congress and the president.

One outcome, which was an important element in the judiciary's increasing willingness to demand results, was the passage of the 1964 Civil Rights Act and the 1965 Elementary and Secondary Education Act. Title VI of the 1964 Civil Rights Act gave the Department of Health, Education and Welfare (HEW) the power to withhold federal funds from segregated schools. Title IV established technical assistance and training programs to provide school districts with help in planning and implementing local desegregation efforts.[10] And the Elementary and Secondary Education Act provided millions of federal dollars to local school districts serving a large number of children from low-income (often minority) families.

With the passage of these pieces of legislation, the plaintiff groups were able, for a short time, to mobilize some of the power of the executive branch of the federal government in the cause of school desegregation (Bullock 1980; Bullock and Lamb 1984). As Wasby, D'Amato, and Metrallier (1977) note:

> Once Congress passed the Civil Rights act of 1964 and the Department of Health, Education and Welfare developed its desegregation guidelines, one had both legislative and executive branches sharing the stage with the Court. . . . The judiciary could be more sure of executive branch assistance to follow up rulings, and more important, there was now executive branch involvement in the early stages of some desegregation controversies. (210)

Once the 1964 Act was passed, it remained for HEW's Office of Civil Rights to issue a series of regulations or guidelines which would develop the criteria for local system compliance with the law. Soon HEW guidelines looked to results rather than to the structure of plans or

10. In addition to centers created through the 1964 Civil Rights Act, other university-based "back-up" centers became important locations for the mobilization of both legal and social science resources. Wasby (1986, 163–164) singles out two organizations for special mention. One is the Harvard Center for Law and Education, funded by the Office of Economic Opportunity and the Legal Service Corporation to assist Legal Service Corporation attorneys in education litigation. In the 1970s it had between five and ten attorneys on its staff, and between 25% and 40% of the cases it handled were desegregation cases. The second organization, headed by William Taylor, was the National Center for Policy Review at Catholic University in Washington, D.C. Funded primarily by the Ford Foundation, it was involved in several desegregation cases, including those in Buffalo, Wilmington, and Louisville.

good-faith efforts. HEW remedies increasingly adopted a public law view. The revised 1966 guidelines said in part, "The single most substantial indication as to whether a free-choice plan is actually working to eliminate the dual school structure is the extent to which Negro or other minority group students have in fact transferred from segregated schools" (Dunn 1967, 62–63).

Over time, however, the major burden of school desegregation once again fell on the judiciary. Substantial local political pressure was applied to prevent the Office of Civil Rights from actually withholding federal funds from local districts. The Nixon administration did not strongly support desegregation efforts, and according to the Commission on Civil Rights, the publicly announced policies of the administration slowed the process of review and enforcement of local district compliance.[11] While it was active, however, administrative involvement had significant direct impact and an indirect impact through the courts. Increasingly, the guidelines were given substantial weight by the courts in determining whether school boards had made progress toward compliance with *Brown*.[12]

In 1968 the Supreme Court moved further toward a public law understanding of remedy in *Green v. County School Board of New Kent County*, 391 U.S. 430 (1968). The question was whether a freedom-of-choice plan adopted in a sparsely populated eastern Virginia county would suffice. The Court provided a 1968 interpretation of what *Brown II* meant.

> School boards such as the respondent then operating state-compelled dual systems . . . clearly charged with the affirmative duty to take whatever steps might be necessary to convert to a unitary system in which racial discrimination would be eliminated root and branch. . . . The burden on a school board today is to come forward with a plan that promises realistically to work, and promises realistically to work *now*. (391 U.S. at 437, 439)

---

11. On the general HEW retreat on enforcement efforts, and the relative advantages of court and administrative enforcement, see Lempert and Sanders (1986).

12. See *United States v. Jefferson County Board of Education*, 372 F.2d 836 (5th Cir. 1966). Judge John Minor Wisdom's opinion in that case and in *Singleton v. Jackson Separate School District I*, 348 F.2d 729 (5th Cir. 1965), and *Singleton v. Jackson Separate School District II*, 355 F.2d 865 (5th Cir. 1966), presaged the *Green* position that school systems have an affirmative duty to integrate. In Wisdom's words in *Jefferson County*, "The only school desegregation plan that meets constitutional standards is one that works. . . . The clock has ticked the last tick for tokenism and delay in the name of 'deliberate speed' " (372 F.2d 836, 847, 896 (5th Cir. 1966)). On the general issue of the relationship between the courts and HEW guidelines, see Recent Cases (1967) and Comment (1967).

In the *Green* case the plaintiffs persuaded the Court that desegregative outcomes, not neutral intentions, were required of school boards. *Brown* did not simply stand for a cessation of discrimination, but rather for the immediate adoption of a plan which would disestablish the dual school system.[13] The private law interpretation upon which school districts had relied—that the Constitution required an end to segregation but did not require affirmative acts toward desegregation—was swept aside.[14]

In *Swann v. Charlotte-Mecklenberg Board of Education*, 402 U.S. 1 (1972) the Court was presented with the question of the scope of permissible remedy. In Charlotte a neighborhood plan would not desegregate the schools. The Legal Defense Fund and the Justice Department parted company when the government brief, written in the Nixon Administration, argued that trial Judge McMillan had abused his discretion by ordering substantial desegregation through the use of busing. The government's position was that remedies should be limited to school pairings, clustering, and redrawing boundaries, even if this meant that some schools would not be desegregated.[15] The LDF brief argued that eliminating identifiably black schools was an essential part of the breaking up of the dual school structure, and that in Charlotte this required the busing of students. Using the *Green* precedent and the opinions of Judge Wisdom in the Fifth Circuit, the LDF argued for a results-oriented, public law view of remedy which would require the substantial physical integration of southern schools.

The Court adopted the Legal Defense Fund's position in *Swann* and moved further toward a public law model of remedy. The Court stated:

> The objective is to dismantle the dual school system. "Racially neutral" assignment plans proposed by school authorities to the district court may be inadequate [if they fail to counteract the effects of past school desegregation]. . . . In short, an assignment plan is

13. During the next Term the Court, against the wishes of the Nixon administration Justice Department, refused to delay plan implementation in thirty-three Mississippi school districts, reaffirming that it was the "obligation of every school district to terminate dual school systems at once and to operate now and hereafter only unitary schools" (*Alexander v. Holmes County Bd. of Educ.*, 396 U.S. 19 at 20 (1969)).

14. As noted earlier, Judge Parker had so held in *Briggs v. Elliott*, 132 F. Supp. 776 (E.D.S.C. 1955), and the school boards had relentlessly urged this interpretation on the courts.

15. For a discussion of the generally antibusing position of the Justice Department during the Nixon and Ford administrations, see Orfield 1978a, chapter 10.

not acceptable simply because it appears to be neutral. (402 U.S. 1, 28 (1971))

The court created an evidentiary presumption that racial imbalance in formerly dual systems constituted a *prima facie* showing that the dual system had not been dismantled (see Fiss 1971). Perhaps the key word is "dismantle"; it implies that an affirmative action is required to alter an organizational structure. Such action is not consistent with private law notions of remedy. In addition, the primary criterion for adequacy in a desegregation plan is not individual opportunity to attend desegregated schools, or presumed individual advantage from desegregation. Rather, it is the distribution of white and black students per se.[16] The court viewed the racial balance criterion of an effective remedy as a question of "macro justice," a public law view. As Fiss (1971) noted at the time:

> The net effect of Charlotte-Mecklenburg is to move school desegregation further along the continuum toward a result oriented approach. . . . The predominant concern of the Court in Charlotte-Mecklenburg is in fact the segregated pattern of student attendance, rather than the causal role played by past discriminatory practice. . . . The Court made no serious attempt either to determine or even speculate on the degree to which it contributes to

16. Several important issues were left undecided in *Swann*. First, the Court refused to decide whether a showing that school segregation is caused by state action other than school board action is a Constitutional violation requiring remedial action by a desegregation decree. This issue reemerged in Detroit, with the Court once again side-stepping the question. As we shall see, the plaintiffs never ceased arguing that evidence on this point was properly part of the issue in dispute in these cases.

Second, at the conclusion of his opinion Chief Justice Burger stated, "At some point, these school authorities and others like them should have achieved full compliance with this decision in *Brown I*. The systems will then be unitary in the sense required by our decisions in *Green* and *Alexander*. It does not follow that the communities served by such systems will remain demographically stable, for in a growing mobile society, few will do so. Neither school authorities nor district courts are constitutionally required to make year-by-year adjustments of the racial composition of student bodies once the affirmative duty to desegregate has been accomplished and racial discrimination through official action is eliminated from the system" (402 U.S. at 31–32 (1971)). The issue left unanswered by this passage is exactly what constitutes a "unitary" system. One point of view might hold that the affirmative duty to maintain a balanced system should never be removed from a formerly dual system as long as continuing imbalance can be avoided (see Judge McMillan in *Swann*, 334 F. Supp. 623, W.D.N.C. 1971). As the last paragraph in the Chief Justice's opinion suggests, however, less rigid interpretations of the state's affirmative duty have been used in proceedings in Baton Rouge, Houston, Mobile, Norfolk, and Oklahoma City to have these districts declared unitary (see Smylie 1984).

present segregation. Nor did the Court attempt to tailor the remedial order to the correction of that portion of the segregation that might reasonably be attributable to past discrimination. The court moved from a) the undisputed existence of past discrimination to b) the possibility or likelihood that the past discrimination played some causal role in producing segregated patterns to c) an order requiring the complete elimination of those patterns. The existence of past discrimination was thus used as a "trigger" and not for a pistol, but for a cannon. Such a role cannot be defended unless the primary concern of the court is the segregated patterns themselves, rather than the causal relation of past discrimination to them. (704–705)

Eventually, the plaintiffs employed a number of expert plan writers to address the problems and tactics of remedy. Their primary task was to come up with plans which would desegregate schools within a district.[17]

Swann marked the beginning of the new stage in the movement to counter school desegregation. During the 1960s there was increasing local resistance to the use of busing as a means to accomplish school desegregation. The countermovement gained force in Congress as the Whitten amendments required that no portion of HEW appropriations could be used to accomplish the busing of students for purposes of desegregation (Bolner and Shanley 1974). As Orfield (1975) notes,

The politics of anti-busing legislation began to change rapidly once the Supreme Court handed down its unanimous and surprisingly tough 1971 decision in the Charlotte, North Carolina case. That decision supporting a requirement for extensive cross-town busing to overcome segregation, galvanized resistance in other Southern cities and spread fears in Northern communities facing suits. (101)

As reaction spread, the antibusing or antidesegregation movement gained new adherents in the urban north, and local community–federal court conflicts escalated to the national branches of government. Senatorial champions of the anti-busing movement were supported by President Nixon's introduction of the Student Transportation Moratorium Act of 1972. Under this pressure, HEW increasingly curtailed de-

---

17. The most prominent plan writers employed by plaintiffs were Gordon Foster and Michael Stolee. Others working variously for plaintiffs, defendants, and judges have included John Finger, Larry Hughes, David Gordon, Larry Hillman, and officials at many Title IV Desegregation Assistance Centers.

segregation enforcement activities, and adopted milder versions of the Whitten amendments as a part of its administrative rules (USCCR 1975). However, given the constitutional foundations of the school desegregation opinions, this countermovement was more effective in satisfying local constituencies and in sending a general message to the judiciary about the opinions of an active part of the citizenry, than it was in affecting the outcome of litigation in specific cases.

In many ways our research begins here. The social science testimony which our social science informants presented in court is largely post-*Swann* testimony. Most of the cases are post-*Swann* cases, and even with respect to those which began before *Swann,* the interviews concentrate upon post-*Swann* hearings and decisions. The interviews show that in *Swann* the plaintiffs achieved a breakthrough in legal theory with respect to the remedy. Remedies would not be limited by the existing racial patterns in a community. They would, instead, attempt to alter these patterns and to structurally integrate black school children. However, it remained to be seen whether this new legal resource could be translated into substantive educational change. The answer depended upon the resolution of questions such as: How willing would school districts be to implement court orders? How willing would the judiciary be to involve itself in the operation of school systems, and, given some judicial willingness, how effective would this intervention be? Most of these questions would be answered in a different part of the Republic. Although many southern cases remained to be litigated, the development of school law was about to move north.

Toward a Public Law of Violation?

The Northern Prelude

Brown was ambiguous as to what it was about a dual school system that constituted a violation of the Constitution. It was possible to read the opinion as saying that dual school systems were unconstitutional because they caused educational and psychological harm to black children. The "harm" theory of *Brown* was attractive to plaintiffs because it appeared to be an argument which might get the courts to sweep away the *de jure–de facto* distinction. The harm would exist regardless of the source of segregation. Such an argument was especially appealing in northern cases, where proof of state segregative action would be more difficult. But in circuit after circuit, northern courts did not find school districts in violation of the Constitution, even though the systems were to some extent segregated, and even though there was some evidence of "educational harm."[18] In these cases the primary theory advanced by the plaintiffs was that black children had been denied equal education instruction. The plaintiffs attempted to advance the public law argument that *de facto* segregation alone was sufficient to require a remedy, because it had the same harmful effects on northern black children that *de jure* desegregation in the South had on southern black children. The private law focus on the intentions of the school district would not be relevant.[19]

However, although plaintiffs could demonstrate inequalities in educational outcome (e.g., test score differences), they could not easily attribute these to school segregation per se (Perry 1977). Better scientific data and theory were needed. During the Johnson administration the plaintiff groups and their allies were able to introduce language into the 1964 Civil Rights Act requiring the United States Office of Education to conduct a national survey on educational opportunity. They hoped that this would generate data which would "prove" that segregated schools caused psychological harm and educational inequality, thus justifying a larger federal role in education and educational change. The Office of Education commissioned a team of social scientists to conduct the study, which ultimately involved a sample of over six hundred thousand students. The research team, headed by Professor James Coleman, produced conflicting results with respect to the harm argument (Coleman et al. 1966).[20] Helpful to the plaintiff cause was the finding that black

18. *Bell v. School City of Gary, Indiana*, 324 F.2d 209 (7th Cir. 1963); *Barksdale v. Springfield School Committee*, 348 F.2d 261 (1st Cir. 1965); *Downs v. Board of Education of Kansas City*, 336 F.2d 988 (10th Cir. 1964); *Deal v. Cincinnati Board of Education*, 348 F.2d 55 (6th Cir. 1966).

19. For an extended discussion of this legal theory by one of its chief architects, see Carter (1965). Other discussions of this point can be found in Schroeder and Smith (1965).

20. The scientific commentary on the Coleman Report is voluminous. A good starting place is Mosteller and Moynihan (1972). A review of the debates can be found in Cohen and Weiss (1977). Although much of the content of the Coleman Report followed in the footsteps of earlier harm arguments, the study was radically different in method and scope. The data came from questionnaires administered to principals, teachers, and students from a large sample of schools in the United States (over 2,000 elementary schools and 600 high schools), and were analyzed using multiple regression techniques. The movement toward a more quantitative sociology in desegregation cases had important consequences. The intellectual and technical tasks facing a lawyer wishing to use such data, and a social science expert wishing to present it, were considerable. Understanding the logic of the analyses and interpretations of the results required training which few lawyers and judges possessed in advance of trial. Given the relative complexity and consequent inaccessibility of the findings, there was increased potential for confusion and

students in mixed race schools did better academically than black students in segregated schools. But several other findings made these data a two-edged sword as far as plaintiffs were concerned. First, the absolute differences in school facilities were not nearly as great as had been anticipated. Second, the achievement differences which did exist were attributed more to the family background and peer-group associations of the child than to the school itself. Third, flowing from the above, most of the academic differences between segregated and desegregated schools could be explained by class-mix rather than race-mix. That is, gains for lower-class blacks (and lower-class whites) were correlated with going to school with middle-class children (whether white or black), not necessarily with white children.

Although the Coleman data were use by plaintiffs in Denver (Coleman himself testified for the plaintiffs) and Detroit, the findings shortly dropped out of the cases, as defendant groups discovered their vulnerability.[21] More important, Professor Coleman and other authors soon refused to testify from the data in support of school desegregation. In fact, one of the researchers on this team argued that plaintiff experts who did use these findings in support of school desegregation were "misusing" the data. A secondary analysis of the Coleman Report data was produced by the U.S. Commission on Civil Rights (USCCR 1967), and it provided more fuel for controversy. This analysis generally affirmed the commission's vigorous support for the desegregation effort, and some of the key scholars (e.g., Thomas Pettigrew) involved in this and in other reanalyses and extensions of the Coleman data continued to testify in support of school desegregation.

With hindsight, we can see that the Coleman Report constituted a watershed for academic opinion concerning school desegregation. Until its publication, the traditional wisdom in social sciences was that schools caused a large part of the difference between white and black

___

obfuscation by witnesses and counsel (see Wolf 1977a).

Beyond the difficulty of communicating these findings, there were methodological limitations. Like all such massive studies, the Coleman Report could use as variables only those things that were relatively objective and open to measurement. The report could measure standard test scores, the number of students in a class, or the number of books in a high school library. It could not easily measure student-teacher classroom interactions or those aspects of learning not tapped by standardized testing.

21. At first, defendant groups had a difficult time obtaining the raw data from the government and in finding individuals who would do an analysis from their point of view. From the shadows of our interviews comes a story of a midnight raid by a defense group, which, over the course of a weekend, took, copied, and replaced the Coleman Report data tapes from the offices of one of the researchers on the staff of the project.

performance, and that schools could be used to reduce these differences dramatically. By casting doubt on both assumptions, the Coleman data helped lead to a split in the academic community. The report led to disputes in the academic literature and broke the nearly united front that social science had presented on school desegregation. Divisions within the academic community were widened as measuring the effects of desegregation became a major area of scholarly interest.[22]

Despite growing academic debate, plaintiffs continued to present testimony on the educational and psychological effects of segregation. Defendants, on the other hand, could find few social scientists willing to say in court that desegregation would not help achievement, and few judges willing to permit it to be said.[23] When some defendants did challenge this interpretation,[24] the appellate courts rejected such testimony as a factual attack on *Brown*.[25] One social scientist we interviewed reported the following experience:

> The legal doctrine is cast in concrete, and that's been one of my frustrations. It's as though the evidence is really immaterial. A legal doctrine makes certain assumptions of facts as to the effects of desegregation. I remember in one case I was talking with the judge from the witness box, and questioning some of the testimony in *Brown*. He asked me, "Are you questioning the facts of *Brown*?" And I said "Yes," and he said, "Well, that's not admissible for you to be doing that." So it kind of stymies a person. The evidence in *Brown* argues that desegregation will change attitudes, increase self-esteem, and improve school performance, when in fact that

22. One significant controversy took shape around David Armor's study of a voluntary desegregation plan in the Boston area. Armor's (1972) initial article, "The Evidence on Busing," which indicated little or no gains in academic performance, was met with a particularly harsh and personal response from Thomas Pettigrew and his colleagues (Pettigrew et al. 1973), leading to a harsh rejoinder from Armor (1973). Subsequently, a long line of research produced studies indicating both positive and some negative academic consequences of desegregation. Among the early efforts were those of Crain and Mahard (1978), Epps (1978), St. John (1975), Weinberg (1975), and Weinberg (1977). Many others continue to this day.

23. David Armor was deposed in the Detroit case on his study, but never testified. As in the earlier southern cases, attempts to introduce this line of findings often met with judicial responses that the data were irrelevant.

24. For a critical review of the testimony and writings of Ernest van den Haag, Henry Garrett, and other experts opposed to desegregation, and for several rebuttals to this review, see Newby (1969).

25. See *Evers v. Jackson Municipal School Districts*, 357 F. 2d 425 (5th Cir. 1964), and *Stell v. Savannah-Chatham County*, 318 F. 2d 425 (5th Cir. 1963).

doesn't happen. We know that it doesn't happen. But there's a difficulty in making that point with the judge.

Evidence on harm continued to be the almost exclusive province of plaintiff experts. Such testimony appeared in ten of the seventeen cases we studied. Table 3.1 presents these data by party. The first row indicates that plaintiffs used six different experts to testify on issues of educational and psychological harm during the violation part of the trial. Defendants used none.[26] Moreover, counting individuals substantially underestimates this difference, because a few plaintiff witnesses testified in numerous cases. Counting person-appearances in the second row reflects this fact. Finally, if cases are used as the unit of analysis, in nine of the seventeen cases plaintiffs presented experts to testify on educational and psychological harm.

Debates about the causes and consequences of desegregation also occurred among legal strategists in the movement. Partly as a result of the Supreme Court's refusal to take any of the early northern cases on *certiorari*, Lewis Steel, a young NAACP lawyer, wrote a scathing article in the *New York Times Magazine* in which he accused the Court, among other things, of refusing "to review a series of conservative lower court decisions which upheld what school officials described as accidental segregation in Gary, Ind.; Kansas City, Kan.; and Cincinnati. As a result the schools of the North have become segregated faster than Southern schools have been desegregated" (Steel 1968). In the ensuing uproar, the NAACP sought to fire Steel. Robert Carter, who had become the General Counsel of the NAACP after the LDF split from the main organization, threatened to resign if Steel were fired. When the NAACP dismissed Steel, Carter and the other members of the NAACP's legal staff resigned, leading the way for Nathaniel Jones to succeed as director of the NAACP Special Contribution Fund. Steel's comments and his firing divided the major participants in the social movement. An American Civil Liberties Union official called Steel's analysis "correct and

26. The terms *plaintiff* and *defendant* must be used cautiously, because the formal position of parties sometimes masks their objectives and true positions. Moreover, their position may change in the course of litigation. Most typically, inner-city school districts, like those in Detroit, Richmond, and Wilmington, may begin and even remain as formal defendants in litigation. But at a later stage, as when cross-district violations and remedies are considered, they may share a point of view with the formal plaintiffs. We have adopted the convention of treating them according to the substantive position they advance at a given stage of the trial. Thus, for example, Detroit school board attorneys bringing experts to testify for the necessity of a metropolitan remedy in Detroit are treated as plaintiff lawyers, although they are, formally, defendants.

Table 3.1. Testimony on Educational and Psychological Harm by Plaintiff and
Defendant Experts at Violation in Seventeen Cases

Types of Testimony	Plaintiff	Defendant
Number of Experts Testifying on Educational and Psychological Effects	6	0
Number of Person-Appearances on Educational and Psychological Effects	11	0
Number of Cases Where Experts Testified on Educational and Psychological Effects	9	0

valuable." However, the American Jewish Congress thought the article had been one-sided, and Jack Greenberg, head of the Legal Defense Fund, in a letter to the *New York Times Magazine*, praised the Court's role in the desegregation effort (Orfield 1978a, 365).

Steel's comments most certainly caused a dilemma for the NAACP. Although the comments may have been well received among parts of the movement's beneficiary constituency, which by this time was being heavily recruited by more militant black groups such as the Student Nonviolent Coordinating Committee and the Congress of Racial Equality, they could not have been well received by other sources of the movement's support. The civil rights groups had come to rely on the courts and on outside conscience constituency foundations for resources to such an extent that the NAACP felt that the better of a bad set of choices was to fire Steel and lose Carter.

In Denver, the LDF, which in *Swann* had pushed for a legal theory merging northern and southern cases, brought one of its few northern cases (Wasby 1986). The LDF based the plaintiff's claim for relief both on intentional acts of the school board (efforts to separate white and black children in the changing neighborhood of Park Hill) and on the "harm theory" ground that the predominantly black schools—the so-called core city schools—provided unequal educational opportunities (Pearson and Pearson 1978). The private law argument was that school boards engaged in acts with the purpose and effect of segregating schools. Such an argument had won early on in *Taylor v. Board of Education of New Rochelle*, 191 F. Supp. 181 (S.D.N.Y. 1961), and it had been part of Judge Skelly Wright's decision in *Hobson v. Hansen*, 269 F. Supp. 401 (D.C.C. 1967). Following that case, it had proved successful in several cities.[27]

27. *Spangler v. Pasadena Board of Education*, 311 F. Supp. 501 (M. D. Cal. 1970); *Johnson v.*

In Denver the trial court and the appellate court again rejected the public law model of violation based upon alleged inequalities in student performance alone and without proof of school system intention to segregate. In *Keyes* the Supreme Court agreed, and by doing so it drove the last nail in the coffin of the harm theory of northern school desegregation (*Keyes v. School District No. 1*, Denver, Colorado, 413 U.S. 189 (1972)). Despite separate opinions by Justice Powell and Justice Douglas, the Court refused to adopt any public law theory of violation based upon the fact of separation per se.[28] The plaintiff had to prove segregative purpose on the part of the school board. Standing alone, the outcome data (e.g., a segregated school system or educational inequality) did not suffice.

Although the Court retained the *de jure* language, through the use of presumptions and burdens it made proof of school segregation relatively easy for plaintiffs. The Court adopted the Legal Defense Fund's position that proof of segregative purpose in part of the system (e.g., the Park Hill schools) was sufficient to meet the plaintiff's burden of making a *prima facie* case with regard to the entire system (413 U.S. at 207 [see Orfield 1978a, 342]). Once the plaintiff had presented a *prima facie* case, the burden of showing that other segregated schools were not segregated by intentional acts of the school board shifted to the board. And, noted Justice Brennan, the rebuttal could not be "some allegedly logical, racial neutral explanation." Rather, the burden required proof sufficient "to support a finding that segregative intent was not among the factors that motivated" board action (413 U.S. at 210).

The LDF had achieved by procedural means what the NAACP had been unable to achieve by a more substantive argument. The Court was unwilling to say, as a matter of substantive constitutional law, that school board intent was irrelevant to a finding of unconstitutional segregation. It was willing to say that once some intentional segregation was shown, there arose a legal presumption that all segregation was the result of school board intention. The use of presumptions is the more cautious course. Presumptions can be changed as events warrant, whereas it is more difficult to change a substantive holding. It is a com-

---

San Francisco Unified School District, 339 F. Supp. 1315 (N.D. Cal. 1971); *United States v. Board of School Commissioners*, 332 F. Supp. 655 (S.D. Ind. 1971) [Indianapolis]; *Davis v. School District*, 443 F.2d 573 (6th Cir. 1971) [Pontiac]; *Bradley v. Milliken*, 338 F. Supp. 582 (E.D. Mich. 1971) [Detroit].

28. A good deal of the academic literature supported abolishing the *de facto–de jure* distinction (Fiss 1965; Goodman 1972; Note 1976; Wright 1965). But for a contrary view, see Graglia (1976).

pliment to the legal skill of LDF attorneys that they were able to exploit this point.

Only one step remained to complete the Legal Defense Fund's strategy of tying the Denver and northern cases to *Swann* and the southern cases. The plaintiff was able to persuade the Court that in proving that Park Hill schools were intentionally segregated, the plaintiffs had shown enough, without rebuttal, to prove that the Denver school system was a "dual school system."

> [W]here Plaintiffs proved that the school authorities had carried out a systematic program of segregation affecting a substantial portion of the students, schools, teachers and facilities within the school system, it is only common sense to conclude that there exists a predicate for a finding of the existence of a dual school system. (413 U.S. at 201)

The key is the "dual school system" finding. Until the Denver case, the common sense meaning and the legal meaning of the phrase were similar. A system was dual where, by law, black and white children were kept in separate facilities and taught by faculties of their own race. Now dual legally meant a district in which some "substantial portion" of schools within the district were in some way affected by school efforts to segregate. The schools did not have to be all black or all white. Nor would all the segregation within these schools have to be attributable to specific school board intentions and actions.

In Denver the Legal Defense Fund was able to avoid the danger of an adverse precedent based upon the harm theory of northern segregation. More important, it was able to develop a theory of the case which allowed the court to retain the *de facto–de jure* distinction, to at least pay lip service to a private law model of violation in school desegregation cases, and yet to open the possibility of northern school desegregation. After the Denver case, the Legal Defense Fund again withdrew from northern school desegregation litigation, leaving the field to the reconstituted NAACP Special Contribution Fund, the Justice Department,[29] and the ACLU.[30]

---

29. The Justice Department had originally brought the suit in Indianapolis, but the Nixon administration had allowed the case to languish. Among our southern cases, the Justice Department was the plaintiff in Austin. During the Carter administration it brought cases in Omaha and Tulsa. It was also asked to intervene by district court judges in a few cases, including St. Louis.

30. The American Civil Liberties Union brought a number of California cases, including the Los Angeles case. In addition, after the local chapter of the NAACP settled the Atlanta

Detroit and Beyond: Social Science Evidence and the Public
Law Model

The choice to litigate in Detroit was ad hoc, forced upon the NAACP
by an unlikely series of events. Compared to other northern cities, Detroit was a minor offender in the area of school segregation. Both the
superintendent of schools and the most recent president of the school
board had been honored by the NAACP for their efforts on behalf of
school integration. However, a movement to decentralize the Detroit
schools, supported by minority groups and led in part by soon-to-be-
mayor Coleman Young, allowed for the election of regional school
boards. There ensued a struggle to draw the regional boundaries, and
fearing that the lines might freeze racial division, the board gerryman-
dered city high-school attendance areas to improve the racial mix. Part
of the political fallout of this effort was a successful recall election of
board members who had voted for this assignment plan. In response
to the recall and in part responding to pressure to sue from the local
chapter, the national staff of the NAACP decided to litigate. The very
fact that this type of pressure could be brought to bear on the NAACP
and on its Special Contribution Fund distinguishes the NAACP from
the LDF. Because it was more completely separated from local chapters
both as a source of revenue and as a source of political pressure, the
LDF found it easier to resist litigation which did not fit into some larger
strategy (cf. Greenberg 1973; Wasby 1984, 124).

In Detroit the plaintiffs were able to prove *de jure* segregation,[31] but
as the case proceeded the NAACP lost further control over the litiga-

city-only case against the wishes of the national organization, the ACLU, apparently
against the objection of other civil rights organizations, pursued a metropolitan remedy
in that city. They lost the case before a three-judge panel in an unreported opinion (*Ar-
mour v. Nix*, Civil No. 16708 (N.D. Ga. 1979)).

31. The proof of violation put on by the plaintiffs was typical of the standard set of
considerations which came to be used to prove a northern violation. It included evidence
of altered attendance boundaries; changes in feeder patterns from elementary to secondary schools; the use of optional attendance areas in changing neighborhoods; location
of new schools; intact busing of black children from overcrowded black schools to empty
classrooms in white schools; and, on one occasion, the cross-district busing of black children from an overcrowded black school to another black school when white schools with
space available were closer. The school board admitted pre-1960 acts of segregation, but
argued that their actions in the ten years preceding the trial did not indicate segregative
purpose. In more recent years, for instance, the board had changed some student assignment patterns and made minor boundary shifts which increased desegregation; it
had revised the open enrollment policy to permit pupil transfers only if they improved
the racial balance of the receiving school, and had required that busing to relieve over-
crowding must be desegregative as well (Dimond 1985; Hain 1978, 228; Wolf 1981).

tion, and watched nearly helplessly as the litigation changed from a city-only suit into a metropolitan desegregation case. As in most large American metropolitan areas, the old core city of Detroit had become increasingly black as whites had migrated to the suburbs.[32] To desegregate the city alone, even under a racial balance standard, would leave the schools predominantly black. Such an outcome would leave much to be desired, or so thought trial Judge Steven Roth. During the trial's city-only phase, Judge Roth found that both the city and the state had unconstitutionally segregated black students (*Bradley v. Milliken*, 338 F. Supp. 582 (E.D. Mich. 1971)). As the case progressed, first a white parent group, the Concerned Citizens for Better Education, and later the Detroit Board of Education, came to favor a metropolitan plan to the NAACP plan which would require reassignment of 100,000 students to bring the ratio of every school in the district near to the districtwide ratio of 65% black to 35% white.[33]

Using his finding against the state of Michigan as a vehicle, Judge Roth pushed toward a metropolitan remedy.[34] Because a Detroit-only plan would make the entire system racially identifiable as black, the goal of a single community would not be served; and insofar as "white flight" and "tipping point" arguments were true, the schools would be likely to become more and more identifiable in the future.[35] To avoid this

32. Farley (1975b,9); Farley et al. (1978); Farley (1984); Taeuber and Taeuber (1965); Taeuber (1975).

33. The NAACP's reservations were partly based on the fact that an attempt to achieve a metropolitan remedy would cause delays. In addition, there were strategy considerations. A metropolitan remedy had been rejected by the court of appeals in a case in Richmond, Virginia, and this judgment had been sustained by a 4–4 decision in the Supreme Court (*Richmond School Board v. Virginia Board of Education*, 412 U.S. 92 (1973)). Whenever there is a tie vote in the Supreme Court, the lower court's opinion is affirmed, but the Supreme Court opinion does not stand as a precedent as would a majority opinion. Thus, the Richmond case did not settle the metropolitan issue either way. Detroit, where the trial record contained almost no evidence on the behavior of suburban school districts, was not the ideal place to retry the metropolitan issue.

34. There was evidence that the state of Michigan had refused to help finance school transportation in Detroit while paying up to 75% of the transportation costs in most counties. This occurred in the aftermath of the effort to gerrymander regional boundaries.

35. On the topics of white withdrawal and tipping points, see Armor (1980); Coleman, Kelly, and Moore (1975); Pettigrew and Green (1976); Ravitch (1978); Rossell (1978, 1985); Wolf (1976, 1977b, 1981). The weight of the evidence now suggests that court-ordered plans do result in incremental white withdrawal, especially among whites scheduled to be bused. Ultimately, demographers became quite sophisticated in their ability to estimate white flight. Reynolds Farley, in a presentation to the court in the Los Angeles case, was able to predict almost exactly the amount of white withdrawal in the first year after a desegregation order.

result, he adopted a plan which included 153 school districts with 750,000 students. Only 25% of the students in this area were black. The Sixth Circuit upheld Judge Roth in June of 1973 in an *en banc* hearing (*Bradley v. Milliken*, 484 F.2d 215 (6th Cir. 1973)).

In a 5–4 opinion, the Supreme Court reversed. Chief Justice Burger held that while in some cases it would be proper to desegregate across district boundaries, this could be done only in a case where the plaintiffs had shown a "constitutional violation within one district that produces a significant segregative effect in another district" (*Milliken v. Bradley*, 418 U.S. 717, 744-745 (1974)). The court found that in Detroit the violations and their effects were limited to the Detroit school district. The action of the state of Michigan did not alone suffice to require a metropolitan remedy.[36]

Although the Detroit case was a setback for the plaintiffs' legal theory, it was a success with respect to their social science testimony. During the trial the plaintiffs introduced social science testimony on the academic and psychological harms of segregation. They also presented testimony concerning housing segregation, which played an important role in persuading the trial judge that Detroit area schools should be desegregated.

If Kenneth Clark represented the first wave of academic involvement in desegregation litigation, Karl Taeuber represented the second. A professor of sociology at the University of Wisconsin, he and Alma Taeuber had written *Negroes in Cities* in 1965. This book dealt not with school segregation, but with residential segregation. The picture it painted was bleak. Unlike other ethnic groups which, over time, slowly "melted" into the general population, black Americans continued, decade after decade, to be discriminated against and to remain walled off in their own communities. Professor Taeuber's area of expertise was not directly probative to the central legal issues in the cases, but it served several purposes for the NAACP. His analyses of the unique situation in which black Americans (and Mexican Americans in the

---

36. Justice Stewart, who joined the majority in the opinion, also wrote a concurring opinion in which he said that although the facts in Detroit showed no evidence of a violation affecting districts other than the city, he would be willing to consider constitutional violations by officials other than school boards or administrators in assessing a remedy. He would expand the realm of issues legitimately in dispute. For example, he noted, schools might be desegregated across district lines if state officials used state housing or zoning laws in a "purposeful, racially discriminatory" manner (418 U.S. at 755). The majority refused to consider the housing case which the NAACP had put on early in the trial because the court of appeals had refused to consider it (418 U.S. at 723 n.7).

Southwest) found themselves laid the groundwork for a new attack on school policies. By showing that numerous social and governmental agencies had acted with segregative purpose, it raised the question of whether the school board had not done the same. Moreover, by indicating that a "neighborhood school policy" inevitably had the effect of perpetuating segregation, it suggested that school boards were at least negligent when the "natural, probable and foreseeable result of their plan was segregation" (*Oliver v. Michigan State Board of Education*, 508 F.2d 178, 182 (6th Cir., 1974)). Thus, it helped undermine a defense that the school board had acted with racial neutrality and done nothing wrong. In addition, it made the point, early in the trial, that the ultimate remedy would have to go beyond neighborhood school policies if significant racial balancing were to occur.

Taeuber became a central part of the movement's renewed litigation effort, testifying in numerous cases for the NAACP and other plaintiffs. In teamwork with Taeuber's testimony about segregated housing, Martin Sloane, a lawyer, often testified regarding state and federal housing policies which had encouraged or perpetuated residential segregation.[37] The plaintiffs presented residential segregation data in eleven of the seventeen cases in our survey. Table 3.2 presents the frequency of residential segregation testimony by plaintiffs and defendants in these cases.

The residential desegregation testimony, even more than the testimony on educational and psychological harm, distinguishes the perspectives and legal theories of the plaintiffs and defendants in the school desegregation cases.[38] Plaintiff counsel employed academic experts more often, in part because they wished to advance a public law view

37. During the early northern years they were joined by Robert Green, who testified on educational issues, including the effect of teacher expectations, social background of students, school resources, and school desegregation on black performance. He often put into evidence the parts of the Coleman Report most beneficial to the plaintiff case (see, e.g., Wolf 1981, part 2). Added to this core group were people such as Gordon Foster and William Lamson, testifying on school board actions with segregative effects. Foster, Michael Stolee, and John Finger often wrote desegregation plans for the NAACP. Self-deprecatingly, some insiders came to call the core group of witnesses the "the dog and pony show" or "the traveling road show."

38. Of course, as the data in table 3.1 indicate, defendants never used educational and psychological harm testimony in any of the seventeen cases, whereas they did use housing evidence in three cases. In the case of the harm testimony, there was a significant barrier to defense testimony from the courts' refusal to permit evidence which challenged the idea in *Brown* that segregated schools were inherently unequal. There was no such barrier here. The lack of defense testimony on housing was more clearly a matter of defendant choice.

Table 3.2 Residential Segregation Testimony by Plaintiff and Defendant Experts at
Violation in Seventeen Cases

Types of Testimony	Plaintiff	Defendant
Number of Experts Testifying on Residential Segregation	6	5
Number of Person-Appearances on Residential Segregation	17	7
Number of Cases Where Experts Testified on Residential Segregation	11	3

of responsibility and therefore of the issues appropriately in dispute.[39] They wanted the courts to understand the position of blacks and other minorities in the context of the historical and structural conditions in society. As one plaintiff attorney noted:

> We use social evidence because it is not possible to talk about or deal with racial discrimination or racial segregation in a societal vacuum. The purpose of segregation was to create, maintain, and protect a sociological, ideological, to some extent a religious and philosophical point of view. Segregation and discrimination became the political and logistical vehicle by which this was done. Therefore, to fully assess and describe the impact of the schools now, segregation as it was created and maintained and carried out by the school system, you have to look at not just the fact of segregation, but its effects as well. We figure it's important for a judge to understand the context within which the individual actions produced the segregation, and to characterize the discrimination that took place. Whether this is testimony having to do with the impact of school segregation on black children's learning ability, or anything else, doesn't make a difference. The effort is to present the full context within which the public officials who created segregation carried out their game plan.

The public law model looks to the school system as part of a larger community and social context, as an organization with a supraindividual structure, with organized policies and programs. These contexts, policies, and programs, not just the discrete acts of the board, are at the heart of the problem. School board policies must be understood

---

39. This does not mean that plaintiff attorneys were unmindful of the necessity of evidence concerning specific school board acts. Plaintiffs did present testimony concerning specific violations. The point is, they also did more.

within the wider structures of American race relations. The matters in dispute are but parts of a larger set of social relations and organizational dynamics affecting school segregation.[40] To quote Fiss (1979):

> These incidents may have triggered the lawsuit. They may also be of evidentiary significance: evidence of a "pattern or practice" of racism or lawlessness. But the ultimate subject matter of the judicial inquiry is not these incidents, these particularized and discrete events, but rather a social condition that threatens important constitutional values and the organizational dynamic that creates and perpetuates that condition. (18)

According to this view, and according to plaintiffs advancing this vision of the issues, the school board should be required to formulate policies and programs designed to counteract these "naturally segregative" processes.

As indicated in Table 3.2, defendants introduced residential segregation testimony much less frequently. Why? In part, as in the case of evidence on psychological and educational harm, they had some difficulty finding experts who would testify for them. But equally important most defense lawyers did not envision a public law defense. They usually envisioned the defense as an effort to meet each alleged occasion of intentional segregation by providing alternative, racially neutral explanations for the given act. Academic expert testimony was seen as unnecessary if it did not speak directly to these acts. Consider these two statements by defense lawyers:

> But in this case the question was, was there [intentional] segregation at all? So social science really doesn't get into that question very much. In fact, we argued that it was inappropriate to have any expert testimony on the educational effects of the segregated schools until it came to the remedy phase, what to do about it if it was.

> We didn't offer experts. We didn't even make a "beachhead" or an issue of the question of whether or not segregation, if it did occur, or racial imbalance if it had ever occurred, was or was not harmful. That just didn't seem to me like that was the question raised at trial.

40. This view is quite consistent with Chayes' definition of a public law model: "In the latter [public law] case, inquiry is only secondarily concerned with how the condition came about, and even less with the subjective attitudes of the actors. . . . Indeed, in dealing with the actions of large political or corporate aggregates, notions of will, or fault, increasingly become only metaphors" (Chayes 1976, 1296).

In support of the argument that defense lawyers generally saw social science as irrelevant, consider a main reason defense counsel gave for using such experts on the rare occasions when they were employed:

> We only used them because the other [side] did. We thought they were full of bull, if you really want to know.

> From a legal standpoint, we felt we had to have a sociologist to counter their sociologists. It just got down to all the sociologists wanted, in my opinion, was to prove their own point regardless of what the premise was to start out with. As long as they could prove their own point, they were happy as larks, they didn't care about anything else. And I thought the whole thing was just a waste of time. I thought we would have been better off if we could agree that they have no sociologists and we would have no sociologists, and we could just present our facts to the court and let it come up with a decision. But you can't do it that way—they have a sociologist and we have to have one.

Not until the mid and late 1970s did the defendants begin to introduce their own testimony own the causes and consequences of residential segregation, and its relevance to school segregation.[41]

The residential segregation testimony, like the Coleman Report before it, eventually came to be a two-edged sword. The testimony of Taeuber and Sloane laid the groundwork for the legal argument that intentional segregative acts by any public agency, not only school boards, should trigger a desegregation remedy. Such a ruling would open the door for metropolitan plans in many cities. However, the position was not adopted in Detroit (*Milliken v. Bradley*, 418 U.S. 717, (1974)), and metropolitan suits have not succeeded except where government officials have been found to act with the specific purpose of segregating schools across districts (Wilmington, Louisville, Indianapolis, and St. Louis).[42]

41. Most of the defense testimony on this issue came after *Dayton Bd. of Educ. v. Brinkman I*, and was designed to address the issue of incremental segregative effect. Only at this relatively late date did the defendants apparently begin to see the advantages of a social science counterattack to the plaintiff's testimony (see Sanders et al. 1981–82). It would be easy to overemphasize the effect of this change in defense strategy for the long-term outcome of desegregation cases, but from a different point of view it was very important. Defense lawyers moved from being what Ackerman (1984, 27) calls traditionalist lawyers, who unquestioningly accepted the legitimacy of the economic and social arrangements of school systems, to lawyers who actively defended the legitimacy of these arrangements in structural terms. One suspects that in the long run this is a more formidable defense.

42. Successful metropolitan cases have usually had a set of "special circumstances,"

Defendants began to adopt the argument that most school segregation was caused by residential segregation, and that residential segregation was fundamentally a matter of the individual housing preferences of white and black citizens. Therefore, school boards could not be held accountable for the results of these choices.[43] Plaintiff experts countered with the argument that one important cause of residential choice was the availability of good schools, and that by segregating schools the board of education helped produce segregated housing.[44] The judicial opinions from Detroit to Columbus reflected the ambiguity of the social science evidence with respect to both the probative value of segregative effect on school board intention to segregate and the causal relationship between residential segregation and school segregation.

The Uncertain Path of the Public Law Model

Part of the plaintiff's purpose in introducing social science evidence on educational and psychological harm, and on residential segregation, was to persuade courts to adopt a public law view of violation in which school board intent need not be proven. The decisions in Detroit and Denver indicate a commitment to a private law model of responsibility. They retreat from an interpretation which assesses the validity of acts based upon their impact on segregation, toward a decision based upon purpose. The Supreme Court solidified its position on the violation issue in two nonschool cases, *Washington v. Davis*, 426 U.S. 229 (1976), and *Village of Arlington Heights v. Metropolitan Housing Development Corporation*, 429 U.S. 252 (1977). In these cases the Court rejected an "im-

---

most frequently some act of a state legislature which has produced an interdistrict violation. Both the special circumstances of the metropolitan cases (Wilmington, Indianapolis, Louisville, Atlanta, and St. Louis) and their varied outcomes make it unclear whether a metropolitan plan can be successful without unique factors proving *de jure* interdistrict segregation.

43. Using data collected by Farley et al. (1978), David Armor and his colleagues attempted to demonstrate in Omaha and Atlanta that black and white housing preferences alone were sufficient to explain almost all school segregation.

44. This argument about the "reciprocal" effect of schools on housing is presaged in *Swann*, where the Court stated: "People gravitate toward school facilities, just as schools are located in response to the needs of people. The location of schools may thus influence the patterns of residential development of a metropolitan area and have important impact on composition of the inner-city neighborhoods" (402 U.S. at 20). This statement reaches well beyond the data available to support it. Yet, the statement itself was accepted in the Detroit case as part of proof of the truth of the argument (Wolf 1981, 278). Again, as when refusing to hear evidence challenging the *Brown* assertion that separate is inherently unequal, the courts substitute judicial authority for scientific fact. To accomplish this is, from an adversary point of view, the goal of expert testimony.

pact" test of liability. "Disproportionate impact is not irrelevant, but it is not the sole touchstone of the invidious racial discrimination" (*Washington v. Davis*, 426 U.S. at 242). Quoting *Keyes* the Court said that the central requirement in school cases was "a current condition of segregation resulting from intentional state action . . . the differentiating factor between *de jure* segregation and *de facto* segregation . . . is purpose or intent to segregate" (426 U.S. at 235).

This set of cases indicate a willingness to assume that school board decisions could be racially neutral even in circumstances where the foreseeable impact of the decisions was segregation (Dworkin 1977). They not only threatened the quality and quantity of evidence needed to prove violation, but raised questions about the appropriate scope of the remedy (Taylor 1978). The Detroit language suggested that at least among school districts the permissible remedy must be limited to the segregation actually caused by *de jure* acts of the state (in this case, school boards). The erosion of the "dual school system" presumption continued in the first Supreme Court opinion in the Dayton case.

In Dayton there had been a tug of war between the District Court and the Sixth Circuit concerning the extensiveness of the remedy. In *Brinkman v. Gilligan*, 503 F.2d 684 (6th Cir. 1974) and 581 F.2d 853 (6th Cir. 1975), the appellate court rejected trial court remedies as being insufficiently broad, and finally ordered the trial court to adopt a system-wide plan for the 1976–1977 year. The record, however, was skimpy as to violation. On this record, the Supreme Court reversed the Sixth Circuit opinion calling for a systemwide remedy. It said:

> The Court of Appeals simply had no warrant in our cases for imposing the system wide remedy which it apparently did. There had been no showing that such a remedy was necessary to "eliminate all vestiges of the state imposed school segregation." (*Dayton Board of Education v. Brinkman I*, 433 U.S. 406, 417 (1977))

Justice Rehnquist stated what was required in such cases:

> The duty of both the District Court and the Court of Appeals in a case such as this where mandatory segregation by law of the races in the schools has long since ceased, is to first determine whether there was an action in the conduct of the business of the school board which was intended to, and did in fact, discriminate against minority pupils, teachers or staff. . . . If such violations are found, the District Court in the first instance, subject to review by the Court of Appeals, must determine how much *incremental segregative effect* these violations had on the racial distribution of the Dayton

school population as presently constituted, when that distribution is compared to what it would have been in the absence of such constitutional violations. The remedy must be designed to redress that difference, and only if there has been a system wide impact may there be a system wide remedy [emphasis added]. (*Dayton Board of Education v. Brinkman I*, 433 U.S. 406, 420 (1977))

One reading of the language of incrementalism implies that contrary to *Swann* and *Keyes*, the remedy need only return a district to the position which would have existed if school boards had behaved neutrally. The Court remanded other cases for consideration in light of *Brinkman I*.[45]

When, upon remand, Judge Rubin reviewed the entire record, he entered a judgment dismissing the complaint. The judge found that although there were instances of purposeful segregation in the past, the plaintiffs failed to prove that these acts, some of which were over twenty years old, had any current incremental segregative effects (446 F. Supp. 1232, 1241, (1977)).[46] The appellate court reversed *Brinkman v. Gilligan*, 583 F.2d 243 (6th Cir. 1978). It concluded that the trial judge had made erroneous findings of fact and had also made errors of law (583 F.2d at 247). The court of appeals interpreted the incremental segregative effect language in public law terms: not that each illegal act should be assessed separately as to its incremental effect, but rather that the nature of northern cases was such that segregation was produced through the incremental effects of many actions. The task of the court was to assess the overall impact of such acts. It was in this posture that the case and a companion case from Columbus came to the Su-

---

45. *School District of Omaha v. United States*, 433 U.S. 667 (1977); *Brenan v. Armstrong*, 433 U.S. 672 (1977). See also *United States v. Texas Education Agency*, 532 F.2d 380 (5th Cir. 1976), vacated and remanded *sub nom Austin Independent School District v. United States*, 429 U.S. 990 (1977). In Milwaukee, Minneapolis, Omaha, Austin, and Indianapolis, hearings were held to measure the "incremental segregative effect" of the unconstitutional school board acts. The lower federal courts proved to be quite resistant to this new direction and to the *Washington v. Davis* direction in the school cases. See *United States v. Texas Education Agency*, 564 F.2d 162, 168–169 (5th Cir. 1977); *Armstrong v. O'Connell*, 451 F. Supp. 817, 824 (E.D. Wis. 1978).

46. In St. Louis, the trial court wrote a similar opinion, with a similar outcome. Judge Meredith found that the plaintiffs failed to show segregative intent and segregative effect sufficient to justify a finding that the schools were unconstitutionally segregated (*Liddell v. Bd. of Educ. & City of St. Louis*, 469 F. Supp. 1304 (1979)). In Austin, Omaha, and Minneapolis, however, upon remand in light of *Brinkman I*, the trial judges found that the systems were segregated and that the defendants failed to carry their *Keyes*-imposed burden of showing that the segregation was not districtwide. They ordered systemwide remedies.

preme Court: *Dayton Board of Education v. Brinkman II*, 443 U.S. 526 (1979), and *Columbus Board of Education v. Penick*, 443 U.S. 449 (1979).

Both the plaintiffs and the defendants recognized that these two cases were to be a critical turning point in the legal theory of the desegregation cases. The Court could either reaffirm the public law remedy theory that the plaintiffs had so laboriously developed over the preceding twenty-five years, or it could abandon *Swann* and *Keyes* and follow the private law path opened in *Milliken*, *Washington v. Davis*, and the first Dayton opinion. Plaintiff groups believed this to be a sufficiently important opinion that for the first time since *Brown* they organized a social science brief in support of the public law view (we presented an excerpt from the appendix in chap. 2).

The Court reversed the trend toward a private law model and adopted the line of argument presented by the trial judge in Columbus. Since the school districts in these two cities were intentionally segregated on the basis of race when the Supreme Court decided *Brown* in 1954, from that time on the school boards had been under an affirmative duty to dismantle the then-existing dual school system. In the key portion of the *Penick* opinion, the Supreme Court held:

> Where a racially discriminatory school system has been found to exist, Brown II imposes the duty on local school boards to "effectuate a transition to a racially non-discriminatory school system" (349 U.S. at 301). . . . Brown II was a call for the dismantling of well-entrenched dual systems, (and school boards operating such systems were) clearly charged with the affirmative duty to take whatever steps might be necessary to convert to a unitary system in which racial discrimination would be eliminated root and branch, Green v. County School Board, 391 U.S. 430, 437–438 (1968). . . . Each instance of a failure or refusal to fulfill this affirmative duty continues the violation of the Fourteenth Amendment. (443 U.S. 449, 458–459 (1979))[47]

The two Ohio opinions provided the plaintiffs with a substantial victory by reestablishing a public law model of remedy in the school cases. The remedy focused upon results.

The Court apparently moved away from a private law model of vio-

---

47. In both cases the appellate courts found that post-*Brown* conduct in some ways increased segregation in the systems. The strongest interpretation of the Columbus and Dayton opinions, however, is that even if all subsequent action had only perpetuated the segregation existent at the time of *Brown*, the school boards would still be in violation of the constitution.

lation as well. In districts which operated a dual system in the *Keyes* sense in 1954 (and one must presume that nearly every system with more than a few minority students did), the obligation was to act so as to desegregate. In Columbus the trial judge stated that adherence to a neighborhood school concept, with knowledge that the predictable effects of such a policy would be segregated schools, was a factor to be considered in determining whether an inference of segregative intent should be drawn (*Penick v. Columbus Board of Education*, 429 F. Supp. 229, 255 (S.D. Ohio 1977)). This is a public law view.

The Supreme Court, however, continued to reject a full public law model of violation. Instead, it reaffirmed the *Keyes* analysis as the central theory of violation. The Court maintained the *de facto-de jure* distinction, and thus in a sense has remained true to the private law model of violation insofar as it is based upon the proof of intended acts.

The Supreme Court decisions in the two Ohio cases approximately coincide with the end of the period covered by our interviews. These two cases also mark the end of the development of the legal theory. The Supreme Court cases decided since that time have broken no new legal ground. This is partly because the social movement organizations that produced this outcome have not been able to exploit the language in *Penick* and *Brinkman*.[48]

48. As noted in chapter 1, there have been recent opinions or litigation in Topeka, Kansas City, Norfolk, Yonkers, and San Jose. Among recent developments is an out-of-court agreement among parties in St. Louis calling for a metropolitan plan which moves children across district boundaries (See *Liddell v. Missouri*, 731 F.2d 1294 (8th Cir. 1984)). Various types of cross-district plans have been proceeding in several other cities, including Benton Harbor, Indianapolis, Little Rock, and Wilmington. An attempt to get an interdistrict remedy in Kansas City was rejected (*Jenkins v. State of Missouri*, 639 F. Supp. 19 (1985), *aff'd*, 807 F.2d 657 (8th Cir. 1986)).

Several school districts, including Mobile, Norfolk, Baton Rouge, Oklahoma City, and Houston, have moved to have their system declared "unitary," since they no longer operate a dual school system. If the district is declared unitary, the majority view is that the supervision of the federal district court is considerably lessened, and resegregation due to demographic patterns will not be remediable. See *Riddick v. School Bd. of Norfolk*, 784 F.2d 521 (4th Cir. 1986). But see *Dowell v. Bd. of Educ. of Oklahoma City*, 795 F.2d 1516 (10th Cir. 1986).

Equally important, the remedy in desegregation cases increasingly avoids mandatory transfers and instead calls for magnet schools and other noncompulsory transfer plans. This is the case in Chicago and Yonkers; *United States v. Bd. of Educ.*, 554 F. Supp. 912 (N.D. Ill. 1983); *United States v. Yonkers Bd. of Educ.*, 635 F. Supp. 1538 (S.D.N.Y. 1986); Kansas City; and, apparently, San Jose (see Gewirtz 1986, 771, n. 148). Whether such plans can achieve significant amounts of desegregation, and whether, over time, they will produce less segregation than mandatory plans, is an open question. For various perspectives on recent events, see Gewirtz (1986), Lively (1986), Rossell (1985), and Terez (1986/87).

This inability may be explained in part by the changing political climate. With the coming of the Reagan administration and the certain opposition of the Justice Department to large-scale desegregation efforts, the national plaintiffs are less willing to risk adverse precedents. Although courts are more immune from political pressure than most governmental organizations, probably the best predictor of legal outcome since the time of *Brown* is the position of the Justice Department. Equally important, however, is that the reach of the legal resource was near exhaustion. The plaintiffs won an important legal victory in Columbus and Dayton, but, as Wilkinson (1979, 132) notes, the legal theory which succeeded was defined by a degree of legalism not to be found in earlier cases. Unless the courts were willing to abandon a private law model entirely, the ability of school desegregation law to reach and remedy school segregation depended more and more on legal presumptions lacking in substantial empirical support.

Conclusion

This review of the development of legal theory and the use of social science evidence in school desegregation cases suggests several themes regarding the interaction between the law and the evidence in these cases. First, the social science evidence presented in school desegregation cases has varied considerably over the years. As the legal issues in school desegregation cases changed, the thrust of the testimony changed as well (Kalmuss, Chesler, and Sanders 1982). The social science issues important in the fifties were rarely raised in the sixties and seventies. Thus, the recent emphasis on demographic data is compatible with plaintiffs' efforts to move the courts toward a public law view of race relations. Data on school conditions produced by institutional arrangements (such as housing and the job market) provide a wider frame of reference within which scholars and litigants can examine how school systems operate.

Second, as the school law pushed toward a public law model, the role of social science grew. Before the *Green* case, social science played a very limited role in determining liability. After *Green* and *Swann* it grew to occupy a central position in the plaintiffs' cases. It became the primary weapon with which the NAACP fought for a public law view of school segregation. Plaintiff experts continued to pursue a structural view, finding the causes of segregation and inequality in the arrangement of public institutions. As moral certainty left the social movement, however, so did the unanimity which defined the early years of social science involvement in the school cases. The plaintiff groups were unable to maintain a monopoly on social science evidence. Defendants slowly gathered experts and data of their own with which to challenge the factual basis of the structural arguments. Their arguments focused on a more individual view of the causes of group inequality (e.g., group culture or family life style accounting for differences in children's academic achievement) and racial segregation (e.g., personal housing preferences of black and white citizens). Increasingly, they questioned whether the courts could successfully desegregate schools and whether desegregation would alter the school experiences of black or white children in significant ways.

Third, in several instances the same social science studies and findings were used by both plaintiff and defense parties to support their arguments. The double-edged effect occurs partly because there are no crucial experiments available in the social sciences to settle such controversies with a universally agreed-upon answer. Some have argued that this is all to the good, and that it is in the very nature of good social science research to raise more questions and explanatory possibilities than existed previously (Cohen and Weiss 1977; Weinberg 1970). When social science is mobilized for a political purpose, however, the lack of agreement is more than a polite academic one. The parties to the litigation actively recruit scholars who represent different positions. Despite the attempts of some scholars to keep themselves and their data above the battle, proponents of various positions sometimes fall into acrimonious debate. This suggests that part of the process of mobilizing social science for courtroom conflict involves tying individuals to positions. Ideas cannot be represented in the abstract. They must have an expert to present them. To become such an expert is to become part of the mobilization effort of the parties. It means entering a role which is uncomfortable for many academics. Therefore, the parties to the litigation who wish to use social science theories to advance their legal theories must deal with the microprocess of actively recruiting and then preparing expert witnesses.

4 Mobilizing Social Scientists as Expert Witnesses

It is a feature of the American trial system that evidence is almost always introduced by a witness. As a result, parties to litigation must find and mobilize individuals willing to testify about facts and ideas in court. Finding experts who could make the best presentation of available data was a constant task for both plaintiffs and defendants in the desegregation cases. Plaintiffs, especially the NAACP, quickly developed a social and intellectual network that located and solicited experts in different cities. Although defense groups were not as well organized in the early cases, they eventually began to gather a list of experts who would testify to their position. Attorneys on both sides devoted considerable effort to recruiting and preparing experts to testify in court, and experts in turn devoted considerable effort to preparing the lawyers.

The individual social scientist who is asked to testify in court in engaging in a type of applied social science, generally to use her social science expertise in a partisan cause. Such application creates numerous problems from the viewpoint of most social scientists. Thus, expert witnessing illustrates and raises important questions about the proper meaning and role of applied social science. This chapter discusses the problems which confront expert witnesses, and then examines the process by which lawyers recruit and prepare experts for trial.

Core Problems in Applied Social Science

Unlike commonsense wisdom, science claims to develop and possess knowledge that more nearly approaches nonpartisan "truth." In fact, social scientists' professional status rests on their ability to generate objective knowledge regarding matters about which many people already know something. They assert that the generation of such objective knowledge relies upon an established set of scientific methods, methods which help control personal and institutional biases and which enable them to stand apart from society's tradition and pressures. The twin ideals of *neutrality* and *autonomy* are encouraged and enforced by the structure of the social science community, and have become operating norms for the profession. They create certain patterns of training and socialization for young scholars; review, reward, promotion, and publication opportunities for older scholars; and preferred notions of appropriate role options and activities for all scholars. Despite their existence and power, there is ongoing debate about whether they are appropriate and feasible guides for all social scientific work. Although some scholars stress pure and formal adherence to these norms, most operate with a series of conscious compromises or trade-offs.

The first norm, neutrality, generally promotes the pursuit of scientific inquiry without concern for its impact on one's values or party loyalties. It is part of the larger commitment to objectivity, to the careful conduct of distortion-free inquiry. Neutrality is a deliberate attempt to avoid the impact of one's commitments to specific causes or parties on scholarly endeavors.

Criticism of the pure neutrality doctrine emphasizes that social scientists are human beings with social identities, beliefs, and values that link them to some causes and parties more than to others. Realistically, the most social scientists can do is to avoid as much partisanship as possible, to avoid overt and visible partisanship, and to avoid deliberate partisanship. In the context of this debate, the core question is, what is reasonable neutrality?

Autonomy promotes the separation of science from the rest of society and its noninvolvement in public policy and action. It has a reciprocal meaning, involving the freedom of science from the intrusion of external political, economic, and cultural forces as well (Frankel 1976; Merton 1938; Shils 1956). An autonomous stance should thus preserve scientists' control of the knowledge-generating process and its products, and not require them to respond to current societal priorities or values. It also supports scientists' ability to pursue basic problems rather than to be so involved as to respond journalistically to pressing events (Gouldner 1962).

There is substantial doubt about the feasibility of complete autonomy as a normative guide. Resources must be allocated to the scientific community on a continuing basis to make its work viable. Science depends upon, benefits from, and is interdependent with extrascientific institutions. Some of these financial allocations have overt or covert strings attached, and these shape what gets studied, even perhaps what is concluded or published from a study. In another vein, Rose (1956) and others have observed that knowledge is a social resource used by societal groups to justify or enhance their power vis-à-vis other groups. Therefore, social scientific inquiries frequently cannot be insulated from society; rather, they may become ammunition in partisan social conflicts. Although debates about exact adherence to these norms occur, they are generally endorsed by the scientific academy. Thus, scholars who argue their infeasibility or undesirability too strongly, or who depart from them too far in practice, are often labeled as deviant and may be sanctioned for their views and activities.

Within the broad area of activity called applied social science, conflict about these norms is even greater. Applied social science promises more involvement in the workings of society and in areas of work fraught with heated disputes among groups with competing interests. To this extent, it is seen, and sees itself, as less autonomous and neutral than "basic" or academic social science.[1]

Because they do not completely abandon core norms, applied scholars still carry these into their work, constantly wrestling with these established referents for proper scientific behavior, and often concerned about being sanctioned by the more traditional scientific community. Such sanctions may include: labeling applied work as illegitimate and unscientific; relegating such efforts to a service category which is seldom weighted heavily in hiring, promotion, or tenure decisions; rejecting such work from first-rate, mainstream social science journals; excluding or isolating applied scholars from the rewards and opportunities of their academic disciplines; and locating applied scholars in professional schools rather than in academic departments.

The opportunities and consequences of their distinctive form of scholarship can create potent problems for applied social scientists. Some of these problems are described below.

Political problems. Applied social science is often carried out in an arena

---

1. Competing terms, each with its own history of plural definitions, have been used to describe applied efforts. They include the following: action research (Lewin 1946), social problems research, sociological practice, policy research (Coleman 1972; Lerner and Laswell 1951), evaluation research (Struening and Guttentag 1975a, 1975b; Weiss 1972), and clinical sociology (Lee 1978; Wirth 1931). Extended discussions of the differences between academic and applied scholarship can be found in various sources, including Coleman (1972), Etzioni (1971), Gouldner (1957), Guskin and Chesler (1973), Merton (1938, 1957), Rein and White (1977), C. Weiss (1976), and J. Weiss (1976).

defined by conflict among groups, and these conflicts may shape the nature of scientific work. Moreover, the audience or users of applied work are often partisan individuals and groups with vested interests in the conflict (e.g., policymakers, practitioners, elite interest groups, challenging groups). How does one manage the demands from and loyalties to competing interest groups when doing applied work involving multiparty conflict? If the groups funding applied work have clear interests, are there conditions for the acceptance of their funds? When most of the scholarly reference group or public community appears to be on one side of a conflict, what are the implications of being on the "other side"? In this study, the problem of being on the "wrong side" is one which defense experts have had to confront repeatedly. We examine the ways in which they experience this problem and the efforts they make to deal with it.

Career problems. The job insecurity and low status created by nonsupport from the scientific mainstream may lead to dead-end or soft-money careers vulnerable to changing public needs and funds. Applied efforts may necessitate voluntary or involuntary movement to different institutional bases for one's work (e.g., from psychology and sociology departments to professional schools or applied research centers). How do applied scholars located in academic departments maintain legitimacy with their disciplinary colleagues? Is the situation different for scholars located in professional or applied schools or departments? In the context of this study, we examine how the experiences of scholars in the traditional disciplines and in professional schools differ.

Skill problems. Social science training generally focuses on acquiring substantive theory and research methods that enable one to work and communicate with academic colleagues. Applied work is often directed to nonacademic audiences and may require a scientific technology that responds to different priorities and criteria and to rapidly changing political conditions. Moreover, applied efforts often focus on the dissemination and use of knowledge, requiring scholars to do more than generate information and understanding. Because few training programs prepare scholars for the variety of efforts discussed here, how does one acquire the skills necessary for various kinds of applied research and action? How does one move beyond generating knowledge to using it or helping others to use it? Within the context of this study, we examine how one learns the attitudes and behaviors associated with becoming a good witness.

Role problems. The established norms of social scientific work require applied scholars to consider carefully their ways of interacting with people on issues in the public domain. How should a scholar act when she has both firmly held social values and scientific knowledge relevant to these values? If research subjects are also collaborators in some process, how does one relate with them as nonsubjects? Are the roles of scholar and citizen separable, and, if so, how are these separations maintained? How does one play out one's role as a teacher in the midst of heated controversy? Although this problem is most acute for our informants during the process of cross-examination, we examine its occurrence and resolution before, during, and after both direct and cross-examination.

Psychological problems. Applied social science is generally viewed as distinct from academic social science. As applied scholars depart from the established goals, norms, and methods of social science, they may have to work alone, probably marginal to the academic community and perhaps even facing scholarly disapproval. How does one deal with feelings of departing from the norms of one's profession and with the negative labeling associated with such practice? How does one create or find an alternative reference group to provide support for applied efforts? How does one cope with embarrassment or challenges to self-esteem? In our study we examine instances of deviance from traditional norms and how scholars adapted to the resultant pressures to conform.

The shape and intensity of these problems vary with the nature of each applied scientific effort and with its degree of departure from scientific norms. Researchers using established techniques to generate scientific knowledge in order to serve the "public good" are probably faced with less explicit and less intense problems than those using innovative methods and active roles to advance the partisan interests of a particular party in the public controversy.

Applied social scientists have played a wide variety of roles in school desegregation, ranging from conducting fairly basic research on educational and social processes through partisan consultation with key school officials or with protesting groups and organizations (Crain and Carsrud 1985). Different roles require different positions with regard to traditional norms of neutrality and autonomy, and encounter the various problems referred to above in different degrees. Programmatic innovations grounded in social science research and theory, and tested with standard research methods, do not depart significantly from established scientific norms.[2] Thus, these scholars are unlikely to have experienced psychological, career, or skill problems. In "enlightenment" activities (Street and Weinstein 1975) or "honest broker" roles (Pettigrew 1971) they may, nevertheless, encounter sanctions that produce psychological or career problems.[3]

However, when social scientists attempt to work with systems to adopt their innovations[4] or to evaluate programs,[5] they become directly involved in political processes and may experience considerable skill problems in dealing with issues of classroom and organizational change. Applied scientists who work with school officials in making educational policy depart more markedly from norms of autonomy and nonpartisanship. If, in addition, such consultation takes the form of aiding low-power groups, rather than official decisionmakers, there is an even greater probability of sanctioning. Psychological and career problems are likely to occur, and these tasks require new roles and skills that are not normally part of scholars' preparation and training.[6] Skill problems are increased when policymakers feel they are under time pressures, need answers, and are impatient with scholarly jargon and caution.

Problems in the Role of Expert Witness

When scholars undertake to apply their knowledge in court as expert witnesses, they face these problems in a unique form (Evans and Scott

2. For example, one type of innovative work involves developing ways of promoting positive interracial contact in the classroom. See Aronson et al. (1975, 1978); Berger and Zeldich (1985); Chesler, Crowfoot, and Bryant (1978); Cohen (1980); Cohen (1973); Cohen, Lockheed, and Loman (1976); Johnson and Johnson (1975); Schofield (1978); and Slavin (1977, 1978, 1983).

3. See, for example, discussions of the honest-broker role of master or monitor in desegregation cases in Dentler (1978) and Dentler and Scott (1981).

4. See Burges (1978); Chesler, Crowfoot, and Bryant (1978); Chesler, Jorgensen, and Erenberg (1970); Forehand and Ragosta (1976); Fulfilling the Letter and Spirit of the Law (USCCR 1976); and Noar (1966).

5. Crain (1973, 1974), Coulson (1976, 1977), and Forehand, Ragosta, and Rock (1976) conducted early large-scale efforts to assess the effects of desegregation. See Armor and Genova (1970) and Gerard and Miller (1975) for examples of studies of particular locales. Qualitative studies have been conducted by Metz (1978) and Rist (1976), among others. Much of the above work has been summarized in comprehensive reviews of the scientific literature on the effects of desegregation (Cohen 1975; Crain and Mahard 1978; Epps 1975; St. John 1975; Weinberg 1977).

6. In the present context, school desegregation plan writers must develop unique skills and deal with unique problems. Exemplary plan writers for plaintiff groups include Gordon Foster, Michael Stollee, and John Finger. Descriptions of the issues and options they may consider in their work can be found in Foster (1973), Hughes, Gordon, and Hillman (1980), and Tompkins (1976).

1983). In particular, the adversary nature and norms of the courtroom threaten experts' ability to maintain a neutral position and adhere to social science norms (Rist 1978; Schwartz 1978; Wolf 1976; Wolfgang 1974).[7] Traditionally, scholars are called by one of the parties to the litigation, which at least structurally identifies them as partisans. In addition, if they are paid for their testimony, it is by the side for whom they testify, creating additional pressures for loyalty and party advocacy. In view of these pressures, some scientists argue that scholars should not enter the courtroom and should not provide testimony in litigation. They often argue that social science evidence is "too soft" to begin with and not a reliable or certain basis for policy decisions. Moreover, in accordance with norms of neutrality, they argue that scientists who do testify should offer only a balanced presentation of facts, including data that might "hurt their side." Finally, they should reflect accurately the complexity of issues, neither reducing them to simplistic dichotomies between right and wrong nor omitting qualifications about the basis, generalization, and certainty of their statement. Simplistic testimony is seen not only as a poor basis for policymaking, but as damaging the image of credibility and neutrality so necessary for the preservation of scientific institutions and for the quality of science itself.

Several scholars have argued that the adversary features of the courtroom create a further structural bias in the selection of expert witnesses (Orfield 1978b; Wolf 1976). Knowledge of adversary pressures may inhibit participation by scholars concerned with objectivity and scientific caution, and encourage participation by more partisan scholars or by those willing to compromise their scientific ideals for the fees or fame associated with the role of expert. Furthermore, in their search for experts, attorneys may not necessarily seek the most competent scholars. Rather, they may seek "predictable witnesses . . . [and a] narrow range of witnesses, strongly identified with particular policy positions" (Orfield 1978b, 171; see also Kelly 1965; Schur 1968). Selectivity on the part of the lawyers who choose the experts, and of the scholars who accept the role, stems from and in turn reinforces the adversary context of the courtroom.

Scholars who participate in litigation may experience political problems as they violate the norms of autonomy and neutrality. Historically,

7. It is important to note that this problem is generic and not limited to experts in school desegregation cases. The problems which the adversary nature of the courtroom pose for the expert have been noted by experts testifying in cases concerning criminal insanity, Indian rights, eyewitness identification, and women's rights, to name but a few examples with which we are familiar.

school desegregation policies tended to be supported by the social science community, which upheld the liberal goals of civil rights, equal opportunity, and racial integration. As a result, scholars who testified for defendant school boards opposing desegregation were often perceived by colleagues as being on the "wrong side" politically. Orfield (1987) points out that this historical trend may have changed in the past few years, and that many social scientists now resist or oppose massive school desegregation efforts. As such, they are prepared to sanction scholars who continue to press for more rapid or extensive desegregation. In either case, when such political problems are accompanied by disapproval and sanctioning, they may result in career problems for some of these scholars. In addition, when social scientists feel that their research compels them to testify against parties with whom they were previously aligned ideologically (e.g., the NAACP, the American Civil Liberties Union, or the Mexican-American Legal Defense Education Fund), they may experience psychological and role problems as well.

The adversary nature of the courtroom also creates psychological problems when it challenges experts' ability to adhere to scientific principles of neutral and balanced presentation. When lawyers encourage experts to omit scientifically relevant complexities, qualifications, and opposing evidence, the incompatibilities between social science and legal-adversary norms may create psychological confusion or role conflict (Pettigrew 1979; Schur 1968; Wolfgang 1974). These problems are intensified under the open and direct attack of cross-examination, a type of challenge to which academics are unaccustomed. Finally, skill and role problems are encountered when attorneys use *ad hominem* attacks and confrontational procedures which are unfamiliar and perhaps uncomfortable for scholars accustomed to social science norms. The heated nature of the desegregation controversy make it even more difficult for scientists to avoid "choosing sides." Whatever personal values scientists have, the pressure of an organized and highly public civil rights movement pushes them toward publicly stating their values in their applied roles, if not in their research itself.

Recruitment of Experts

If the parties to a lawsuit wish to use social science as a resource, they must recruit and prepare social scientists to be expert witnesses. From the beginning of school desegregation litigation, the parties to litigation experienced difficulties in this central mobilization task. Before turning to the young, relatively unknown Kenneth Clark in the South Carolina case, NAACP attorney Robert Carter approached a number of leading social scientists. Several prominent individuals expressed general sympathy with the NAACP position, but, for various reasons, refused to testify. William H. Kilpatrick, a native of Georgia, and the successor to John Dewey at Columbia Teacher's College, refused because he believed that abolition of the dual school system was premature. Elsa E. Robinson, a psychologist at NYU, refused because she had concluded, after reviewing the experimental evidence on the effect of segregation, "that there is as yet no scientifically verified material of an empirical nature which bears directly on the issue" (Kluger 1975, 336). Gordon Allport, Harvard psychologist and past president of the American Psychological Association, perhaps the person most associated with the "contact hypothesis" concerning the effect of racial separation and racial interaction on prejudice, refused because he felt that he "would not be the type of effective witness" that the NAACP needed (Kluger 1975, 336). Otto Klineberg, who had originally led Carter to Clark, first promised to testify, but withdrew two weeks before trial, pleading a heavy workload at Columbia.

These responses reflect various reasons scientific experts still give for refusing to testify: disagreement with the party's objective, a belief that they do not have the right temperament for testifying, the idea that testifying is incompatible with their scientific role, and a general fear of the unknown of the witness stand. They also represent, respectively, the political, skill, role-based, and psychological problems of applied social science. The only problem that the scholars who were originally invited did not face was the one related to career concerns, perhaps because they were already very senior academicians and at the top of their professions when they were invited to appear.

Some of these reasons also highlight a paradox concerning the recruitment of expert witnesses: the paradox of scientific prestige. The advantage of having leading experts in a field provide testimony is obvious. Their prominence, and the prominence of their institutions, makes it more likely that their testimony will be influential. Thus, other things being equal, testimony from a prestigious expert is a more valuable resource. However, the very factors that make such witnesses desirable—earlier basic research on a problem, full professorships at prominent institutions, leadership roles in their discipline—are factors that are likely to increase their reluctance to set aside the ideals of autonomy and neutrality, and to make them experience some of the problems normally associated with testifying.

The ability of plaintiff groups to link up with a network of elite social scientists remained a key to their effective mobilization of this resource. Plaintiffs' advantage over defense attorneys in this regard stemmed in part from their superior organization and experience. Precisely because they usually were a part of a social movement organization, plaintiff lawyers were able to make use of the NAACP's nationwide contacts as well as of national and local representatives who could do the legwork. Moreover, 75% of the plaintiff attorneys we interviewed had prior experience in school desegregation litigation, compared to less than 20% of the defense lawyers. Galanter (1974) distinguishes between parties to litigation who are "repeat players" and parties who are "one shot" players, arguing that repeat players have a number of advantages in litigation. Some of these advantages we have already seen, such as the ability to play for rules over a series of cases. Another advantage Galanter mentions is ready access to specialists and expertise (98), sometimes through other lawyers who have access to experts. Over time, a trust relationship may develop between lawyers and experts, making it easier to recruit experts for the next trial. Two plaintiff lawyers described the situation as follows:

> We've used a number of social scientists. Every case, every school case in which we're involved, we'll use social scientists because we really can't conceive of a school desegregation case that is one-dimensional. And therefore, we have developed over time a knowledge of the field. We know who is active, we know who is doing what, we know those who have written analytical work, who have conducted surveys and studies. We know who the people are.

> There's a real good network of social scientists set up for plaintiffs. These are people who have consistently been there. If they can't do it, they know a lot of others.

Thus, new cases did not necessarily require a whole new set of recruits, learning, and trust relationships. With a semiorganized group of experts available and willing to testify, the plaintiff lawyer did not always have to repeat the difficult tasks of finding the social scientist, determining what she had to offer, and then preparing her for the stand.

Defense attorneys suffered under the additional handicap of being relatively inexperienced in this area of law. Typically, the school board was represented by a major law firm in the defendant city, a firm chosen because it had represented the school system in the past. This past work typically involved such matters as managing labor relations, acquiring property, drawing up contracts, organizing pension funds, helping the board draft legislation, and the like. Rarely did it involve federal court trial work, and rarely did it deal with civil rights issues.

In the absence of any formal social movement organization for defendants, most defense attorneys had to do their own nationwide legwork. Some eventually constructed an informal network of attorneys who had been involved in desegregation litigation, and through this network they were able to contact experts who had worked for defendants in previous cases. According to one defense attorney:

> We had a network of attorneys from about all the big school systems in the U.S.A., and not only the 7 northern ones. Everyone was looking for consolation, so we consoled each other. At this late date I can't tell you precisely what prompted us to go to a particular individual or source for a particular kind of evidence or testimony, but you almost have a network of communication which reminds me of the Revolutionary War. We were on the case that was on the hot seat, or the prime candidate, or the first guinea pig. And as a result, we were somewhat the focal point of that organization. We had experts from Detroit, Cleveland, you name it, we had them. As a result we had quite a cross-pollination of thoughts about what should be proved, how it could be proved, who the prominent people were and things like that. It was very effective.

Although slowly growing in sophistication, this network was not as successful nor in place as early as the plaintiff network, and a relatively small percentage of the defense attorneys we interviewed were connected to it.

The defense lawyers we interviewed said that they had encountered bias within the academic community which they believed resulted in high costs to any academically-based expert willing to testify for a school board.[8] They mentioned occasions where experts, both prominent and less well known, refused to testify because of feared effects on collegial associations or job prospects. Social scientists' reports of such pressures indicate that they experienced both political and career problems. Their reactions are presented in detail in chapter 8.

The potentially chilling effect of such problems and perceived pressures were outlined as follows by two defense attorneys:

> [Expert X] was one of the few people who would be willing to talk to us even though we were on the "wrong side." It's not fashionable to be defending these lawsuits. It's fashionable to be on the other

---

8. Kluger (1975, 344) reports some of the early difficulty confronting defense counsel in the *Brown* cases in this regard. The first and best choice for the defendants in the South Carolina case was Howard Odum, sociologist from the University of North Carolina. Among the reasons for his refusal was his concern that testifying on the segregationist side would reflect badly on the university.

side. After talking to one or two of the local sociologists, we did not find somebody who would go along with us. We would find people who, because of peer pressure, did not want to testify for the defendant regardless of what the facts were or anything else. . . . We were told, off the record, that if they did work for our side they were categorized as defense witnesses. Their access to grants, promotions, to new relationships in their professions, would be greatly jeopardized. If a man is doing a study showing how blacks are being mistreated, that's great. The Ford Foundation will give money, the government will give money, so forth and so on. If they are doing a study, not quite as bad as Dr. Shockley, but a study showing that blacks deserve what they get, no money will be forthcoming. I thought it was fear on their part.

We weren't going to get any sociologists that were going to agree with us. Although we looked around and tried some folks, we were not successful.

This perception of defense expert unavailability was shared by some of the plaintiff lawyers as well.

I'd have to say there is a little bias in the field. If you testify on behalf of plaintiffs then you aren't as nasty a person as somebody who testifies on behalf of the school boards. . . . I certainly picked that up just talking to experts at various universities. There's a certain distaste about people who will help a school board out. I'm sure it goes back to this whole claim that there are constitutional rights and these are discriminators you are helping. [Expert Y] is a guy that loves minorities. That makes you very unpopular in some circles, but in a court of law there is nothing dishonorable about someone who's trying to help the downtrodden. That works to our advantage, there's no question about it.

These problems confronting the defense further explain the striking difference in plaintiffs' and defendants' recruitment and use of academically-based expert testimony. Table 4.1 aggregates the data in tables 3.1 and 3.2 to show the total difference between plaintiffs and defendants.

Table 4.1 Plaintiff and Defendant Use of Academic Experts at Violation in Seventeen Cases

Use of Experts	Plaintiff	Defendant
Number of Experts	14	5
Number of Person-Appearances by Experts	33	7
Number of Cases in Which Experts Appeared	11	3

Until relatively late in the history of the school desegregation cases (1975 and after), the defendants found it much harder to recruit the social science resource than did the plaintiffs.

Preparation of Experts

Once an expert is found who is willing to testify, or at least to discuss the possibility of testifying, there remains the task of preparing the expert for court appearance. We might profitably think of this as the micromobilization of social science. The courtroom is foreign territory to many social scientists and there is much to learn about this new and different setting. However, experts were not naive pawns, to be manipulated or used by lawyers. From the beginning of their relationship most lawyers and experts are involved in a set of mutual exchanges through which they influence one another. Our informants identified three different kinds of preparation: psychological, factual, and strategic.

Psychological preparation. Court proceedings can be intimidating. Witnessing is a type of "fateful action" (Goffman 1967). There is something important at stake which one can fail to do well by becoming flustered, nervous, or inarticulate. Psychological preparation of the expert attempts to minimize the chance of such responses and to reduce some of the psychological, role, and even skill problems noted earlier. In such preparation, lawyers explain to potential witnesses the rules and procedures of the courtroom, and most important, forewarn them of the rough and tumble of cross-examination. As one attorney noted,

> It's a matter of preparing them for what the process is, and then giving them techniques that assure their survival, and survival as a whole person, within that context.

An expert noted in turn:

> Especially in the beginning, [my lawyer] would try to explain the rules of evidence and my freedoms and lack of freedoms when I'm on the stand. In effect, he would train me in the process of being a witness, which I needed in the beginning.

In particular, scientists and their attorneys agreed that scientists needed to understand the nature of the adversary process in the courtroom.[9] One attorney's comments about such preparation include the following:

9. In chapter 6 we indicate the choices scholars exercised about how they played out

We would first educate him/her on how the adversarial process worked. What I generally try to explain to people in that field of expertise is that they need to understand that the legal process of searching for truth and the academic process of searching for truth are entirely distinct and different. The legal process is adversarial and the academic process is cooperative. It's really not their job to find ultimate truth or to attain it sitting in the witness stand; their job essentially is to play a role in a play.

One cannot play a role effectively unless the entire play is understood.

In addition to general explanations of courtroom processes, attorneys' preparation of experts often included more specific advice about how to prepare oneself psychologically to function as a witness. One scholar, speaking about the necessity of an expert to remain in control, remembered his attorney telling him,

> Of course you've never testified before and you do have to understand something about the adversarial situation. . . . The one thing you have to realize is that in the adversarial situation you cannot give a simple yes or no answer.

However, different attorneys may give different advice:

> I tell people to try to give testimony that is as direct and as responsive as possible—yes and no answers are best, but not to the point of absurdity. On the other side of that point is to be aware of the question that is so deliberately vague or deliberately ambiguous that it promotes information that may lead to argumentation they don't want. I try to encourage short answers.

Another specific aspect of the psychological advice that scholars were given focused on their ability to control themselves:

> The most important advice I give people is to remember that your sense of time as a witness is distorted. The period of time in which you're not saying anything seems like an eternity, but it really isn't. You can stop and not say anything. That kind of timing or maintenance of the timing of the response is extremely important in surviving strong cross-examination. . . . Whatever the question, no matter how innocuous it is, think of your answer in your mind before you say it and count to three.

---

their roles in the adversary setting of the courtroom. Almost all scientists agreed that they needed to understand how the adversary process worked in order to make effective choices, and perhaps to reduce the conflicts and tensions associated with testimony.

It is not always easy for the expert to adhere to these suggestions. One scientist discussed his frustration, and the need to establish control over his propensity to "lose his cool," in the following terms:

> The next time I am under cross I am going to write up a card and I am going to put it in front of me where I can see it and it is going to say on it—"Stop!" And any time that I get a question that upsets me I'm going to stop, and I am going to sit, and I am going to wait until I have figured out what I am going to do, and then I am going to answer. I am not going to be rushed and I am going to try to keep my cool. Somebody else could write "Be cool." I am going to have to write "Stop" because "Be cool" is not strong enough.

Some attorneys agreed that even the best preparation does not guarantee a smooth performance. Ongoing assistance designed to reinforce these preparatory messages was contemplated by several attorneys.

> It helps if the lawyer who had put you on knows how to protect you from attack that is not a proper attack. Well, if your witness is being badgered with lots of quick questions, not being allowed to finish, the guy is stepping on his lines and so forth, and then restating testimony, not quite the way he said it. . . . If the guy is not an experienced witness, an experienced trial lawyer who has put him on the stand is going to stand up and object, make the attorney ask the question, let the witness finish the answer. You say, "I believe that statement mis-characterized the previous testimony." You alert the witness to the games the lawyers play. To some extent you should have done that in advance but like any public presentation there is a certain amount of nervousness that takes place and you have got to figure that anyone is going to drop 30% of their preparation, it is just going to go, they can't even remember where it was. It is your job to go pick it back up and remind them of it and you can't do that only by waiting until you get to re-examine.

> The best technique that I know [to protect your witness] is to warn your witness. I guess it is not the most honorable technique, but to stand up and make an objection and say something in that objection that tips him off as to what is going on or where he ought to look out for it.

In addition to the provision of advice, and promises of future support, the psychological preparation of witnesses proceeded according to other techniques. Some attorneys established role-plays or walked through the actual testifying scenario with their experts.

What we would do is, we would role play, we would dry-run a case if we had time. The night before I testified, the lawyer would take me through the kinds of questions he was going to ask.

Well, I think it was simply a conference session where we would go through this direct testimony and play the devil's advocate type of thing and ask him very tough questions that we expected that they would ask on the other side. This is a fairly common way of doing that. We did that with each other in preparation for oral argument primarily before the appellate courts, because judges are known to ask some pretty searching and direct questions. In order to be prepared for those you have just about got to think about them in advance. Sometimes there wouldn't be an answer, but sometimes they would at least be prepared for the question and say I don't know, which is the best answer you can give if you don't know.

For the preparation for cross-examination we helped them antici-pate all likes of possible cross-examination questions and tactics. We ran through it with them.

Some attorneys gave their prospective witnesses transcripts of other witnesses' depositions or copies of court testimony. Others requested that scholars sit in the courtroom to hear other experts testify, learning from firsthand observations. In addition, some scientists reported that they had talked to their colleagues who had testified, and had asked them what it was like in the courtroom. Various forms of psychological preparation represented more or less conscious efforts to help scientists anticipate and respond to the psychological and role problems accom-panying applied efforts. They also dealt explicitly with some of the skill problems of scientists who needed to practice being in the unfamiliar role of expert witness.

Substantive factual preparation. Substantive preparation is the heart of the attorney-expert interaction. At the outset, attorneys and experts must come to some minimal agreement on the subject matter to be covered. The intended factual basis of testimony, as well as experts' credentials, are reflected in the following partial witness list filed by the defense in the Cleveland litigation:[10]

---

10. From "Tentative witness list of defendants, *Briggs v. Board of Education*" (filed 11/24/

Dr. Nathan Kantrowitz, Professor, Kent State University, Kent, Ohio. He will testify, as an expert, as to ethnic and racial segregation in Cleveland and its causes and its relation to school segregation.

Dr. Nathan Glazer, Professor, Harvard University, Cambridge, Massachusetts. He will testify, as an expert sociologist and educator, on the adverse effects of the forced quota allocation of students, by race, with regard to academic achievement, self-esteem, aspirations and racial polarity.

Dr. Margaret Fleming, Director, Research and Development, Cleveland Public Schools, She will testify as to the Cleveland Schools' testing procedures, the various efforts to eliminate the adverse effects of racial isolation made by faculty, Board and staff, the compensatory education program, the correlation between poverty and achievement, the comparability reports, the evaluations of the disadvantaged pupil program funds, the various evaluation abstracts under Title I of the Elementary and Secondary Education Act of 1965, the educational and sociological effects of forced quota allocations of students, the impossibility of using 1970 Census data to project school population, mobility data, and various other research findings and reports bearing on the absence of segregative intent in specific Board and staff conduct. Dr. Fleming will also testify as an expert sociologist and educator on the adverse effects of the forced quota allocation of students by race with regard to academic achievement, self esteem, aspirations and racial polarity.

And for the plaintiffs in the same case:

Robert Green, Ph.D., Dean of College of Urban Studies, Michigan State University, East Lansing, Michigan. Educational psychologist. To testify on community perceptions toward segregated schools.[11]

William Lamson, Demographer, NAACP. To introduce plaintiff's exhibits 75 through 98, map of school boundaries of the Cleveland Public Schools, 1940, 1945, 1950, 1955, 1960, 1965, 1970 and 1974.

---

75), and "Plaintiffs' reserved list of witnesses" (filed 11/20/75), United States District Court for the Northern District of Ohio (Eastern Division).

11. It is worth noting that by the time of the Cleveland trial in 1975–1976, Professor Green, while part of the team of plaintiff experts used by the NAACP, was no longer directing his testimony toward the academic and psychological effects of segregation and desegregation on students. He, too, had become part of the effort to relate school segregation to other types of community demographics and racial isolation.

Gordon Foster, Ph.D., Professor of Education, Director, Title IV Desegregation Center, University of Miami (Florida). To testify on the effects of policies and practices utilized by the Cleveland Board of Education.[12]

Willard Richan, DSW, Dean, Department of Social Administration, Temple University, Philadelphia, Pennsylvania. Principal Investigator of a study sponsored by the United States Civil Rights Commission which culminated in report: Racial Isolation in the Cleveland Public Schools, published by Case Western Reserve University, 1967. To testify on findings of his study of the Cleveland Public Schools made pursuant to the above report.

Martin Sloane, Esq., Former staff member, United States Civil Rights Commission. Presently General Counsel, National Committee Against Discrimination in Housing, Washington, D.C. To testify on the effects of national and local housing practices and policies.

Karl Taeuber, Ph.D., Professor, Institute for Research on Poverty, University of Wisconsin, Madison, Wisconsin. To testify on pattern of residential and school race segregation throughout the country and in Cleveland, and the causal factors which contribute to both, and their dynamic interaction over time.

Constructing this list is in part the result of lawyer-expert interaction about the substance of the case and the presentation of relevant credentials.

Both lawyers and experts bring certain resources to the case. Sharing and integrating this knowledge is a cooperative task. Lawyers bring knowledge of the legal issues involved and of the local community and school system. Local knowledge is especially critical for the expert who

---

12. Dr. Foster was primarily a plan writer. Earlier in his career he worked for the Office of Education in the Department of Health, Education and Welfare. There he helped hammer out the first set of Office of Education standards designed to bring some uniformity to southern desegregation and to eliminate the tactics (e.g., freedom of choice) used by southern districts to block desegregation for the first fourteen years following Brown (Radin 1977, 104 ff.). He became, perhaps, the premier plan writer of the desegregation era, and in this capacity was frequently used by the NAACP at the remedy stage of trial. Here, however, he and William Lamson helped to build the case on its merits. Foster's task was to help show the segregative effect of school board policies and practices concerning things like school siting and drawing of attendance zones, and to show that the alternatives would have been less segregative. His was the key task of helping to prove de jure segregation by arguing that their cumulative segregative effect would allow one reasonably to infer that the decisions were taken with knowledge of their segregative effect, and, by implication, with a desire to segregate.

must use raw information to draw up plans, calculate rates of white withdrawal, or analyze local residential patterns. Unless the expert has some local knowledge, opposing counsel is likely to attack her as an outsider with nothing to contribute to the specific case. Attorneys are likely to encourage the expert to make as many visits to the jurisdiction as possible, and to ride around looking at the physical plant. Regarding this aspect of expert preparation, two attorneys noted:

> Make sure the expert is just as familiar as he can possibly be with the school district, because that is one thing that school board people often dwell on, this person is an outsider, right? So he has to be familiar as possible with the school district. The court will take an opportunity to disallow an expert's testimony on that basis.

> For our preparation we wanted them [the experts] to know as much as possible about the physical facts of the case, i.e., the number of classrooms, the proximity of schools, the availability of transportation, etc.

The experts also bring resources which the lawyer must master. First, of course, experts bring the general methods and substantive knowledge of their discipline. This includes a general knowledge of research results in the field and statistical and other procedures for aggregating and analyzing data. The second kind of information some experts bring is the results of specific research they have conducted: for example, a study on achievement effects in some desegregated setting, perhaps even in the local school district. The lawyers must achieve a minimal mastery over these technical materials if the examination is to be successful. Moreover, the attorney must be able to relate these findings to the legal theory he is advancing in the case.

After choosing his own experts and discovering which experts may appear for other parties, many attorneys read what those experts have written on the topic of their testimony. Sometimes they read almost everything on the subject. When an expert has testified in previous cases, the attorneys must prepare themselves for trial by examining the transcripts of those cases.

> We would make sure we understand our experts' exhibits and the general principles behind their research.

> Many of us attorneys read all the material we thought was necessary background. We read the Coleman Report which is awful, it is like Marx's *Das Kapital*, it is deadly reading. But we read it . . .

as we thought it was important. We also read Moynihan's book on education that came out about that time. Some of us lawyers, myself chiefly, probably read a lot of background sociological material.

In preparing for cross-examination of experts on the other side, you take their deposition, which we did for each and every one of them. Then we got their vita, we got the list of each and every publication that they had, and we got their views. And we got them to specify what their views were on certain points. We got them to formulate an opinion on everything, everything that could possibly come up during the trial, so that if they changed one word of it we would hit them over the head with that page of the deposition.

For all but the most experienced attorneys, an unassisted reading of this type of material has its limits. For instance, one of our respondents defined a trial attorney's knowledge of the subject matter of his suit as a mile wide and an inch deep. Because a deeper understanding requires assistance, an attorney's own expert can be helpful in expanding this understanding. As one expert pointed out:

Your role is to teach him social science in one day. In each case my time is spent 100% trying to teach them. Because I do quantitative research, basically I try to teach them statistics.

And as two lawyers remarked:

I grew in terms of my own thinking about the problem. The more I talked, I just kept learning and learning and crystallizing what I thought more and more and more. It really helped me, not only in his preparation, but it helped me tremendously in the cross-examination of the other guy.

The truth of the matter is that they [the experts] prepared us [the attorneys]. Just by telling us what their positions were, in terms of educational theories that should be brought out. An expert witness, really because of his or her expertise, is not one that you would prepare like you would prepare any other witness. With these experts, you just really ask them hypotheticals, and also ask them to assume certain things. You ask, do you have an opinion as to that impact of this situation on the issue? And they just talk.

Not all of this preparation happened prior to the trial. In several instances, attorneys' preparation for cross-examination of opposing experts was facilitated by having experts sit with them at counsel table.

These scholars assisted attorneys by noting possible questions as the testimony developed. Said one scholar:

> I am used in another way during the trial. When the attorney I am working with is about to cross-examine a very important witness for the school board, for example, he will have me sitting next to or near him to coach him and I will be writing questions. I can ask questions or write a question to really throw a witness in panic. For example, suppose a witness is reporting on the use of a particular kind of standardized test. I'll write him a note, to tell him to ask what were the reliability estimates or coefficients for that test at the time the test was administered? Did the sample include blacks and females? If I write that question out and hand it to him and he raises that question to the witness they often go into a state of panic.

One should not conclude that the substantive preparation between attorney and expert proceeds with total cooperation and agreement. The two have a common interest, but they also have sources of potential conflict. The expert may often be unwilling to say what the attorney would like him to say, and the attorney may refuse to pursue a line of evidence that the scientist feels strongly about. The actors must find a mutually acceptable ground, however, and the difficulty of this process depends upon the nature of the testimony wanted by the lawyer and the degree of caution exhibited by the expert.

This process of exploration or negotiation may take several forms. In one form, the attorney asks the witness to carefully think through his testimony, to make sure he has accounted for all possible arguments and has gathered all the relevant theory and/or data before trial. As one lawyer described the process, it was a detailed exploration of the factual evidence and arguments that the expert could provide.

> I would ask a question and say, OK what do you think, and most of this was by phone. He would give his answer and then I'd say but how would you explain X? And he might say, well I hadn't thought about that, let me think about it. And then he would think about what body of knowledge he had at hand to address that question. I will not tell them what to say. I just want to know what they're going to say to that question.[13]

---

13. This particular discussion, or series of discussions, was done over the telephone. Depending upon travel costs and degree of prior acquaintance, this was not an unusual medium for preparation.

A second form of this process involved a greater degree of negotiation concerning which issues experts would or would not cover in testimony. The ideal outcome of negotiation is a body of testimony which supports a set of legal arguments and which in turn is supported by existing social science knowledge. Two experts described the negotiations with their lawyers as follows:

> Yes, we negotiate. The lawyers say, "Here are the points we would like to make. We are looking for an expert witness who would agree to this kind of testimony." I say, "Well, I can go this way but I can't go that way." It is very honest and straightforward. The lawyers understand about roles pretty well. They don't have any problems with my saying I can do this but I can't do that.

> It turns out to be a negotiation process. . . . I used the phrase as an alternative to consensus. It is a push and pull—a real negotiation process, and that's one of the reasons why the briefing preparation is terribly important. Occasionally you have to tell the legal counsel, "No way will I give that kind of response to that question," or "I'm not your witness on that point and you have to get some other witness if you want that point made." You place limitations on what you're willing to say or are able to say authoritatively. There are two kinds of limitations I make. First, it might be that you're being asked to say something which you honestly don't believe and as a professional person you aren't at liberty to do so. In other instances I honestly feel that my expertise does not cover that particular point of learning and I can recommend some other persons sometimes. Often I'm asked to testify to demographic data and I think that demographers are much better qualified to do that than myself and I'll tell that to the lawyers.

Attorneys experienced the process of negotiation in a like manner:

> One has to call the expert on the phone and discuss the desired testimony, what we are trying to prove, and ask him or her whether she would be able to testify to that conclusion. The conversation goes on to see in what way she would be able to verify and validate it, what exhibits would be useful to graphically illustrate that conclusion, etc.

> When I talked to him I asked several questions. What is this and what is that and what is this and what is that? What do you think about that? Is this a valid approach and is that a valid approach? I

just asked him questions. And the answers that were favorable, we then worked into his deposition to some extent, and to some extent we fished around in his deposition. And he was very willing to talk about methodology, and very honest. And if anyone asked him to completely repeat everything I ever said to him, and he ever said to me, no one would be embarrassed professionally or in any other way. That is a much different process than hiring someone and sitting down and saying, well, if we use this approach we will get the number to sixteen; how about if we use that approach, will it be seventeen or will it then be fifteen? Well, we won't use that approach. How about his approach? This is a different process. You work together as a team to advocate a point of view. And I'm sure that some of the experts sat down with some of the lawyers and said, "No, you better not get into that one, you better not look at it that way." Or, "If you get into this one you are going to get into that trap."

In general, scientists want to tell the truth as they see it, and attorneys want their experts to tell the truth as they perceive it. In many cases, both sides may understand that the expert has abandoned the role of the purely neutral social scientist, but this does not mean that either the expert or the attorney expects the expert to abandon truthfulness or professional integrity. Negotiations help both parties understand the bounds of acceptable testimony in this complex situation.

Experts and lawyers must also negotiate what to do about information which does not support or benefit their position. Several lawyers seemed to let a preponderance of evidence decide whether to include some social science finding. If it helped their position more than harming it, they included the testimony. But if negative evidence exists, it may be important to bring it out before opposing experts and attorneys do so. For example, in *Briggs v. Elliot* the defendants admitted that the state of South Carolina did not operate an equal school system for black and white students (Kluger 1975, 347–348). This admission substantially neutralized a whole series of experts that Thurgood Marshall was prepared to examine on inequality in Claredon County schools. One expert we interviewed emphasized this point:

You want to know the knowledge in the field for you and against you, because you want to know how to argue something that you have to concede.

Several attorneys addressed this issue even more explicitly, stressing the preparation required to know what they had to admit to as a weakness ahead of time.

> If there is anything that is vulnerable, you don't want to wait until cross-examination. You want to take the wind out of the defendant's sails by asking about it yourself.

> You want to cover what they testified to in other cases. You always want to be careful if they testified to something that might be harmful, in another case, that would be harmful if it were brought up in your case. You want to know about that. There is a lot of work involved in all that.

A correlate to this "rule of admission" is that a point may be particularly powerful if made during cross-examination rather than during direct examination. A skilled witness's ability to do this successfully depends in part upon good legal and scientific preparation. It also required good psychological preparation, so that he can keep his head during cross-examination, refusing to let opposing counsel alone set the agenda for what is to be discussed. Decisions such as what harmful facts to raise during one's own direct examination and whether to try to score "bonus points" during cross-examination move beyond substantive preparation to the tactics of presenting evidence. Although most experts were limited to psychological and factual preparation, a few did move on to a more interactive involvement in the case. By examining the type of social science data that was available and feasible, they helped formulate the legal strategy of the case.

Strategic preparation. Lawyers usually develop the theory of a case, or the set of arguments to be presented to the court, without the assistance of social science experts. However, on certain occasions experts have played an important role in developing legal strategy. Kenneth Clark clearly played such a role in helping prepare the Supreme Court brief in *Brown*. More recently, Pettigrew (1979) has commented that

> The legal and social science intellectual maps are sharply different. . . . This makes "the fit" between them vital but difficult. Often the same legal point can be. drafted in any one of several ways, all of them equally meaningful in legal terms, but only one of which shows directly relevant social scientific evidence. Likewise, the same social scientific conclusion can have diverse legal implications depending on its phrasing and content. Early involvement of the expert witness, then, allows this "fit" between the two fields to be made in the underlying fabric of the brief's argument. (6)

Several of the scholars we interviewed had been involved in such strategic preparations. As one stated,

There are a number of issues in school desegregation cases that lawyers don't see that a good expert ought to see. If an expert is worth his or her salt in any kind of litigation, they ought to be able to point out areas that lawyers can cast in legal terms and I think that is where my help has been and the help of a good expert ought to be.

It is at this level of preparation that social scientists are most likely to identify with the social movement objective of desegregation litigation. They are no longer merely dealing with the problems of testifying in court, but are working as committed advocates, helping to craft a "winning" way to use social science evidence as part of legal strategy.

Two groups of witnesses are most likely to be used in the strategic preparation of a case: local experts and inner-circle experts. Local experts may be included early because of their accessibility and their knowledge of particulars in the local community. One expert involved in this stage of preparation commented as follows:

I was involved in over-seeing, advising and consulting on what kinds of data to get, how to put the data together. We had lots of sessions on what kinds of legal issues did they want to make and then we looked at what kinds of data are available.

A second group of experts likely to participate in developing or refining the legal approach is the movement's inner circle. The inner circle is composed of experts and lawyers who have worked together on many school cases. They are repeat players who are familiar with the issues and committed to their party's cause. Some of these scientists have not only appeared in court, but have prepared *amicus* briefs that have been presented to appellate courts. These are the people who, in 1978, put together the social science brief in *Penick* concerning the substantial "incremental segregative effect" of past school board actions. Key scholars also tried to advance the state of knowledge in this arena in other ways. For instance, in a special issue of the *Annals of the American Academy of Political and Social Science* (Roof 1979), seven of the thirteen articles on "Race and Residence" were at least partly authored by scholars who had been expert witnesses in these cases.[14] Moreover, requests were

14. See the following articles: D. Garth Taylor, "Housing, Neighborhoods, and Race Relations: Recent Survey Evidence" (27–40); Nathan Kantrowitz, "Racial and Ethnic Residential Segregation: Boston, 1930–1970" (41–54); Reynolds Farley, Susanne Bianchi, and Dianne Colasanto, "Barriers to the Racial Integration of Neighborhoods: The Detroit Case" (97–113); Thomas Pettigrew, "Racial Change and Social Policy" (114–131); Franklin

made to federal agencies for research funds to investigate this matter empirically, essentially to test or demonstrate the empirical validity of the "reciprocal effects" phenomenon (see Pearce, Crain, and Farley n.d.). The legal needs of the social movement often led to attempts to mobilize additional social science resources to meet those needs.

In the late 1970s defense attorneys in several cases began to rely upon an inner circle of their own. They report a similar preparation process, including some assistance with expert data collection. Said one attorney,

> We sought their answers good or bad, favorable or unfavorable, to our case that would provide solutions to these puzzles that we were presented with. And they didn't have any immediate answers. But they were interested in the field and they were interested in doing further research. Of course, we had to pay them for their time, and I think that we enabled them to do research that they might not otherwise have gotten around to doing without a grant or some kind of assistance.

Style and depth of preparation. Ideally, preparation would involve psychological, factual, and strategic elements. As noted earlier, it may also include extended interviews, courtroom observation, review of transcripts, and role playing. However, the interviews indicate substantial variance in both the depth and the style of witness preparation. These two reports from lawyers represent two extremes:

> We didn't have any preparation. They were on their own.

> Our preparation was a two man job. For the first couple of weeks we took a couple of days each week and discussed the theories and facts of the case, and then the next few weeks for the same amount of time, we went over the direct testimony, and then the next two weeks the cross.

What accounts for these variations in depth and style of preparations? Table 4.2 indicates considerable agreement among attorneys and scholars that plaintiff witnesses more often receive extensive prepara-

D. Wilson, "Patterns of White Avoidance" (132–141); Karl E. Taeuber, "Housing, Schools, and Incremental Segregative effects" (157–167); and Juliet Saltman, "Housing Discrimination: Policy Research, Methods, and Results" (186–196).

Table 4.2. Attorneys' and Scholars' Reports of the Preparation of Expert Witnesses

	Preparation of Experts		
	Extensive	Minimal	(N)
Reported by:			
Plaintiff Experts	69%	31%	(32)
Defense Experts	55%	45%	(20)
Reported by:			
Plaintiff Attorneys	55%	45%	(20)
Defense Attorneys	36%	64%	(14)

tion from their lawyers than do defense witnesses.[15] Fifty-five percent of the plaintiff attorneys said they gave their witnesses a good deal of preparation, whereas only 36% of the defense attorneys said so. More plaintiff witnesses than defense witnesses also reported receiving extensive briefing from their attorneys.

The data also indicate that the more times experts testified, the less often they received extensive briefing. Almost 70% of the experts who testified once or twice reported receiving extensive briefing, whereas only 55% of the scholars testifying in three or more cases reported such continued preparation. In these latter situations, apparently, experts had already worked out the mechanics of their testimony with their attorneys, and needed only to be brought up to date on local legal or evidentiary specifics.[16] For instance, as one well-traveled expert witness recalled:

> [The lawyers and I] developed a genuine rapport: they knew where I was coming from and I knew where they were coming from. We got to where I could arrive at the airport, drive to the hotel, meet them there, and go immediately into the deposition. They would have sent me materials in advance, but we had no rehearsal of any kind.

When the expert and the lawyer are new to desegregation litigation, or to each other, the preparation is likely to be more extensive in nature.

15. "Extensive" preparation, covering all three forms of preparation discussed in this chapter, meant more than an hour or two of casual conversation. It often involved at least one full day of specific preparation for a given trial.

16. This general relationship between experts' experience and extensiveness of preparation was maintained regardless of the party for whom testimony was being provided. Because defense witnesses in general received less preparation, this finding is attenuated among experts who testified often, but the small sample size prohibits any finer discriminations. Repeat players, for plaintiff or defense, received less extensive preparation than first- or second-time testifiers.

Those attorneys who did the least by way of witness preparation were either local lawyers trying the case while maintaining a regular law practice or defense lawyers who saw little real use for expert testimony. The content of the expert testimony also affects preparation time. If the reason for using experts is only to testify to the local realities, not much legal preparation is necessary—the expert has to get the data together and present it. However, if what is needed is a coherent empirical and theoretical argument to alter judicial conceptions of the case, or of racial and educational matters generally, more extensive preparation is needed. Thus, the more complex the legal strategy and argument, the more preparation is needed, at least for first-timers.

Conclusion

In this chapter we have examined the process of mobilizing social science evidence as a key resource for school desegregation cases. When social scientists involve themselves in applied work, expecially in the role of expert witness, they face psychological, political, career, and skill problems. Anticipating these problems, some experts refuse to testify. Psychological and factual preparation can help experts overcome their fears or lack of skills and their discomfort regarding testifying, and enable them to cope with the unfamiliar role and procedures of the courtroom.

In a legal system where evidence is almost always presented through a witness, recruiting and preparing experts are essential parts of the national plaintiff's mobilization strategy. The macro goal of mobilizing social science evidence can only be achieved through the micro process of mobilizing the individual social scientist. In the next several chapters we examine this micromobilization in greater detail.

5   Characteristics of a "Good Witness"

In considering the weight to be given to the testimony of all of the witnesses, the Court has considered their qualifications, experience, interest or lack of same in the outcome of the litigation, their bias if any, as well as their actions upon the witness stand, and the weight and process of the reasoning by which they supported their respective opinions and testimony, and all other matters which served to illuminate their statements.[1]

Thus did Judge Merhige explain why he agreed with the experts who testified that greater educational equality would result from a metropolitan school desegregation plan in Richmond, rather than with defense experts with opposing views.[2] He noted the characteristics of expert witnesses that impressed him and that potentially influenced his willingness to believe and/or seriously consider their testimony.

General Characteristics of a Good Witness

The most basic characteristic of a good expert witness is his or her credibility. As Judge Merhige's quote suggests, one aspect of credibility is

---

1. Memorandum, U.S. District court for the Eastern District of Virginia, Richmond Division, *Carolyn Bradley v. The School Board of the City of Richmond*, Virginia (1/15/72. Judge Merhige (p. 89).

2. One could read Judge Merhige's opinion as a reflection of his predispositions; he believed the plaintiff witnesses because there was an ideological congruence between their testimony and his judgment. If one believes that this is the sum total of judicial decision making, that the outcome of trials is basically *policy-driven* and not *evidence-driven*, much of the discussion in this chapter may appear trivial (Sperlich 1985, 346). We argue that judges' opinions are influenced both by their policy preferences and by the nature and quality of the evidence and the witness presenting it.

relative neutrality. The judge is looking for a witness without a stake in the case, a witness without biases. The lawyer, knowing this, must nevertheless find a party witness, a person who supports his view of the case and is willing to testify for a party to a lawsuit. Balancing these contradictory objectives is the core of what it is to be a good expert. As one of the lawyers we interviewed noted, "A credible witness is hard to find." This, of course, doesn't keep attorneys from using experts, nor does it prevent scientists from trying to be credible witnesses.

We asked lawyers and experts to name the attributes which make an expert credible. In general, both groups named the same factors. As noted by McCormick (1984), the interviews suggest that a good expert may not be a good witness. Credibility may be broken into two inter-related factors: (1) the general knowledge, background, and experience of the expert which constitute the substantive base of his or her *expertise*, and (2) the presentation and demeanor of the person, the appearance of what we call *persuasiveness*.[3] The two factors are clearly related, for a totally uninformed expert is less likely to feel comfortable on the stand, and therefore less likely to make a poised presentation. But they are not synonymous, and both have to be weighted carefully. As one of the judges interviewed noted:

> Perhaps you are impressed with the credentials and expertise of a particular witness. I tried to listen to all the evidence, but there are always some witnesses who weigh their knowledge, their expertise, differently. They appear to be more credible than other evidence or other testimony.

In many instances expertise is equal, or is equal at least as far as the lay observer (including the judge) can tell. One judge indicated how hard it is to deal with opposing expertise.

> This is our daily problem, a choice between two experts, both perhaps exceptionally trained, and both with many skills and experiences. One expert tells us one thing and another seemingly equally qualified expert testifies to the contrary. It's a difficult problem and if we're overwhelmed by a mass of statistical data somebody still has to make the choice. It's the judge in a court case, and

3. Choosing a term to describe the nonsubstantive component of being a good witness was difficult. Although the term *presentation style* captures most of what is involved, it connotes that what is at stake is simply a matter of "style"; that is, a question of presentation of self. What is involved is deeper than a question of style. It also concerns what the expert is willing to say and not say on the stand.

Table 5.1. Characteristics of a Good Witness

Characteristics	Mentioned by Scientists ($N = 43$)		Mentioned by Attorneys ($N = 49$)	
	N	%	N	%
Expertise				
Have good credentials	5	5	18	10
Have good data/experience	7	7	14	8
Know the local area	7	7	26	14
Persuasiveness				
Communicate clearly/specifically	11	11	25	14
Don't use jargon or highly technical materials	11	11	9	5
Stay within area of expertise	11	11	14	8
Admit ignorance	6	6	12	6
Don't be adversarial	14	14	6	3
Maintain integrity	12	12	15	8
Don't get rattled or hesitant	8	8	19	10
Be courteous	3	3	21	12
Respond to questions	5	5	4	2
Total	100	100	183	100

Note: The figures in each left-hand column indicate the number of times a characteristic was mentioned; the right-hand column indicates the per cent of all responses for each characteristic represented. Only 43 scientists and 49 lawyers, compared to the number of "full and complete" interviews previously identified, answered this question. Some attorneys and scientists were never asked about general characteristics of good witnesses, and others discussed specific witnesses, but not the general question.

the integration cases are all court cases and not jury cases. The judge has to make that choice. It's not always easy, but somebody has to make a decision.

If the expertise of different witnesses is relatively equal, those scholars who make a better self-presentation and who "appear to be more credible" may make the difference in a decision.

In table 5.1 we report the characteristics which lawyers and scientists associate with "good witnesses." We have grouped them according to whether they address matters of technical knowledge (expertise) or skills and tactics of presentation and style (persuasiveness).[4] In general,

4. In asking this question in the interview we did not offer the options reported in the table, nor did we prestructure the responses. The two major categories of expertise and persuasiveness, as well as the characteristics within each category, emerged from our reviews and grounded coding of the interview material.

attorneys provided more detailed answers to this question than did scientists (3.7 characteristics per informant for attorneys vs. 2.3 per informant for scientists). Perhaps this reflects their greater experience and sophistication about witness characteristics. Moreover, more attorneys than scientists mentioned characteristics relating to expertise (32% of all attorneys' responses compared to 19% of the scientists'), especially having good credentials and knowing the local area.[5] Perhaps scientists assumed that their own and others' expertise was of high quality, and therefore not a particularly noteworthy issue; attorneys may have been much more cautious and therefore attentive to these characteristics of their witness.

Although there is substantial agreement between experts and attorneys on the persuasiveness dimension, 14% of the scholars emphasized not being an adversary, as opposed to 3% of the attorneys. More scholars (11%) than attorneys (5%) mentioned not using jargon in court, and the need to be courteous was recognized more by attorneys (12%) than by experts (3%). The overall pattern, however, is one of broad consensus between experts and lawyers about what constitutes persuasiveness. This may be partly due to the factual and psychological preparation discussed in the previous chapter. This process may bring the attorney and the social scientist into a general agreement about how the expert ought to try to present himself.

Table 5.2 presents a breakdown of the attorneys' responses by party representation. Plaintiff attorneys mentioned more characteristics than defense attorneys (4.6 per plaintiff informant vs. 2.9 per defense informant), and also stressed some different specific factors. Defense attorneys placed greater emphasis on "knowing the local area." This was probably a result of their focus on specific local features and their desire to find scientists who could testify to the absence of segregation, or to the absence of an intent to segregate, within the local school system. Percentage-wise, defense lawyers were also more likely than plaintiff lawyers to stress the importance of witnesses admitting ignorance, not being an adversary, and maintaining their integrity. Plaintiff attorneys also mentioned these attributes, but not as often as defense attorneys did. In turn, plaintiff attorneys more often stressed the need for courtesy, for staying within one's area of expertise, and for witnesses not to get rattled or hesitant under pressure.

---

5. The chi-squared statistic comparing the distributions of attorneys' and scholars' responses in the two major categories of expertise and persuasiveness is statistically significant ($X^2 = 4.56$, df $= 2$, $p < .05$).

Table 5.2. Characteristics of a Good Witness as Mentioned by Attorneys

Characteristics	Mentioned by Plaintiff (N = 25)		Mentioned by Defense (N = 24)	
	N	%	N	%
Expertise				
Have good credentials	11	10	7	10
Have good data/experience	10	9	4	6
Know the local area	13	11	13	19
Persuasiveness				
Communicate clearly/specifically	14	12	11	16
Don't use jargon or highly technical materials	7	6	2	3
Stay within area of expertise	11	10	3	4
Admit ignorance	6	5	6	9
Don't be adversarial	1	1	5	7
Maintain integrity	7	6	8	12
Don't get rattled or hesitant	14	12	5	7
Be courteous	17	15	4	6
Respond to questions	3	3	1	1
Total	114	100	69	100

Scientists' responses to these questions about characteristics of good witnesses are shown in table 5.3. Defense scientists more frequently mentioned the importance of maintaining integrity (as did defense attorneys).

When the scientists' responses are recategorized in terms of the amount of experience witnesses had in testifying, first-time witnesses more often stress the avoidance of jargon, staying within one's area of expertise, and not being adversarial. Repeat players more frequently mention maintaining integrity and not getting rattled. Experienced witnesses seem to understand that the real issue is integrity (and perhaps coolness under fire); if integrity is maintained and demonstrated, the other accoutrements of style may be less important. Thus, for the experienced witness, jargon may at times be useful, and going outside one's credentialed area of expertise may be acceptable for an acknowledged expert.

Expertise

Expertise is factual knowledge in a field. This knowledge is first demonstrated in a courtroom through the listing of credentials, usually consisting of a Ph.D. and publications in the area. It is more valuable if one has conducted research on the specific issues under discussion (e.g.,

Table 5.3. Characteristics of a Good Witness as Mentioned by Scientists (by Party Affiliation and Experience)

	Party		Experience Appeared	
	Plaintiff (N = 27)	Defense (N = 16)	Once (N = 23)	Two + (N = 20)
Characteristics	N %	N %	N %	N %
Expertise				
Have good credentials	3 5	2 6	2 4	3 7
Have good data/experience	5 8	2 6	4 7	3 7
Know the local area	5 8	2 6	3 5	4 9
Persuasiveness				
Communicate clearly and specifically	7 11	4 12	6 11	5 11
Don't use jargon or technical materials	7 11	4 12	8 14	3 7
Stay within area of expertise	7 11	4 12	9 16	2 4
Admit ignorance	5 8	1 3	2 4	4 9
Don't be adversarial	10 15	4 12	10 18	4 9
Maintain integrity	6 9	6 18	5 9	7 15
Don't get rattled or hesitant	6 9	2 6	3 5	5 11
Be courteous	2 3	1 3	2 4	2 4
Respond to questions	3 5	2 6	1 2	3 7
Total	66 103	34 101	55 99	45 100

studies on white flight) or has had experience working with these issues (e.g., school administration or drawing up desegregation plans). Ultimately, an expert is one whose peers believe him or her to be an expert, and this peer reputation is developed and validated through degrees, publications, and research grants (see McCormick 1984, sec. 13).

Several judges indicated their concern with these same issues of expertise. For instance, the importance of scholarly credentials was expressed in the following terms:

> Well, I consider all of his educational training, all of his experience in employment, and whether I'm convinced he really studied the matter.

> I'd like to know how long he's devoted himself to studying the problem.

> If you have to highlight something, it's best to highlight it with the strongest witness you can, as strongly as you can. When you have a man who comes out of Washington, and has a background in this,

whatever is there, it seems to me, will be more impressive than if you had some second-year student from the university come out and tell me.

One frequently controversial aspect of expertise concerns the question of local knowledge, which, as noted earlier, is seen as an especially important issue for defense attorneys. The great majority of courtroom experts are not from the immediate area under litigation, and their knowledge of particular facts and conditions in local schools is quite limited. A credible expert often has to take steps to acquaint herself with the particular school district, and perceptive local attorneys help prepare their witnesses on this dimension. In particular, plan writers and witnesses testifying to school board intentions must be able to exhibit local knowledge if their expertise is to be believed. Researchers testifying to equal status interactions or educational harm may not need to tie their testimony so clearly to the local area.

Several judges emphasized the importance of local relevance and experience.

> Credible social science must be by a local person who knows the situation. However, a social scientist was more credible when he was far enough away from home so that no one knew him.

> The more you know the more you are able to make decisions. In this case the one person who really studied the community thoroughly before he ever came to court made the most sense.

But most judges were also impressed by generalized and comparative knowledge, as well as by witnesses' ability to connect it to the local situation.

> We're in new areas all the time and so we don't have the expertise, and we're finding our way and perhaps groping. We have consultants and a number of traveling experts who have been helpful too. They've testified in five, maybe six, cases and their testimony has been accepted, and I think this is probably true of some of the special consultants as well. They work perhaps in New York or they worked in Florida or they worked in California, and they can modify their recommendations according to the problems of the particular area.

> I thought some of the testimony was highly relevant and helpful. I thought [X] was helpful when he was able to look at our system and suggest some other ways this could have been done reasonably, which the board could have reasonably been aware of. I thought

some of [Y's] studies concerning what happens when a school turns black in a neighborhood was interesting. It showed the reciprocal effect. And I thought our local people who were the long-timers here, and who had some actual data on what happened in this town, were extremely helpful in how the suit developed.

You not only have the data involving the school system, but you had by way of comparison the data involving other large school systems around the country.

Ultimately, the key issue on expertise is that the evidence must make sense to the judge. It must make "common sense" on its own terms, and in the mind of the judge. Following Judge Merhige's example, other judges reflected on how they assessed witnesses' expertise and how they balanced the different kinds of information presented.

The defense witnesses showed little regard, if any, toward the choice of neighborhood living related to the factor of a given school. They're certainly valid people and have given this a tremendous amount of study and research. But I have thought it was a highly important factor which they didn't give enough consideration to. Whereas, on the other hand, the plaintiffs had several well qualified experts, other than sociologists, who testified that in their experience in the real estate field, schools played a very important part as to where folks wanted to live and where they wanted to move to and move from.

The business of neighborhood contacts makes some sense. My life experience tells me that is true. My life experience tells me that I am capable of doing a hell of a lot more because I can pick up the phone than if I were to come cold into an area and spend a year or two developing contacts. If I have a contact which I have developed at school or in my neighborhood or so on, then my life's chances, that is his phrase, are immeasurably enhanced. I think he is right.

Obviously what is important is the feeling I get as to whether what he says is sensible. Common sense plays an important, in fact a vital part, in any trial. And I try to use my common sense the best I can to as whether that expert makes sense to me and whether the reasons he gives for his conclusions make sense.

As we have noted, most experts have expertise, at least at the level of formal credentials and experience. In several cases one party or the other contemplated using advanced graduate students who were working on dissertations directly concerning some issue in the case, but we know of no cases where graduate students actually appeared as witnesses. The primary reasons lawyers gave for refusing to use students involved matters of expertise; for example, the student was not yet a doctor or professor. Therefore, differences among experts who do testify are subtle and not always easily ascertainable by the judge. In our sample of 17 cases, there was a rough balance of quality in credentials between expert witnesses for both the plaintiffs and the defendants, and substantial differences in expertise were rare.

Persuasiveness

Given these comments on expertise, it is not surprising that when asked what makes some witnesses more credible than others, most lawyers, judges, and experts dwelt upon the issues of style and demeanor. It is here that the adequate witness and the good witness part company. Which elements of style lend credibility? In general, they involve the skill and role problems that academics face when they enter an applied arena (see chap. 4).

Clear communications and jargon. A basic skill problem confronting social scientists is that they, like all scientific experts in all walks of life, are often distrusted by laity not conversant with their special language and assumptions. Physicians speak of contusions and abrasions instead of cuts and scratches; lawyers speak of parties of the first and second part instead of you and me; and social science experts speak of multiple regressions and correlations instead of cause and effect.

The first element of a good style is to translate the special language of the discipline into words and ideas which reside in the working vocabulary of lay persons (in this case judges and lawyers). A number of experts underlined this ability as a key characteristic of a good witness.[6]

> I purposely refrain from using academic jargon. I try to talk in language the judge will understand and I refuse to get involved in detailed methodological questions that I think are of no value or interest to the judge.

6. There are also occasions where experts may purposely use jargon to obscure issues raised by opposing attorneys that they feel are harmful to their testimony/side. As one scholar noted: "I sat in when [X] was being cross-examined and I thought he was helpful except when someone asked him a question that would hurt his side. Then he lapsed into jargon so no one understood him." In chapter 7 we present some examples of testimony which can best be described as deliberate use of jargon for purposes of obfuscation.

> My own feeling is that social scientists should try to be as accurate as they possibly can, while couching it in language the judges will understand.

Lawyers agreed with the line between style of witnessing and communication skills.

> A good witness is clear and articulate and does not use scientific lingo, so any intelligent person in the field can understand what he is actually saying.

> A good witness is someone who can communicate with lay people and is not someone who is going to couch everything in technical jargon.

Several judges commented on the issue of jargon as well.

> Oh, I had a lot of fun with cohort group. I had some trouble with multiple regression analyses and finally I figured out that what you do is, you freeze the factors and work on one factor. When I realized that it was elementary. Maybe I didn't understand it as well as I should, but I thought I understood it. I just thought the whole idea created too much uncertainty and I just wasn't impressed with the evidence.

> Well, I think they got down to earth better and laid things out a little more simply and a little more understandably.

Some jargon is simply that, jargon, serving neither clarity nor brevity of expression. Other sorts of expert language, however, do serve a clarifying or specifying function, and to abandon them for "lay language" is to engage in simplification and invite absurdity. Nevertheless, experts who refused to abandon such terms have not been frequent testifiers.

Adversariness: admitting weaknesses and maintaining integrity. A second central element of credibility involves the role problem which confronts the social scientist when she becomes an expert witness. The expert brings one critical attribute to the court which poses a great threat to her credibility: she is, typically, one party's witness. Thus, every expert is expected from the start to testify in a way that will advance the interests of the party that called her, and to attack or rebut points made by the opposition. It is not uncommon to hear judges, lawyers, and, indeed, social scientists speak of some experts as "hired guns" or "whores." The expert's solution to this problem cannot, however, be a total retreat to nonpartisanship. The party did not hire her to be a witness for the opposition. The expert's problem is to find the appropriate balance between party advocacy and neutral presentation. It is important to note that although appearing nonadversary is partly a matter of style, it also involves the substance of what the expert says (and does not say) on the stand.

According to lawyers and experts, persuasiveness can be enhanced if the witness can indicate that she is not simply supporting a side, regardless of the facts or merits of the case. As one expert notes, the key is to "maintain your integrity and neutrality." Another expert concurs:

> It seems to me that if you're going to have any credibility at all, you've got to tell the truth as well as you can.

And a judge argues:

> Credibility comes from a balanced approach. Where every answer supports the person who hired [the expert], you get suspect.

The expert must walk a fine line with regard to qualifications and admission of problems, for she is a party witness. Her effectiveness as a witness for a party will be limited if she presents all sides of every issue with equal force. However, she will also be ineffective if she loses credibility due to a blatantly one-sided presentation. This is how lawyers describe the tenuous balance between partisanship and neutrality:

> He [the expert] has to be willing to concede points, but in the opposite spectrum he cannot be malleable as putty, which makes him utterly useless. He can't be afraid of offending anybody.

> Tell both sides, but stress one side.

> The expert should not appear to be the adversary.

As this last quote suggests, appearances are important. Judges attempt to determine a witness's partisanship or neutrality because a fully partisan witness will have little to add in which they can put their faith. As the following judges' comments indicate, however, it is not easy to weave one's way through expert testimony in order to ascertain excessive adversariness.

> You use the traditional tools in any evaluation of a witness. How the witness appears on the stand, whether or not his demeanor

suggests he is speaking truthfully, just like you'd believe a person in ordinary life. I don't think that any of the witnesses in our case were lying; everyone was telling the truth from his perspective. What a judge in a case like that is trying to do is to say, "What is this guy really getting at? I know he's from the university, but what kind of ax does he have to grind?" That's not too difficult for me. Well, it's always difficult for any fact-finder, you never know whether you're viewing people correctly. But after all the experience I've had watching people on the witness stand, I get some perception of what's happening.

Well, listen, I am not a maiden on desegregation cases. And secondly I am not a maiden when it comes to witnesses. You know, you get to the point after a while when you develop your own attitude about what you think is plausible and what you think isn't plausible. After many years now, and some varied experiences, you get to the point where you recognize what is advocacy and what it is based upon. The problem with all witnesses is you have to be very careful in finding their biases or assumptions. Once you determine what the man's assumptions are you don't have to listen to the balance of the testimony. You know exactly what is going to happen. You do that when you read academic papers. You know where he is coming from and if you feel this is the same old stand you know good and well by the time you get to the end of it what the answer is going to be.

And in an extreme case . . .

Either the Rockefeller or [the] Guggenheim Foundation has picked up this fellow and as a public service they send him to confer with local school boards. We had to hide him in the hotel. He didn't come to a meeting and confer with us, but the Superintendent and I (before I was a judge) and two other board members went over. He was a traveling troubadour paid for by liberal foundations, at least in those days, come to keep the peace.

These judges are reporting the criteria for assessing certain aspects of persuasiveness, especially with regard to adversariness. Their comments stress an inquiry into a witness's special "interest in the outcome" or "ax to grind," but they also touch on "demeanor," apparent "advocacy," and so forth.

Under these conditions, it is obviously important for witnesses to avoid the appearance of outright advocacy. The most frequently used tactics in appearing nonadversary are to admit weaknesses in one's position and to admit ignorance when one doesn't know the answer to a question.[7] Several lawyers stressed the importance of this tactic as follows:

> A witness will hurt the credibility of his testimony if he never budges from his stance in court.

> A good witness will say "I don't know" when he doesn't.

> I felt he was ineffective by refusing to admit simple things, through appearing not to give an inch on anything.

Judges commented on the same issue in their interviews.

> The ones who weren't good witnesses were the ones who obviously refused to consider the possibility that they may be wrong in their conclusions, that their data base is wrong, or that that particular factor they are considering is wrong. For example, I thought [X] really believed what he was doing, besides making money out of it. But I felt that here was a man who was blind. He couldn't bring himself to say that white withdrawal based on intolerance was a racist thing.

> He did what he could within the limits he had. But to come out with the conclusions, as strongly as he did, discredits them in my eyes anyway. Now that is why I was fond of the other guy. When he comes on and talks about it, he admits the possibility that you have to make a choice. You are faced with white flight. The method of desegregation which minimizes white flight most effectively is voluntary reassignment. Well, everybody knows that. But some guys won't go to the next step and ask, say how much desegregation will you get if you do that? The other guy took the next step. He said, you won't have much white flight, but you also won't desegregate anybody. And when he tells me that, my responsibility becomes very strong.

Don't get rattled or hesitant, be responsive. The tension involved in maintaining the balance between partisanship and neutrality is at its greatest

---

7. As we noted in chapter 4, some lawyers prepared their witnesses on precisely this point. Whether the resultant behavior is truly nonadversary, or only strategically so, is hard to determine, both for us in trying to code data and presumably for a judge trying to assess the credibility of a witness.

during cross-examination, because the opposing counsel wishes either to portray the expert as an adversary or to cause her to make fundamentally damaging concessions in the name of objectivity and neutrality. In the face of this attack the expert must not become rattled but must remain cool and responsive under fire (see chap. 7). Two scholars pointed out some of the difficulties of demonstrating these characteristics.

> It's very difficult to maintain neutral expertise [during cross-examination] when one's results and data are being challenged.

> I didn't enjoy cross for a single moment, because of what [the opposing attorneys] were trying to do. I really detested it. [The opposing attorneys] had to find whatever weaknesses there were [in my data] and play upon them and blow them out of all proportion.

Attacking credibility is the cross-examiner's stock-in-trade, and experts must understand and effectively manage such attacks. As one expert commented:

> You just can't give up simply because the opposing attorney is bearing down on you, because that is what they are going to try to do. It is the lawyer's job to somehow get you to agree that you didn't say what you said.

Under such circumstances, total neutrality may harm credibility, especially if the expert appears hesitant or seems like a person with no opinion. Opinions, honestly and forthrightly delivered, are what experts are for. As several experts put it:

> Do not be too extreme in your testimony or it will hurt your credibility as an expert witness. Instead take the middle of the road. *However,* take a stand, and do not be cloudy by answering too many questions with "I really don't know."

> The world is very complex, but the courtroom requires that if you are going to be effective, . . . act as if the world is simple. Answer questions in yes and no terms.

Most experts try to find a balance between the two roles of scholarly expert and expert witness: thinking and communicating in a specialized and technical jargon, with generalized and theoretical knowledge, and also being a party witness with a particular side to present and a particular loyalty.

Conclusion: The Witness's Relationship with the Judge

The purpose of being credible is, ultimately, to persuade the judge about the correctness of one's position.[8] Even judges who have already formed the basic outlines of the decision are often looking for information about the particulars of the violation or the specifics of a good desegregation plan. In both situations the judge may turn to what he believes to be the credible expert testimony for assistance. As one judge noted:

> I compare the evidence and reread the record and choose the fellow who impressed me the most. I have my clerk take notes and I carefully watch the witnesses while they testify. It's intangible, what I look for. It's partly content, partly sincerity, and partly a good grasp of information.

The advantages of having a credible witness are perhaps best demonstrated in situations where a judge, having decided that a witness is credible, turns to her for additional help on some issue. In such situations the judge abandons a passive role and actively intervenes in the proceedings. In the following example, the defense counsel challenges the plaintiff expert's knowledge of the local area and the appropriateness of applying his considerable research to the local situation. The witness testifies that intermixing students of different races in school can lead to positive outcomes, and qualifies this statement by saying that the gains will be limited unless a number of other actions are taken as well. The cross-examining attorney tries in vain to simplify the issue to one of mixing, per se without other actions. When he tries for a simplified "yes" or "no" answer a second time, the judge intervenes.

> DEFENSE COUNSEL: All right. Just to sum up, then, tell me whether or not all of those things apply if this corridor is broken

8. Persuading the trial judge is not the only point of view from which we might judge a witness. Another important part of expert testimony is building a record for appeal. Thus, even if an expert does not persuade the trial judge, his testimony may provide an appellate judge with the factual basis for some ruling. In this regard, it is as important to build the record before a "friendly" trial judge as before a hostile one. It could be argued that the ultimate reversal in *Bradley v. Milliken* was in part due to the failure to build the record on cross-district segregation in Detroit. Judge Roth never provided the plaintiffs a full opportunity to make this case, and Justice Stewart, the swing vote in the Supreme Court, ultimately said that although he might support a metropolitan desegregation remedy in some cases, the record in Detroit did not justify a finding of a cross-district violation (*Milliken v. Bradley*, 418 U.S. 717 (1974)). This aspect of expert witnessing is very important for the parties, but this chapter focuses more narrowly on what it means to be a good witness within the context of the single trial.

up and the citizens are intermixed with the rest of the community? WITNESS: The first step is the pure intermixing. Certainly benefits will accrue from that. The real benefit is the challenge of the school district, the administrators, and principals, and teachers, to turn that process of desegregation into the most positive, affirmative, creative situation possible. There is a great benefit merely in mixing. There is greater benefit if the School Board and the school district take strong affirmative action. It can become an exemplary school district for the whole United States.

DEFENSE COUNSEL: Doctor, I am not sure, was your answer "yes" or "no" to my question of whether or not these things happen in the event that the corridor is broken up and we achieve a unitary system here? That is your conclusion?

THE COURT: His answer was that it depends on the intent of the School Board and the administrators in breaking it up as to positive action. I believe the children are taught by example, as well as anything else. If the School Board, the way I understand it, does it on its own, positively, affirmatively, with good grace and good intentions, that example will permeate the entire student body. Then the quality of integration, which he is talking about, will be improved more than just shoving bodies around.

WITNESS: That is exactly right. I will add, just the mere shoving of bodies around is better than what we are doing

Sometimes the judge will take the lead in asking witnesses questions. In one case, the judge asked a plaintiff witness a question about the relation of segregation to evidence of harm or violation.

THE COURT: I believe in the *Brown* case in 1954 that the Supreme Court of the United States, as well as possibly the lower courts, relied quite heavily on the testimony or studies or the findings of Dr. Kenneth Clark. Do you recall that to be true?

WITNESS: I believe it is, Your Honor.

THE COURT: Can you review for me briefly what Dr. Kenneth Clark's findings were on that date?

WITNESS: Yes. He had given a group of children in New York City a doll test wherein they had . . . these were black children . . . they had a choice between playing with a white doll or a black doll, and they found that black children rather consistently wanted to take the white doll instead of the black doll. The white doll was a more desirable plaything—just little children. Then after they had played, Dr. Clark asked the children if they would draw pictures of the two dolls and rather consistently the white doll was drawn as a larger and more attractive looking thing and the black doll was drawn smaller and less attractive. Dr. Clark, as a social psychologist, concluded from that that the segregated school system had really given the black children a sense that black people were smaller, less desirable looking, and so on, than whites. And I suspect, Your Honor, that this is part of the thing that led the court to use the words "damage them in heart and mind in a way never to be undone."

The most experienced witnesses understand that this type of interaction provides them with their greatest opportunity to persuade the court to adopt their position. A final comment by a social scientist who is widely thought to be a "good witness" summarizes this issue:

Testimony is designed to persuade one person, namely the judge, and there's always a question in the minds of the witnesses as to whether or not the judge understands and is listening to what is being said. I attempt to place my responses in different words, or on the next opportunity expand upon an answer which I felt was not communicated well at an earlier point. Periodically, I've simply asked the court for an opportunity to make a statement. At the beginning of the day I might say, I'm not sure that I communicated well when I responded to the last question yesterday, and I'd like to elaborate, is that alright your honor. I didn't do that until I'd been a witness in court several times and developed a little more, shall I say poise, as a witness. Frequently now, the court will turn to me as a witness and ask me to elaborate. I encourage and enjoy that kind of opportunity, because then I know that I'm talking directly to the person who is listening.

6   Social Scientists' Experiences as Expert Witnesses
Roles and Role Conflicts

> A court is inherently an adversary proceeding. Scholarship is in-
> herently not an adversary proceeding. . . . There is no way you can
> go into a courtroom and testify without testifying on one side or
> the other. I'm not interested in sides. I am interested in how the
> world works. . . . I'm not interested in advocacy but am very in-
> terested in objectivity. So, I find the court antithetical to my pur-
> poses, which is as objective an analysis as I possibly can make of
> how the world works.

This statement by a social scientist who refused to testify in a school
desegregation case illustrates some of the value problems inherent in
the role of scholar-expert witnesses. Many experts anticipate that they
will experience skill and role problems if they testify as party witnesses
in court (see chap. 4). The academic sphere is generally believed to be
fundamentally different from the applied sphere of the legal arena, and
these differences frequently create conflicts for academic experts. The
adversary nature and norms of the courtroom strain scholars' ability to
remain detached and disinterested. At the same time, they have voluntarily taken on the role of expert witness, and seek in some way to
be of service to the parties in dispute. The normative and psychological
problems that scholar-experts face are rooted in having to negotiate the
conflicting norms and role demands usually attributed to the academic
and legal spheres.

   A number of writers have noted the courtroom pressures to adopt a
legal adversary stance. Pettigrew (1979) argues, in fact, that social scientists must make major compromises and adjustments in court, because they are operating in a legal and not an academic context.
Scholars trained and experienced in the scientific system cannot easily

jettison their commitment to scientific norms. The subsequent role conflict is summarized as follows by Schur (1968):

> As a scientist, the sociologist is supposed to conduct objective value-free research, yet when he enters the case he must ordinarily represent one side. As a scientist, he should always note the basis for and limitations of his findings. . . . When he takes on the quite different role of participant in an adversary proceeding, which principles (those of the academy or those of the courtroom) govern his behavior? (187–188).

In this chapter, we describe and analyze empirically some of these potential conflicts in applied scientific roles. First, we record and examine the comments of scholars who testified in court to understand the extent to which they expected to experience discrepant normative pressures during their involvement in desegregation cases. Second, because expectations regarding differences between legal and scientific norms may be too abstract and not be actually experienced by scholars in courtroom testimony, we examine these scholars' interviews for actual experiences of normative discrepancies. Third, we examine the interview data again to see whether these encounters with normative discrepancies actually produced role conflict. Fourth we analyze how scientists coped with or resolved such conflict when it did occur, examining whether the expert adopted a normative stance involving a neutral, social science approach or a more legal-adversary approach to the courtroom experience, and the effect of this choice on the expert's experience in court. Finally, we analyze some of the factors influencing experts' choice of normative stance, basically their disciplinary back-

Figure 6.1. Flow of Analysis

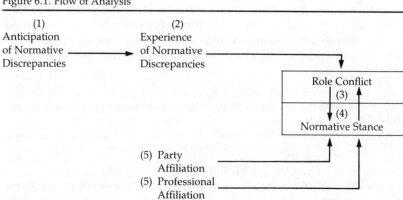

ground (professional affiliation) and their relationship to the parties in the desegregation controversy (party affiliation). The flow of the analysis is diagramed in figure 6.1.

The Content of Normative Discrepancies

If a scholar noted a difference between legal-adversary and social scientific norms, it was coded as a normative discrepancy. After a thorough reading of the interviews, we grouped the normative discrepancies reported into fifteen categories.[1] The fifteen issues can be grouped into four general categories, and are presented below.[2]

Relationships with attorneys

1. Experts' goals for their testimony differ from those of their attorneys.
2. Attorneys encourage experts to omit qualifications.
3. Attorneys encourage experts to omit complexity.
4. Attorneys encourage experts to omit opposing evidence.
5. Attorneys subtly try to shape the content and style of expert testimony without considering the constraints imposed by social science norms.
6. Attorneys encourage experts to make statements that go beyond the data or the experts' area of specialization.

Testifying for one side

7. The role of testifying for one party strains the neutrality of the expert.
8. Experts have to choose between presenting all the relevant evidence and helping their side win the case.

---

1. See Appendix B for the interview schedule. Questions 2,3,4,5, and 10 in the social science interviews solicited comments concerning possible sources of tension and conflict in the role of expert witness.

2. Two caveats are in order about the coding of normative discrepancies. While some specific issues may reasonably be coded under several categories, they were coded only under the issue which came closest to capturing the main idea of the respondent's comment. Even with fifteen categories, not every comment fit clearly within a category. Where statements of normative discrepancy seemed to fit no category exactly, they were coded under the category which seemed to best fit. Moreover, even when an issue might fit into more than one of the fifteen categories, it was coded as a single normative discrepancy. In the quantitative analysis which follows we use only the total number of discrepancies as the measure of normative discrepancy and role conflict (see Kalmuss 1980)

9. Experts feel pressed to please their "clients," who are paying for the experts' testimony.
10. Experts blur the distinction between personal opinions and social science evidence in order to help their side.

Control of courtroom presentation

11. Experts are not able to control their presentation and interactions as they do in academic contexts.
12. Experts are unable to include relevant information and sufficiently expand their statements.

Cross-examination

13. The combative nature of cross-examination strains the neutrality of experts.
14. Cross-examining attorneys try to baffle or confuse experts, thus reducing their ability to present material in a coherent and professional manner.
15. In the heat of cross-examination, experts make statements that do not accurately reflect their data or conventional scientific wisdom.

Almost all informants (96%) expected or anticipated some of these fifteen discrepancies between social science and legal-adversary norms. The mean number of anticipated discrepancies reported per informant was 3.84, with 54% of the informants reporting four or more examples. Obviously, scholars believed that there would be major differences between the norms of the courtroom and those of scholarly enterprise.

Anticipated and Experienced Normative Discrepancies

It is important to distinguish between scholars' expectations or anticipations that these normative discrepancies may exist and their actual experience. A lack of behavioral experience with specific roles and normative discrepancies may make one unaware of normative discrepancies or cause one to anticipate more discrepancies than are actually experienced. Discrepancies between social science norms and legal-adversary norms that informants reported actually experiencing in the role of expert witness are called *experienced normative discrepancies.*

It is relatively easy to distinguish between anticipated and experienced discrepancies. For instance, among the examples of anticipated discrepancies are the following:

> I was prepared for the lawyers to push my testimony further than
> I was willing to go as a social scientist (#6)[3]

> In court I thought you would not be expected to qualify as you
> would be in an academic forum. (#2)

Experienced normative discrepancies, on the other hand, had to be
phrased in the first person and focused on experience rather than on
anticipation. For example,

> [In an academic forum] I frequently couch my findings and con-
> dition them with all the cautions that go into social science re-
> search. It's very difficult to present in that sort of fashion, the
> fashion that you would in a journal article, in the role of expert
> witness. Particularly in cross-examination the adversarial situation
> stimulates one to omit caveats. (#2)
>
> Somehow [testifying] doesn't feel natural. It's not as natural as
> going to a professional meeting and delivering a paper. . . . There,
> you're simply transmitting information. Theoretically that's all
> you're doing in court, but the adversarial process changes that to
> some extent. (#11)

As the data in table 6.1 indicate, most informants (90%) reported
experiencing as well as anticipating discrepancies. However, they reported an average of 1.61 fewer experienced than anticipated discrepancies, and this mean difference is statistically significant. Eighty-one
percent of the informants reported experiencing fewer discrepancies
than they had anticipated or believed to exist.

Table 6.1. Aggregate Difference in the Numbers of Anticipated and Experienced
Normative Discrepancies

	Reporting no discrepancies (%)	Reporting 1–3 discrepancies (%)	Reporting 4 or more discrepancies (%)	Mean Number
Anticipated Discrepancies	4	42	54	3.84
Experienced Discrepancies	10	75	15	2.23

Notes: $N = 52$; t statistic $= 7.52$; df $= 51$; $p < .001$.

3. The numbers in parentheses refer to which of the fifteen issues the comment was
coded under. This comment was under issue 6, "Attorneys encourage experts to make
statements that go beyond the data or the experts' area of specialization."

The different rates of expected and experienced discrepancies suggest that the conflict between social science and legal-adversary norms may not be as pervasive in practice as they are in theory. These data lend support to the argument in chapter 4 that the process of witness preparation is not a relentless effort to make them partisans.

Role Conflict

Role conflict refers to discrepancies that created unpleasant feelings for experts. Informants had to explicitly link tension, conflict, anxiety, frustration, or similar feelings to a normative discrepancy for it to be coded in this fashion. The following statements are examples of such conflict:

> Testifying is certainly nothing like doing research or even teaching, where you try to show both sides more clearly and forcefully than you do in court. For that reason, it's a bit uncomfortable for me.

> I have always had a problem in the past on cross-examination. I tend to be sort of agreeable and friendly. . . . This is not a good thing to do. I mean it is an adversary proceeding and you shouldn't be too friendly. If you are doing this business in order to make a point, you have to play the adversary thing. I didn't know that in the past and felt uncomfortable.

> I always experience a certain amount of tension in the process of testifying. The conflict is between whether I am testifying for the people who hired me or whether I am a servant of the court, and am simply supposed to answer questions and however the questions come up, the answers fall where they will.

Quite clearly, all three informants were "uncomfortable," experienced "tension," or had a "problem."

On the other hand, many experts reported experiencing discrepancies that they did not associate with conflict and that did not create discomfort. Some scholars have noted that situations with highly incompatible normative expectations often do not produce conflict for the individuals involved (Gerhardt 1973; Sieber 1974), and that role conflict cannot be assumed simply on the basis of exposure to discrepant expectations (Stryker and Macke 1978).[4] For instance, the scientist quoted

---

4. Informants generally did not report conflict associated with anticipated discrepancies. There is no reason to assume that anticipated discrepancies are not capable of creating conflict for individuals. However, given the empirical constraints of this study, and

Table 6.2. Extent to Which Normative Discrepancies Involved Role Conflict for Expert Witnesses

	Discrepancies never involved conflict (0%)	Discrepancies sometimes involved conflict (10–90%)	Discrepancies always involved conflict (100%)
Number of informants	22	13	12
Percent of informants	47	28	25

at the end of chapter 5 reported normative discrepancies between his role of witness and his role of social scientist, but these did not cause him to experience role conflict while on the stand. He enjoyed his courtroom activity.

The findings regarding role conflict support the distinction between conflict-free and conflict-laden discrepancies. As indicated in table 6.2, nearly half of the informants (47%) who experienced discrepancies reported no role conflict.

Obviously, many of the acknowledged discrepancies between social science and legal-adversary norms did not involve conflict. Why?

Scientists' Selection of a Normative Stance

One of the ways in which people negotiate competing role demands (and thus reduce or avoid role conflict) is by making a clear choice between them, in this case by adopting a dominant normative stance to guide their courtroom behavior. Fifty-three percent of the expert informants indicated that they had selected the set of norms to which they would adhere before they testified.[5] Many of these individuals ap-

our inability to discern this issue from retrospective interviews, we limited our operationalization of conflict to reports of discomfort associated with discrepancies that were actually experienced.

5. Because of the cross-sectional nature of our data, there is no way other than respondent self-reports to assign causal priority to the experience of role conflict or the selection of a normative stance by social scientists. As the figure on page 108 indicates, we have chosen to think of the choice of stance and the experience of conflict, at least in the aggregate, as being in reciprocal relationship. With respect to specific experts, causal priority may run in either direction. If an expert comes to witnessing with a well-developed stance, he may never experience role conflict. Or the experience of normative discrepancy may cause the expert to choose a clear stance in an effort to reduce conflict. Moreover, there are other solutions to role conflict beside choosing a normative stance: an expert can refuse to testify. These cautions should not keep us from noting the interesting ways in which the selection of a normative stance and the experience of role conflict are related, and what this tells us about being an expert witness in a heated social controversy.

parently chose a style during their recruitment and preparation. The process is illustrated by the following statements:

> I feel that many witnesses are drawn out beyond their depth and that the lawyer pushes them to make statements with greater certainty than they really feel they know, and they get sucked up in it. I was afraid of getting sucked into that, so I thought it was very wise to stake out my ground. . . . [I told the lawyers] that I had some relevant data and was willing to make some fairly strong statements in that area. But there were many other issues which surrounded the case that I did not feel that I knew more about than other people and I was not willing to extend beyond what I thought I knew.

> I talked to people who had testified to figure out what principles they had learned from being on the stand. . . . I had also attended a conference on law and social science. Before the conference I felt that I did not fundamentally understand what expert witnesses were supposed to be and what their status was, and after the conference I felt that I did. And then, sort of to solidify that, I did a bunch of reading on expert witnesses and social science and taught classes in it, just to make sure that I could explain it to other people, before I went into court.

Making a clear choice relieves one of the necessity of making a new decision every time behavior or interaction occurs. What is such a choice like? Consider these two statements, each reflecting a different choice between two normative stances.

> Adherence to professional standards is the only thing that justifies you being in court. . . . I stayed within the boundaries of a social scientific presentation in the sense that I didn't say what I said for my client's sake.

> Generally you reluctantly provide information that's helpful to the other side. To the extent that that's in conflict with your commitment to knowledge and inquiry, yes, there is an inherent conflict. My style is to reluctantly provide information that would help the other side. You don't get trapped into dishonesty, and you don't say things that you can't live with after you leave the courtroom. You know the rules of the game. You know that you're not going to be paid to help the other side. And if you honestly believe that you're on the right side of the courtroom, you're going to provide

> information that will support that argument, and you're going to withhold information that would help the other side.

The first quote indicates a commitment to a social science normative stance. The respondent is unwilling to compromise the "professional standards" of his profession (neutrality and autonomy) for the sake of the case. The second quote recognizes that the role of expert witness may lead to pressure to behave in ways in conflict with the scientific values of open inquiry and a search for knowledge, but accepts a legal-adversary normative stance as the appropriate way to behave.

In determining informants' normative stance in court, three kinds of statements in the interview were used; direct reports about normative stance, reported courtroom behaviors, and informants' analysis of some of their courtroom behavior. The two preceding quotes were direct statements about normative stance, as are the two following statements:

> Well, I'm inclined to follow the scientific norms. And that's what I did.

> I would say things on the witness stand that in my real life I was not quite sure of. But I was not engaged in a professorial dialogue. I was in the role of an expert and an expert is just not unsure. . . . You omit all the qualifications one would give in the classroom or with colleagues. This is a different arena, you don't do that here.

Reported courtroom behaviors were also used to indicate normative stance. The following reported behaviors were coded in the social science category:

1. Telling the whole truth and not omitting evidence that might harm one's side
2. Qualifying statements in terms of level of generalization, degree of certainty, and the degree to which they are based on established social science knowledge
3. Confining one's testimony to one's area of expertise
4. Confining one's testimony to hard facts or data
5. Securing approval from one's lawyers to adopt one or more of the above behaviors in court, before agreeing to testify or while formulating one's testimony.

The following reported behaviors were coded as reflecting legal-adversary norms:

1. Volunteering only the part of the truth that supports one's side

2. Omitting opposing evidence
3. Omitting mention of problems or flaws in one's data
4. Scanning the data and selectively presenting the portion that most strongly supports one's side.
5. Not fully qualifying one's statements
6. Presenting opinions or positions before one feels all the research on the issue is in
7. Including statements that are not based on social science research or data
8. Attempting to dodge questions, score points, or impeach whatever points the opposing attorneys raise in cross-examination

The final measure of reported normative stance included informants' analyses of some of their courtroom behaviors, or their own reflections on the reasons for their actions. Two particular sets of behavioral analyses were the most difficult to code: adversary behaviors interpreted by respondents as backsliding, and social science behaviors that they interpreted as strategic.[6] Both of these codes involve an effort on our part to interpret the subjective meaning that actions held for experts, rather than to code the actions themselves.[7] Backsliding included reports of legal-adversary behaviors by scholars who had otherwise adopted a social science stance. They were distinguished from typical legal-adversary behaviors because experts reported discomfort associated with their occurrence, and labeled them as deviant due to their departure from social science norms. Informants attributed such backsliding behaviors to the adversary pressures of the courtroom and not to their own values. Because their reactions to or analyses of these behaviors reflected a concern about deviance and a general adherence to social science norms, they were coded as consistent with these norms.

> I did not feel good [in a particular case] because I had pushed my data beyond its limits, because of the adversarial pressure of the courtroom. And experts become uncomfortable when their opinion, method, or conclusions are stretched too far beyond their normal standards of what is a credible scientific position.

6. On the face of things, it is difficult to distinguish backsliding or strategic behavior from more direct normative statements and choices. Thus, in conducting this coding procedure we used a contextual analysis of experts' reports, examining otherwise discrete comments in the context of the rest of the interview.

7. Such coding is subtle, and admittedly open to interpretation, but we believe that it more fairly reflects the reality and complexity of how what goes on in court affects expert witnesses.

> The lawyers want you to say that you're absolutely sure of statistical results. And you can never be absolutely sure. And I think the real danger is when you give in to the lawyer's desire to state them as if you were absolutely sure. I'm sure there were cases where I stated things with a higher degree of certainty than I would have under other circumstances. Yeah, that tension makes me uncomfortable.

Strategic acts were social science behaviors reported by scholars whose other behaviors and statements reflected legal-adversary norms. They were distinguished from regular social science behaviors because experts clearly identified them as strategic. That is, at least part of the explanation for the behavior was to score points, gain credibility, or protect oneself in an adversary interaction. Because the asserted purpose of these behaviors was strategic, they were coded as reflecting a legal-adversary stance.

> The technique is to qualify and I do qualify most of the things I say. It is the extreme statement that is to be avoided. It is the extreme statements that get the speaker in difficulty in cross. And I've seen it trap very experienced witnesses.

> An expert witness isn't supposed to be an expert on the law, so if anybody asks you about the law, right away you say, "It's not up to me to deal with that question." It doesn't mean that sometimes you don't intentionally jump the boundary, but you wouldn't feel the necessity to be an expert on law. If anybody asked you a question you didn't want to answer, you just could exclude it. See, one of the things an expert witness becomes expert at is excluding things.

Each statement referring to normative stance in court (direct statements, reported behaviors, and behavioral analyses) was coded as following social science or legal-adversary norms. An index score of each informant's normative stance was computed using the following formula:

$$\text{Normative Stance} = \frac{\text{Total Number of Statements Reflecting Dominant Normative Stance}}{\text{Total Number of Statements Reflecting Any Normative Stance}}$$

For example, an informant who made five statements about normative stances (a direct statement, three reported behaviors, and one behavioral analysis), four of which reflected adherence to legal-adversary norms, would have an index score of 4/5 or 80% legal-adversary.

Table 6.3. Expert Witnesses' Adoption of Social Scientific or Legal-Adversary Norms

	Percent of Reported Behaviors Indicating Adoption of Social Science (Legal-Adversary) Norms					
	0%	1–24%	25–49%	50–74%	75–99%	100%
Percent of Respondents	25	14	4	11	11	35
N = 52	13	7	2	6	6	18

The distribution of informants' normative stances indicates that 60% of the informants reported a totally consistent set of behaviors (35% were totally social scientific and 25% totally legal-adversary (table 6.3). When predominant categories are combined, 85% of the informants reported a clear or primary normative stance. Only 15% reported approximately equal numbers of behaviors from both normative sets. About half of the informants (46%) could be identified as primarily social scientific, because 75% or more of their statements fell into that category, whereas 39% could be identified as primarily legal-adversary. Most experts, then, did choose a dominant normative set, either social science or legal-adversary, to guide their courtroom behavior.[8]

8. In six cases, we checked the reliability of this choice by examining transcripts of informants' actual courtroom testimony (direct and cross-examination). We analyzed six court transcripts, three of experts who reported adherence to social science norms and three of experts who reported adherence to legal-adversary norms. Three of these experts testified for the defense and three testified for the plaintiff. A coding scheme was developed which categorized statements and interactions between experts and attorneys as reflecting adherence either to social science norms or to legal-adversary norms. This scheme was similar to that discussed on the preceding pages, except that it referred to actual dialogue and interaction, not solely to reports of actions. For example, the inclusion of methodological or substantive qualifications, the inclusion of opposing evidence or alternative conclusions, and easy concession of points on cross-examination were coded as social science behavior. On the other hand, reluctance to concede points or a tendency to be "combative" on cross-examination were coded as legal-adversary. "Combativeness" was reflected in not answering and in hedging or dodging questions posed by the cross-examining attorney, as well as by directly antagonistic responses.

The results of the analysis of courtroom transcripts indicated that scholars' reported normative stances were reliable indicators of their actual normative stances in court. In each case, the overall stance reflected in the court transcripts was the same as the normative stance reported in the interviews.

The court transcripts also indicated that informants' reports did simplify their courtroom behavior to some extent. In the interviews, they tended to portray a higher level of consistency between their preferred stance and their behavior than existed in the record, and to assert a level of control over their behavior that was not reflected in the transcripts. The observed differences between experts' reported and actual behaviors are probably a

Table 6.4. The Relationship between Experienced Role Conflict and Pure or Mixed Normative Stance

Normative Stance	Role Conflict		Total
	Yes	No	
Pure	45% (14)	55% (17)	100% (31)
Mixed	52% (11)	48% (10)	100% (21)
Total	48% (25)	52% (27)	100% (52)

Notes: $\chi^2 = 0.261; p < .61;$ df $= 1; N = 52.$

In order to test the notion that the selection of any clear normative stance might in itself reduce conflict, we recoded all subjects who reported 100% legal-adversary or 100% social science behaviors into a *pure* category, and all other respondents into a *mixed* category. As table 6.4 indicates, pure normative stance was not significantly related to whether one experienced role conflict.

If adoption of a clear normative stance does not reduce role conflict, is adoption of a particular stance (legal-adversary or social science) associated with less role conflict? Table 6.5 indicates that it is.

Sixty-two percent of the experts who adopted a social science stance experienced at least some role conflict, compared to only 25% of the

Table 6.5. The Relationship between Experienced Role Conflict and Normative Stance

Normative Stance	Role Conflict		Total
	Yes	No	
Social Science	62% (15)	38% (9)	100% (24)
Mixed	62% (5)	38% (3)	100% (8)
Legal-Adversary	25% (5)	75% (15)	100% (20)

Notes: $\chi^2 = 6.93; p < .03;$ df $= 2; N = 52.$

function of cognitive tendencies to filter out inconsistencies and ambivalence in the recall of past experiences, as well as caution about openness and presentation of self in an interview setting. Despite these minor variations, the court transcripts support our use of scholars' normative stances reported in the interviews as a good indicator of their actual stances.

Despite the small number of transcripts that we analyzed, we have no reason to assume that the experts whose transcripts we analyzed exhibited more consistency between their reported and actual normative stances than other experts. Although it would have been preferable to examine more transcripts, financial considerations alone made this impractical. Transcripts of expert testimony in school cases typically run to hundreds of pages, costing fifty cents to one dollar per page. Our primary sources of transcript materials were attorneys in the case who were kind enough to provide us with a transcript for free or for the cost of photocopying the material.

experts who adopted a legal-adversary stance. We have no direct measure of the intensity or magnitude of role conflict, but we do have a count of the number of times role conflict was reported by each informant. The mean number of conflicts mentioned by experts choosing a legal-adversary stance was 0.45, whereas for experts choosing a social science stance it was 1.2. Thus, in the aggregate, a legal-adversary stance appears to be associated with significantly less role conflict than a social science stance. These results support the point made by Pettigrew (1979) and Wolfgang (1974), who argue that court procedures place pressures on experts to adopt legal-adversary norms. Part of the pressure comes from the relatively higher levels of role conflict associated with an attempt to maintain a social science normative stance in court.[9]

It appears that the adversary nature of the courtroom makes a social science stance less effective than a legal-adversary stance in reducing conflict. Obviously, however, reduction of role conflict is not the only factor affecting the choice of normative stance. If it were, we would not expect half of our respondents to choose a social science stance. Some experts obviously feel a strong commitment to nonadversary social science values, regardless of their comfort in court.

Moreover, the choice of normative stance is not determined entirely by social psychological factors. The choice is in part a response to political and career problems confronting the applied social scientist. This choice must be examined within the political context of the wide variance in values of the different social sciences, and with the realization that by taking a side in the school desegregation cases, one became part of a heated social movement controversy.

The Effect of Party Affiliation and
Professional Affiliation on Normative Stance

Almost all witnesses providing testimony appeared on behalf of one or the other of the parties to litigation. Such affiliation constitutes structural partisanship, and can generally be associated with pressures toward party loyalty and advocacy. Complete neutrality is very unlikely under these circumstances. An expert witness who truly believes that there are persuasive arguments on both sides of the case, and who is determined to present both of those sides to the best degree possible, is very unlikely to appear as a witness for either side. Of course, most experts are chosen because they do not believe that the arguments on both sides of the case are of equal strength.

---

9. However, there are clear limits to this argument: nearly 40% of the informants who adopted a social science stance reported *no* role conflict.

Table 6.6 The Relationship between Party Affiliation and Normative Stance

Normative Stance	Party Affiliation		Total
	Defense	Plaintiff	
Social Science	73% (16)	27% (8)	46% (24)
Mixed	9% (2)	20% (6)	15% (8)
Legal-Adversary	18% (4)	53% (16)	39% (20)
Total	100% (22)	100% (30)	100% (52)

Notes: $\chi^2 = 10.89$; $p < .004$; df $= 2$; $N = 52$.

Problems of neutrality and of autonomy are intensified when experts are paid for their testimony by the side that they represent. Payment fosters a tendency to earn one's keep, to testify in a manner that satisfies one's employers, and to be loyal to one's comrades. For example:

> You start off with the main obligation to present the most balanced account of the evidence. . . . Now, that's going to be hard anyway because you get pulled into the team, one side. Now suppose that the team's paying you $10,000 to help them win their case. You get an output (testimony) under a much stronger sense not to qualify [your answers]. You know you're not going to be paid to help the other side.[10]

> There's a natural process that since they're paying you, there may be an unconscious tendency to slip into their side and depart a little more than you would have if you were speaking before a neutral panel somewhere.

> There's a tension between professional standards and commitments to the clients in the case because you always want to be nice to the people who have been so flattering as to ask you to testify. So there is this kind of thing.

Because these pressures affect both plaintiff and defense experts, one might expect them to move toward a legal-adversary stance in equal numbers. Table 6.6 indicates that this is not the case.

Almost three-fourths of the defense informants reported that they

10. Contrary to this comment, few, if any, experts in these cases made large amounts of money, and several refused to take more than expenses. No one admits to having been influenced personally by the economic rewards of testifying. Actually, paying experts is not necessarily a bad strategy for the parties. An expert who works without pay is likely to be challenged as a zealot who is part of a cause and who would stretch the evidence to support the cause.

adopted a social science stance. Plaintiff experts displayed considerable variation, with over half adopting legal-adversary norms and the other half divided between a social science and a mixed (social science and legal-adversary) stance.

Plaintiff experts' more frequent adoption of a legal-adversary normative stance reflects the effect of the values they bring to court and of their roles as part of a social movement. The experts' professional affiliations also differed. Some worked in academic social science departments such as sociology, political science, and psychology, whereas others had their primary academic base in schools of education. Seventy-two percent of the defense experts were social scientists, as compared to 58% of the plaintiff experts.

At a structural level, the disciplines of social science and education endorse and reward somewhat different notions of appropriate scholarly behavior. Education is a more applied field than sociology and psychology, the dominant social science disciplines of witnesses. Research focuses on a particular institution, on how it operates and how it can be improved. Concerns about implementing knowledge inevitably link education scholars to nonacademic audiences (e.g., teachers, policymakers, and parent and student groups), and such applied efforts are expected of them. Social scientists are generally not expected to apply their knowledge; they are expected to concentrate on the generation and dissemination of knowledge through established academic channels (e.g., journal articles, books, academic presentations, and teaching).

The following statements by educational scientists and social scientists reflect the different patterns of institutional rewards associated with these disciplines. Commented some educational scientists:

> In order for me to practice in my field, I cannot sit in a musty library and read and publish occasional articles. My professional role is in the field and that's where I belong if I can be of use there.

> I'm terribly disappointed with social scientists in terms of their lack of help in the field of education. . . . It has to do with the academic reward structure. Social scientists get no reward for involving themselves in education, except insofar as the research goes back into the social science mainstream. Then it's okay. I serve as a consultant in lots of different ways. In my system I put it on my activity reports, and I get merit increases in terms of my consultant role. We're supposed to go in for outreach and public service. Not the sociologists or psychologists.

Table 6.7. The Relationship between Professional Affiliation and Normative Stance

Normative Stance	Professional Affiliation		Total
	Social Science	Education	
Social Science	70% (21)	26% (3)	46% (24)
Mixed	12% (4)	21% (4)	15% (8)
Legal-Adversary	24% (8)	63% (12)	39% (20)
Total	100% (33)	100% (19)	100% (52)

Notes: $\chi^2 = 11.35$; $p < .003$; df $= 2$; $N = 52$.

And two social scientists said:

> Yes, there are going to be costs of my applied work, but I'm not going to stop doing it either. . . . I don't talk about it with my colleagues at the university. I simply don't share those activities with them because it has negative consequences; and that's how I handle the role conflict, just by not talking about it.

> I think those people who control our discipline, who regard themselves or are regarded as pure social scientists, think poorly of applied work. They consciously manipulate the discipline to try and keep graduate students from going in that direction. They give rewards to grad students who are in their image. This is conscious on their part.

As a result of these different disciplinary pressures, we can expect social scientists to have a greater commitment to a social science normative stance.

Table 6.7 shows the relationship between professional affiliation and normative stance. Sixty-three percent of the educational scientists adopted legal-adversary norms and 26% adopted social science norms, whereas 24% of the social scientists adhered to legal-adversary norms and 70% to social science norms.

The choice of normative stance can also be influenced by other professional attributes, beyond disciplinary orientation, that experts bring with them to the courtroom. These attributes include values concerning the proper role of applied scholarship. At one end of a continuum of applied scholarship, one may address applied issues but limit dissemination to traditional academic channels such as professional meetings or journals, or disseminate information directly to policy makers and interested groups. Movement from these relatively passive postures may involve making recommendations based on research findings, or even by explicitly using scientific knowledge and skills to create, implement, or resist change. The traditional style of relatively passive intervention of academics in the policy arena approximates Max Weber's vision of the citizen-scholar who, while in the scholarly role, should attempt to remain outside politics (Weber 1946). The following are comments of informants who held a passive applied role conception:

> I think it is possible to do applied research without being an advocate. Being an advocate is something else altogether. To some degree, I would argue that a researcher is only there to put his research out. That is not to say he can't have any other roles, such as advocate. But in the role of researcher, he is there to put his research out and have somebody else pick it up.

> As social scientists become advocates and present their opinions as science, that compromises the credibility of science.

> I'm uncomfortable with social scientists endorsing particular solutions to social problems. They should generate knowledge and then they may apply it to a particular problem and real-world situation. If a solution is suggested from that application, they should present their work and the suggested solution to policy-makers. They should not advocate for that solution. They should merely present it as part of the knowledge package they have generated.

These informants do not consider active intervention and advocacy that compromise the principles of autonomy and neutrality appropriate forms of scholarly activity.[11] Rather, they view the scholar's task in the applied arena as sharing expertise and transmitting information to decision makers.

By contrast, active intervention in the policy sphere involves some attempt to implement a given policy or policy direction; that is, some degree of partisanship. It generally involves an overt relationship between personal beliefs and applied scientific endeavors. The following informants' statements illustrate a more activist conception of an applied scientific role:

> My orientation to social science was always based on the idea that knowing something places on the individual a responsibility for its application. Being a social scientist placed on me the responsibility of utilizing that knowledge in a way to achieve certain kinds of goals. The goals must be consistent with my own values and beliefs.

---

11. The concepts of scholarly autonomy and neutrality are discussed in chapter 4.

I use my social science knowledge in ways to further my own values.

Social science is active, it has effects when it is committed and engaged, when it is serving some actor or set of actors in a social interaction. Social science can do perfectly good work in the service of some cause. . . . The way social science knowledge finds its way into action is when people care deeply about it and when people care deeply about things, they're inevitably partisan.

Social scientists have a responsibility to use their knowledge to make certain kinds of changes. The more important an issue is to the social scientist, the more responsibility he has to utilize this knowledge in the area.

Scholars who endorse active intervention in the policy arena reject a pure form of the citizen-scholar distinction and accept advocacy as part of the applied scientist's role. They are involved in the desegregation effort and see their role as actively advancing the movement's interests.

We coded our interviews with witnesses for statements reflecting positive or negative views of an active or advocacy style of intervention. Statements coded as reflecting an activist role conception had to express one or more views: (1) endorsement of active intervention in the policy sphere; (2) endorsement of advocacy as appropriate scholarly behavior; and (3) endorsement of a direct relationship between personal values and scholarly endeavors.

Informants who did not express these views were coded in the non-activist category.[12] As expected, table 6.8 shows that educators tended toward an activist role conception and social scientists toward nonactivism.[13] Applied role conception helps to explain the data in table 6.7

---

12. These informants did not necessarily assume a totally antiactivist conception. Many nonadvocates would limit their role to only sharing information with policy makers. Some nonadvocates, however, adopted a middle ground. They would recommend policy to decision makers, but would not be advocates for the policy. Separating nonadvocates into these two categories does not alter the conclusion in the text.

13. The adoption of a more activist role conception is reflected in the other behaviors of educational scientists and social scientists. We asked each expert to fill out a questionnaire asking for a listing of other roles that the expert had played in desegregation efforts (see Appendix B). We also asked each expert for a copy of his or her current vita. Using these two pieces of information, we determined whether each scientist had played some other active role beside being an expert witness. Educational scientists were substantially more likely to have done so ($\chi^2 = 8.03$, $p = < .05$, df $= 1$, $N = 52$).

Table 6.8. The Relationship between Professional Affiliation and Applied Role Conception

Role Conception	Professional Affiliation		Total
	Social Science	Education	
Activist	45% (15)	90% (17)	62% (32)
Nonactivist	55% (18)	10% (2)	38% (20)
Total	100% (33)	100% (19)	100% (52)

Notes: $\chi^2 = 9.87$; $p < .003$; df $= 1$; $N = 52$.

showing a relationship between professional affiliation and normative stance.

In table 6.6 we saw that party affiliation is related to normative stance. Table 6.7 indicated that professional affiliation is related to normative stance, and, as we noted in the text, professional affiliation is related to party affiliation. The relationship between party affiliation and normative stances may exist because plaintiff experts are more likely to be educational experts and therefore more likely to adopt a legal-adversary normative stance. Does this background variable explain all of the normative stance–party affiliation relationship? Or is there still a party effect controlling for professional affiliation? To address this question, we examined the relationship between normative stance and party affiliation within categories of professional affiliation.

When we look only at social scientists (the left half of table 6.9), experts who testify for the plaintiffs remained significantly more likely to adopt a legal-adversary stance than experts testifying for the defense. The difference in normative stance between plaintiff and defense educational-science experts is not statistically significant, but the basic pattern is the same. Overall, the relationship between party affiliation

Table 6.9. The Relationship between Party Affiliation and Normative Stance Controlling for Professional Affiliation

	Professional Affiliation			
	Social Scientists[a]		Educational Scientists[b]	
	Party Affiliation			
Normative Stance	Defense	Plaintiff	Defense	Plaintiff
Social Science	87% (14)	41% (7)	33% (2)	8% (1)
Mixed	0% (0)	24% (4)	33% (2)	15% (2)
Legal-Adversary	13% (2)	35% (6)	33% (2)	77% (10)
Total	100% (16)	100% (17)	100% (6)	100% (13)

Notes: [a]$\chi^2 = 8.31$; $p < .02$; df $= 2$, $N = 33$.   [b]$\chi^2 = 3.57$; $p < .16$; df $= 2$; $N = 19$.

and normative stance remains significant when controlling for professional affiliation.[14]

The remaining relationship between party affiliation and normative stance can be explained by the differences between the parties in the desegregation suits. To be an expert for the plaintiffs (especially for the national plaintiffs) was to play a role in a broad social movement. Plaintiff lawyers viewed the cases as a challenge to the unconstitutional organization and operation of the school system and other governmental organizations. The organization and the movement legitimated a more adversary position among all its participants.

In fact, among plaintiff experts a legal-adversary normative stance was significantly related to an absence of role conflict.[15] Following are two quotations from experts relating their choice of a legal-adversarial posture to the reduction of role conflict:

> I understood the partisan nature of the courtroom and I realized that I would be on the stand arguing for a position without also presenting evidence that might be contrary to my case of side. But you see, that didn't bother me, because I knew that the other side was also doing that.

> I think that a lot of the conflict said to be associated with social scientists participating in the courtroom neglects the fact that the courtroom is structured quite differently. And that it is not the role

14. Because of the small N, we collapsed normative stance into two categories (social science and legal-adversary) by allocating the "mixed" individuals according to their dominant preference. We then conducted a log linear analysis with normative stance as the response variable, and professional affiliation and party affiliation as independent variables. Below are the results of a restricted model including only main effects for the two independent variables.

Analysis of Variance Table

Source	DF	Chi-Square	Probability
Intercept	1	0.58	0.445
Professional Affiliation	1	9.16	0.002
Party Affiliation	1	6.37	0.012
Residual	1	0.16	0.686

Both main effects are significant. As the nonsignificance of the residual indicates, the main effects model is a good fit to the data. There is not a significant interaction between professional affiliation and party affiliation.

15. Because of the small N, we dichotomized normative stance into legal-adversary and social science categories. $\chi^2 = 8.17$, $p < .01$, df $= 1$, $N = 30$, Gamma $= .82$.

of the witness to define the case, to call attention to everything that could possibly be said about a subject. . . . I guess I accepted the idea that I am serving one side and that resolved potential conflicts.

Although defense experts also had to deal with the adversary nature of party witnessing, they did not have the additional social-movement incentives to adopt a legal-adversary stance. Unlike plaintiff experts, almost none of the social scientists testifying for the defense viewed their side of the case as part of a social movement. One way to deal with conflict was to adopt a neutral stance regarding the merits of the litigation and act as an objective social scientist disseminating information. The following remarks reflect such a choice:

> I experienced no role conflict because I did what I told myself I would, and that is restrict myself to statements on which there was evidence.

> My thoughts about role conflict helped me define my role. . . . I defined my role very narrowly to avoid such conflict.

Among defense experts, the choice of a normative stance was not significantly related to the experience of role conflict.[16] Unlike plaintiff experts, a substantial minority of defense experts adopted a social science normative stance without experiencing role conflict.

Role Conflict in Applied Social Science: How Different Are the Courtroom and the Academy?

Social science norms and legal norms are not quite as discrepant as the literature (Caplan 1979) or our informants first assumed, and the role of expert witness may not necessarily be laden with constant conflict. The situation, at least in the school cases, may be better explained by a model that accepts the possibility that at times the legal sphere can be relatively nonadversary and the academic sphere adversary.

The courtroom is not relentlessly adversary. Often it may not represent a drastic departure from the academic sphere, and thus may not create role conflict for expert witnesses. As we saw in chapter 4, an expert's own lawyer often has an interest in having the expert behave as much as possible as a neutral, objective expert. Although this may be done for strategic reasons, it may also reduce the experience of role conflict. Even cross-examination, probably the most consistently ad-

---

16. Because of the small N, we dichotomized normative stance into legal-adversary and social science categories. $\chi^2 = 0.04$, $p < .80$, df $= 1$, $N = 22$, Gamma $= .11$.

versary courtroom activity, is not inevitably so. In some cases attorneys feel there is little use in attempting to discredit expert testimony in cross-examination, and therefore they do not offer much of a challenge. This may be especially likely when scholars present clear and simple facts and figures that leave little room for dispute. As one expert commented:

> In some sense they couldn't impeach my testimony because the tables were right there and anybody could see them. All I was doing was saying, these are the tables and this is what the numbers mean. By delimiting my testimony so much into observable facts, I'd given them practically no ground to go on.

In addition, attorneys may not conduct a particularly adversary cross-examination when they believe that the scholar's testimony is irrelevant. For instance, when experts testify on minor points or on matters only indirectly related to the case, opposing attorneys may consider their testimony unimportant or too trivial to attack. A relatively nonadversary cross-examination may diminish the extent to which experts experience the courtroom as fundamentally different from the academic sphere. This in turn reduces the role conflict caused by such differences. Defining the adversary nature of the courtroom as a variable rather than as a constant permits an understanding of why role conflict is not inevitable for all expert witnesses.

Just as the legal arena may sometimes be nonadversary, the academic sphere may occasionally be quite adversary. The dialectical approach to truth that informs the basic organization of American court procedure is not an alien idea in social science. Controversies among individuals or groups of scholars within the academy often escalate beyond the level of polite intellectual debate. Some would even argue that "normal" science is often a process of testing competing theories through competitive replications by biased scientists (Campbell 1977; Loftus 1986). Many of these disputes emerge from recognized and ongoing cleavages within the academic sphere. Such competing orientations can be theoretical (consensus vs. conflict), political (conservative, liberal, or radical), professional (basic vs. applied), epistemological (positivist vs. phenomenological), or methodological (qualitative vs. quantitative).

Academic controversies are typically aired at seminars, in journals, and at professional meetings. Occasionally these disputes become heated enough to be publicly labeled as adversary (e.g., the controversy regarding Arthur Jensen's work on the genetic basis of intelligence, and the debates as to whether academic organizations should take a public stand against the Vietnam War). Like the question of intelligence, school desegregation has been an area with a high level of controversy. A number of heated academic controversies have arisen over the evaluation of school desegregation programs (Armor 1972: Pettigrew et al. 1973) and analyses of "white flight" (Coleman 1976, 1975; Farley 1975a, 1975c; Orfield 1978b, 1975; Pettigrew and Green 1976; Rossell 1975/76). These debates sometimes surfaced in academic journals and professional meetings prior to emerging in school desegregation cases.[17] Such scientific disagreements were often no less combative than a typical cross-examination in the courtroom. For example, Pettigrew et al. (1973) began a "discussion" of an article by Armor (1972), which reported negative evaluations of busing programs and questioned the effectiveness and wisdom of court-ordered busing, with the statement:

> David Armor's "The Evidence on Busing" presented a distorted and incomplete review of this politically charged topic. (88)

In reply, Armor (1973) stated:

> I cannot agree with the assumptions behind this reasoning [presented in the Pettigrew discussion], with the kind of morality that it represents or with the implicit suggestion that social science should be used only when it favors the values of the social scientist. (129)

The conflict has continued into more recent times. Responding to an article by Harold Gerard questioning the quality and accuracy of the 1954 social science brief in *Brown v. Board of Education* (Gerard 1983), Stuart Cook, an original signer of the brief, said:

> In his article . . . Gerard asserted that the Social Science Statement's central conclusions have been "questioned," alleged that it "myopically" omitted critical information about the difficulties of desegregation, and attributed to it discredited predictions about the consequences of school desegregation. . . . In this article, the basis for questioning the statement's conclusions is shown to be untenable, the "myopic" omissions are shown to be irrelevant to

---

17. As the social science consensus on issues surrounding desegregation began to break down, defense groups sought out experts for their side. Thus, in Boston, the defense introduced an affidavit and a report from James Coleman arguing that white flight would occur if a city with a high percentage of black students was desegregated when the suburban ring was not desegregated and was of a different racial composition (*Morgan v. Kerrigan*, 530 F.2d 401, 420 (lst Cir. 1976)) (see Loh 1984, 137). In 1976 Coleman also addressed the Massachusetts State Legislature with a similar argument. (Coleman 1979). In response to this white flight argument, the plaintiffs were required to mobilize counterarguments (see Pettigrew and Green 1976).

the constitutional issue before the Supreme Court in 1954, and the discredited predictions are shown to be missing from the statement altogether. (Cook 1984, 830)[18]

Perhaps the most noteworthy example of the social movement controversy spilling over into the academy was the response to James Coleman for his views on white withdrawal (Wilkinson 1979, 181). This included an attempt to have him censured by the American Sociological Association partly because of his allegedly inappropriate behavior concerning the school desegregation controversy. These examples illustrate the adversary nature of what are often framed as academic debates. They are relatively extreme cases, whereas most public disputes are more controlled and focused on scientific criteria (e.g., critiques of a researcher's assumptions or of research designs.) As a result, their adversary quality remains hidden to the public, but strongly felt within the academy.

However, the academic sphere is not entirely an adversary arena, nor do all its disputes or decisions reflect an underlying adversary base. Moreover, discussion of the nonadversary nature of some cross-examination does not argue that the courtroom supports a social-scientific style. Our research indicates that it is incorrect to assume that there is a constant and polar difference between the two environments.

The overlap between the academy and the courtroom is especially large when the controversy litigated in court is the topic of an important social movement. The fact that school desegregation was an important issue in society at large meant that the academy was drawn into the controversy just as the courts were. The reason for mobilizing social science findings was, from the point of view of the parties, to find arguments to support their case. Those experts who were mobilized in support of or opposition to court-ordered school desegregation ultimately carried this conflict beyond the court and into the academy. The harshest words and gestures were reserved for those who had involved themselves directly in the controversy as expert witnesses and were delivered by others who were themselves involved in the controversy as experts. The attacks and counterattacks within the academy were themselves part of the social movement debate.

---

18. The conflict goes beyond the data to disagreement about the proper role of social science information. Part of Professor Cook's rebuttal to Professor Gerard is that certain alleged omissions in the 1954 brief were irrelevant because they did not address the "constitutional issues" of the time. This, of course, is a different criterion for inclusion than one which would argue that the role of social science is to present the best insight that the academy might offer about the prospects and problems of school desegregation, regardless of their legal relevance.

7 Strategies of Cross-Examination

The most adversary aspect of the courtroom experience is cross-examination. When dealing with his own attorney, during both preparation and direct examination, the expert rarely confronts the full adversariness of litigation. Opposing counsel, however, is the lead agent in arguing against the witness's version of reality. In so doing, attorneys often strive to portray the opposing party's expert as an ideologically committed or incoherent adversary. Thus, it is during cross-examination that social science evidence can most clearly be seen as a resource to be mobilized by one party, and, if possible, countered or discredited by the other. The cross-examination process also most directly challenges the skills, roles, and value stances of many social scientists, and creates psychological stresses that magnify underlying problems confronting the social scientist/expert.

The Purposes of Cross-Examination

Most legal scholars view cross-examination as an essential aspect of the attorney's role. For instance, in objecting to the use of what he believed was weak or inadequate scientific evidence in the early desegregation cases, Cahn (1956) indicated that opposing lawyers failed in a critical duty.

> More important, however, it is a lawyer's duty to conduct thorough and searching cross-examinations of adversary experts. In this way, he serves more than the interests of his own client. Vigorous cross-examination serves the larger social interest (a) by exposing fallacies in the expert evidence and (b) by deterring experts from making assertions that will not hold water. If the prospect of skilled cross-examination can deter some laymen from committing per-

jury, it may also deter some experts from passing off wishes as facts. (193)

Several experts we interviewed agreed that the purpose of cross-examination is to clarify issues and to challenge questionable statements.

> The function of the cross-examination is to sharpen what's been said, to make sure the witness says what is in fact true and consistent with reality. It's done to ensure validity, and it's terribly important. It is not used to discredit the witness: the attorney who tries that is in trouble.

Most experts, however, saw cross-examination as a means of discrediting one truth in order for another to persevere. Although the purpose of cross-questioning is to "get at the truth," the truth is to be understood within the context of an adversary proceeding. To get the truth is to simultaneously undermine the opponent's truth and the resource that supports it. These experts felt, therefore, that cross-examination was a partisan attempt by opposing attorneys to undermine their testimony via attacks on their credibility. Consider these reflections by scientists:

> The purpose of the cross-examination is to destroy the credibility of the witness.

> The lawyers are trying to make you look bad and less competent than you are. They will try to make you contradict yourself, and will try to discredit you personally if they cannot discredit your social science data or testimony.

Attorneys agree that one purpose of cross-examination is to gain admissions favorable to their side of the case, even if those involve discrediting the witness (Haddad 1979). Most attorneys we interviewed concurred with scholars' observations that they tried either to challenge the credentials of their opposing witness or to discover weaknesses or holes in their arguments that might destroy their credibility. For instance:

> I guess you would say that a good cross-examiner had to destroy the credibility of a witness.

> It was easy to cross-examine him and to affect his credibility because he had a tendency to make a lot of statements that he didn't really have any knowledge about. That they were really opinions

Table 7.1. Percent of Experts' Role Conflict Occurring during Cross-Examination

Percent of Role Conflict Occurring During Cross	Experts Experiencing Role Conflict	
	N = 25	100%
Less than 50%	5	20%
50%–90%	6	24%
100% (all)	14	56%

that he held without any basis in fact or in articles that he had read or whatever.

My cross-examination of expert witnesses is to hold them to the area of their expertise and to prevent their trying to spread the aura of legitimacy from an area in which they might be legitimate and unchallengeable experts into an area where they are just somebody else talking.

This view of cross-examination creates particular stress for experts, especially for those anticipating attacks by opposing attorneys. Experts expressed far more discomfort and conflict related to cross-examination than to any other aspect of witnessing. The data on role conflict, discussed in the last chapter, support this point. Table 7.1 demonstrates that over half of the informants who experienced role conflict noted that all (100%) of their conflict occurred during cross-examination, and 80% of the informants specified that most of the conflict they experienced occurred at this stage of testimony. These results are the same for scholars adhering to legal-adversary norms as well as for those following social science norms.

It appears that a primary source of the stress related to cross-examination is the struggle for power and control that occurs between scientists and attorneys.[1] Direct examination offers several opportunities for experts to structure and control their testimony. First, once they have decided to testify, scholars generally enter a negotiation with their attorney(s) as to the exact content and style of their testimony. Second, because they may select the lawyers for whom they will testify, one criterion may be whether a particular attorney will allow them to behave consistently with their preferred normative stance. Cross-examination

1. This is not the only source of stress, of course. Another is the drain on energy caused by the sheer length of time witnesses spent on the stand, being the object of constant scrutiny and potential attack. Witnesses often spent several hours under cross-examination. "It required 100% concentration all the time. I found it stressful to face a lengthy and boring set of questions with an expected yes/no response."

does not offer the same opportunities for structuring normative adherence. Prior to entering the courtroom, experts cannot select the lawyers who will cross-examine them; nor can they structure their testimony, because they rarely know exactly what questions will be asked. Consequently, experts often felt that they would not be in control of the lawyer-witness interaction during this phase of testimony, and therefore not in control of their own personal reactions, scholarly resources, and impact on the court.

> It was not the kind of thing an analyst or researcher is used to. It's easy to get trapped into saying something you don't want to.

> As college professors we are used to asking the questions, and you cannot do that in court. You can't fight back.

> There is kind of the danger of losing control . . . of being emotionally coopted.

> It is a little mini-war that the expert-witness plays with the lawyer. And once the lawyer makes you look like an ass, you say, "Boy, next time I get on the witness stand, the lawyer's going to look like an ass."

The control theme is echoed even by those scientists who claimed that their cross-examination experience was not stressful. Scholars who thought that they had not lost control of the expert-lawyer interaction felt they had won.[2]

> There is no way the lawyer can know enough social science to even come up to your knee in their ability to cross-examine you.

> The lawyers are sufficiently unskilled in social science evidence and they can't trap us.

> The first 10 minutes [of cross] were very stressful. But that was because I really didn't know what was coming at me, what kinds

2. As is demonstrated in this chapter, feeling that you have won or can win can be a dangerous assumption. Some witnesses seriously underestimated the skill of opposing counsel, and were subsequently harmed by their overconfidence. As more than one lawyer indicated: "Really, I really do try to come off as a nice guy in the deposition. I'm just stupid, I don't know anything. You tend to get the experts to really let it out and say things they wouldn't say if you were being really offensive with them. Then they tend to be a bit careless."

of questions were going to be asked. . . . And then I began to realize that I'm the expert on the stand on this issue and that I know more than [the opposing attorney] will ever know. So there's no reason for me to be afraid of this guy. Once I realized that, there was no problem. It was a cat and mouse game. . . . He'd ask me questions and I'd sit there and play games with him and toy with him until he asked a question the way I wanted it to be asked, and then I'd load up on it and sit back again.

The adversary nature of cross-examination creates special difficulties for those scholars who choose to adhere to social science norms in court. Note the comments of the expert quoted above, who experienced a good deal of stress about his ability to control the situation until he purposely chose to treat cross-examination as a "cat and mouse game" and adopt a legal-adversary stance. One expert who was generally committed to a social science normative stance stated that prior to cross-examination, she managed to remain detached and neutral. However, during cross-examination the combative behavior of the opposing attorney made her feel like an advocate, defending a position and a side of the case. Another expert stated:

As the case progressed I became more convinced that our side was right and I'm going to fight it to the last breath I have. But how much of that could have been conditioned by some attorney cross-examining or blasting you in a polite way, saying that for a buck you'll testify to anything, I'm not sure. Being human, I could have been influenced by that sort of thing. Damn it, I'm going to get in there and show you.

Yet, the combative or challenging behavior of opposing attorneys may make it difficult or dangerous for experts to blatantly adhere to legal-adversary norms as well. Whereas lawyers may desire partisan commitment from their own witnesses, they seek out signs of it in opposing experts, and use such evidence to undermine the expert's credibility. An expert may be labeled as "biased," a "hired gun" for one of the parties, or a "carpet-bagger." As one expert reported:

That made me almost angrier than anything when he implied that the way I was reporting the data might have had something to do with hiding the facts. Especially since I felt that I had been very much up front in the beginning, that the facts were the facts regardless of how I felt.

Such labels can undermine the credibility of any witness. Thus, legal-adversary experts are as interested in appearing credible as social science experts, for if they lose their credibility they can no longer help their side win its case.

The following section presents several strategies by which attorneys attempt to label the expert as an advocate, and to show his testimony to be wrong, biased, or both. Some of these approaches are focused upon discrediting the *expertise,* the credentials or knowledge base, of the witness. Others are focused on limiting or discrediting his *persuasiveness,* the manner in which he appears as reasonable. We also indicate how experts attempt to fend off such attacks. In the process we see examples of good (and bad) expert-witnessing in action.

Attorneys' Strategies of Cross-Examination

The strategies of cross-examination, and indeed of any courtroom examination, are the subject of a body of how-to books and articles written by successful trial attorneys (Bailey and Rothblatt 1971; Imwinkelried 1982; Jeans 1975; Keeton 1973; McElheney 1974) and often presented in journals oriented to practicing attorneys (e.g., *American Journal of Trial Advocacy, Litigation, Trial,* and *The Practical Lawyer*). Much of this advice is summarized by O'Barr (1982). Beyond general tactics, there are five particular strategies that attorneys may have pursued in the attempt to undermine opposing experts in the school desegregation cases:[3] (1) challenging the witness's credentials and substantive knowledge, (2) challenging the witness's knowledge of local issues, (3) implying special interest (gain) or bias, (4) searching for admissions of legitimacy of opposing views, and (5) exposing contradictions in testimony. All of the examples provided here are taken from a review of over 2,500 pages of transcripts of courtroom testimony offered in the school desegregation cases.[4]

---

3. The current leading book on how to cross-examine the opposition expert is that of Imwinkelried (1982). Although the topical headings presented here came from a review of our transcripts, in most cases they are paralleled by discussions in his book. For example, chapter 9 is on "Attacks on the Scientist," and covers fifteen different possible attacks on the witness's credibility, neutrality, and competence. Chapter 10 is on "Attacks on the Theory or Technique" used by the expert; and chapter 11 concerns "Attacks on the Facts or Data Analyzed."

4. These excerpts from courtroom testimony have been edited to preserve anonymity, but we have tried not to alter the meaning of any particular testimony. Although these excerpts are, we think, illustrative, we caution the reader to remember that, as in all interaction settings, abstracted bits of dialogue and behavior can never convey the full meaning of underlying events.

Challenges to Witnesses' Academic Credibility

Several attorneys indicated that it was fruitless to directly challenge a scholar's academic credentials. If a person is admitted as an expert and has the requisite degrees and publications, this type of challenge is rarely productive. Frontal attacks on the credibility of witnesses are often not only futile but also dangerous to the attorney's cause. In the early desegregation trials, cross-examination of plaintiff witnesses was often particularly disparaging, sometimes to the discredit and tactical disadvantage of the opposing counsel. As Cahn (1955) indicated in his review of Isadore Chein's testimony and cross-examination:

> In the Virginia trial [one of the cases which became part of *Brown*], the defense appeared particularly inept. Far from caring to concentrate on the doll test and its scientific validity, the lawyer for the defendants was preoccupied with other lines of cross-examination. He had a different set of values to display. Why concern himself with dissecting the experts' logic and the correctness of their inferences? Instead questions were asked which would convey disparaging insinuations about a professor's parents, his ancestral religion, the course of his surname, the pigmentation of his skin, or the place of his birth. . . . As any healthy-minded person reads the Virginia trial record, it is impossible not to contrast the altruism and sober dignity of the scientists with the behavior of the defendants' counsel, who by his manner of espousing the old order, exposed its cruelty and bigotry. (165)

It is rare to discover such crass cross-examination in later school cases. A more typical challenge to witnesses' academic credibility raises questions about their particular experience and knowledge of the field. As one attorney indicated in an interview:

> I don't challenge their credentials. I don't need to do that. . . . You just want to make clear what it is that forms the basis of their testimony. It's important for the judge to know whether this person who is brought forward as an expert knows what the hell he's talking about.

Consider the following examples of attorney challenges to one educational scientist's limited experience as a school superintendent:

> COUNSEL: You yourself have not been the superintendent of any large city—
> WITNESS: That is correct.

COUNSEL: According to the newspaper you were the superin-
tendent at some district in the state at some time.
WITNESS: They were two separate districts.·
COUNSEL: How big a district was the first?
WITNESS: Oh, small. Enrollment at the time was under a thou-
sand, but I can't remember the exact number.
COUNSEL: Any blacks?
WITNESS: No.
COUNSEL: How large was the other one?
WITNESS: Somewhat larger. I am trying to remember. If you give
me an honest man's leeway, I would say a thousand, give or take
some.
COUNSEL: And were there any blacks there?
WITNESS: No.
COUNSEL: Is that the extent of your experience as an administra-
tive head of any school district?
WITNESS: Yes.

Other challenges to a witness's credentials may include examination
of prior testimony or scholarship, particularly if the scholar has testified
in other cases. In the following excerpt, the attorney has read to the
court passages from a social scientist's own early work, in an attempt
to show that his current testimony is different:

COUNSEL: My point is that you now repudiate it. You're now saying you repudiate—
WITNESS: I would now soften what I said here when I said, "virtually unknown empirically," because there have been empirical
studies on the question that tend to show that, as is the case for
whites, black housing sites tend to follow black job opportunities.

Several attorneys indicated that it was easier for them to conduct a
cross-examination of witnesses who had testified many times before.
Their statements were on the record; it was easier to predict what they
would say, to prepare to challenge it, and perhaps to even find an embarrassing admission or error in pages of prior testimony.

He had never testified before, which you can understand is a benefit in that he didn't have a million pages of cross-examination to
pull out the mistakes that he had made before.

When an expert had not testified before or did not have a personal track
record, different challenges were necessary.
In addition to challenges focusing on the witness's own experience

and research, attacks of a more indirect sort were made on the source material a scholar cited. Here the attorney attempts to challenge the witness by implying that sources not appearing in a refereed journal may not be quite acceptable, legitimate, or fully scientific.

> COUNSEL: Was that published in a refereed journal?
> WITNESS: It was a special report by the Department of Geography.
> COUNSEL: Was it published in a refereed journal?
> WITNESS: No.

Later, the witness turns the tables, and raises the same issue regarding one of the attorney's sources.

> WITNESS: Has this article been published?
> COUNSEL: Yes, I believe so.
> WITNESS: Where was it published?
> COUNSEL: It was published by the Survey Research Center of the Institute for Social Research. . . . I don't know if it's been published in a refereed journal. It's a hard cover book I have been advised.

The game continues. Now the attorney "reduces" the witness's reference to a much less credible source, a graduate student's doctoral dissertation:

> COUNSEL: Was it a book?
> WITNESS: It's a dissertation.
> COUNSEL: Was it published by a commercial or academic publisher?
> WITNESS: No.
> COUNSEL: So this is what we call a student doctoral dissertation?
> WITNESS: Yes.

Attorneys can also challenge a witness's credibility by noting that they have not studied the precise issue about which they are testifying. Granting the witness general expertise in the area of residential segregation, the attorney below closed in on the expert's publication record regarding the role of schools in this process (known as the "problem of reciprocal effect").

> COUNSEL: In fact, Doctor, everything that I have read of yours, including your articles . . . at no place mentions school *de jure* segregation as a cause of racially segregated neighborhoods, is that a fair statement?
> WITNESS: I don't know whether there is some reference to it in

the materials of the kind you mentioned, about, but I have not studied that aspect specifically.

COUNSEL: You came here to testify about it, though?

WITNESS: Certainly.

COUNSEL: My point is, can you refer the Court at any place in
your various publications where you attribute segregated racial patterns to education and assignment of pupils by an educational system. You cannot, can you, Doctor?

WITNESS: No, I can't.

COUNSEL: And yet you have written literally thousands of pages
on the question of residential segregation in course of your career?

Challenges to Witnesses' Knowledge of Local Issues

A second major strategy used by attorneys challenges the relevance,
applicability, and validity of the national scholar's general data to the
circumstances of the local arena. Although social scientists' ability to
generalize across individuals and local situations is central to the development of their discipline, this focus may make them vulnerable in
a court proceeding concerned with local facts, local violations, and local
remedies. Gardner (1979) has stressed the importance of this strategy
for defense counsel in employment discrimination cases, and Pettigrew
(1979) has reported its common use in school desegregation trials. As
noted by one attorney, some scholars are easy to cross-examine because
they lack time on-site, experience in the specific locale, or even knowledge about the case or school situation at hand.

> He, on the other hand, was an easy cross because he had no fa-
> miliarity with the city. He had no familiarity with voluntary pro-
> grams. He had no familiarity with mandatory programs. He was
> basically laying out a line. So he just came here and pontificated
> and it wasn't too hard to deflate that.

One example of the use of this strategy follows:

> COUNSEL: Can you tell us where the initial placement of a school
> in this city has influenced the initial character of the neighborhood?
>
> WITNESS: No, I can't.
>
> COUNSEL: Since you can't tell us one, then you are not telling the
> Court that the initial location of schools in this city has influenced
> the racial character of the neighborhoods?
>
> WITNESS: No. I am not adducing any specific examples about this
> city, and in particular, I would be uninformed about the initial
> placement, because most of my studies have dealt with a period

when the city was largely built up—had more to do with relocation and redesignation of the character of schools.

COUNSEL: Doctor, I inquired of that because you were tendered by your attorney as an expert in the field of racial residential urban segregation, especially in this city, and that is what you purport— you do purport that to be your field of expertise.

WITNESS: Yes.

Another example of this general approach comes from cross-examination in which the witness clearly anticipates the line of attack, and attempts to distinguish his observations ("refamiliarizing myself") from his investigations ("scholarly study"):

COUNSEL: Your study of this school system, if I have got it correctly—first, your study of the plan is limited to your driving tour of the schools, right, on two separate occasions?

WITNESS: My study of what?

COUNSEL: Of the plan.

WITNESS: Of the school plan, yes

COUNSEL: And you didn't go in the schools?

WITNESS: No sir. Not on that tour. I have personal acquaintance among many teachers and I must say I have conversed with some of them.

COUNSEL: But your investigation did not include conferences for that purpose with any teachers or principals or administrators?

WITNESS: You are speaking now of my tour?

COUNSEL: Yes.

WITNESS: Yes, and I think you dignify it to call it an investigation. I was refamiliarizing myself with the schools in this system.

COUNSEL: And you haven't made any study of the type of programs which are being advanced, taught, in each of the various schools?

WITNESS: No, sir.

COUNSEL: Nor of the particular training which particular teachers have received for particular programs in the particular school?

WITNESS: No, sir.

A particularly interesting example of this form of challenge, and the court's response to it, is provided below. It is taken from testimony and cross-examination in which the witness's studies of minority education have already been referred to several times. After testifying to these studies, the witness has indicated that he spent a little time observing and talking with educators in the local school system. He has just characterized one school as a "minority" school, one of the best he has seen; he has also characterized another school as a "white" school, one of the best he has seen. Counsel challenges the witness on his limited observations, and addresses the court with a concern:

> COUNSEL: I think we are entitled to show that it takes time to accurately evaluate a school and that unless you have a preconceived notion as to what you are going to find . . .
>
> THE COURT: He says it is based on what he saw here, but what he saw here supports his factual basis and former investigation of students in all the region, and his visits here to the schools, for a very short time, only support what he has observed in years of study.
>
> COUNSEL: What we want to demonstrate is that it is recognized that you can't make any valid conclusion at all about how a particular school or class is conducted without considerably more visits than the witness has made.
>
> THE COURT: He has not testified how the school is conducted or how it was evaluated. He just says that his short visit here substantiates his previous findings on a study of "minority" schools, that these schools which were either minority or white, fell in the same pattern and substantiated or verified his previous conclusions which he made from studies.

Now the judge elaborates his point to the examining attorney:

> THE COURT: That is where you are misconstruing the testimony. He didn't testify he reached the conclusion from looking at the school for an hour and a half. He said his studies teach him certain patterns that exist in segregated schools, He said the short time in an hour and a half of what he saw substantiated the studies he made which shows when you segregate children in that percentage of eight-five minority, certain patterns are going to exist.

While this dialogue is occurring between attorney and judge, the witness sits back and waits. After all, the judge is responding to the challenge to the witness's expertise.

A similar dynamic occurs in the following passage, although on a different topic. The witness has just testified to the problems of teacher prejudice against minority youth, and to the potential impact of such attitudes on student performance.

> COUNSEL: Did you talk to any teachers? You said you did not talk to any teachers in this city to see if this is a prevalent attitude?

WITNESS: I said I talked fifteen minutes to one teacher. I also said I drew no conclusion from that. I said that is a general characteristic across the nation.

THE COURT: Do you think you can ask the teacher or superintendent, or the School Board Member, or a Doctor of Education, or a housewife, or a Federal Court Judge, if they are prejudiced and they will say they are?

WITNESS: It is impossible. There is no instrument to measure that.

COUNSEL: I presume a man of your qualifications who has been making surveys can make questions of a particular individual to get some indication about how they feel?

WITNESS: Honestly, I think you can, and this is, of course, what I did. And I automatically got the stereotype. I am not talking here and now about throughout the nation, but I will stand on it that we have tapped the real feelings so that I consider the more important thing is not the attitude and not the perspective, but the behavior. The behavior is observable, it is recordable. If I were to study this city it would take me a year, probably, and what I would do is establish check sheets on the behavior of teachers: how many times does X teacher or teachers as an aggregate call on minority children as related to such and such, how much reinforcement, how much reward, what kind of reward? I would use some kind of interaction scale. I think it is a dead issue to look toward prejudice. What I said is [that] teachers in minority schools tend to be pessimistic about the ability of their children to learn. I refer you to "Dark Ghetto" by Dr. Kenneth Clark to support what I say about the black population, and so forth. He has not studied this city either.

Buoyed no doubt by the judge's intervention and apparent sympathy (with his expertise, if not necessarily his stance on the issue), the witness subtly attacks back in his last comment. Kenneth Clark has not studied this city either!

Implications of Special Interest or Personal Bias

A third strategy of cross-examination attorneys employ is to suggest, or gain admission, that the scientist has somehow been compromised by his or her personal interests or biases in the case. (Haddad 1979; Kalmuss 1981). Kornblum (1974) and Shubow and Bergstresser (1977) have identified some of the specific indicators of bias for which attorneys should probe. Personal bias may take the form of strongly held values on the issues in litigation, friendship with or loyalty to the attorney or party in the case, monetary gain, publicity seeking, consistent alliance with or allegiance to a particular party in a series of cases (plaintiff or defense), and strong theoretical or ideological predispositions. Attorneys are generally rather cautious about how they employ this strategy. A direct approach might have them labeling all experts as "hired guns," "whores," or "party shills." Rather, a more subtle and indirect series of inquiries and implications is usually used.

Innuendos and direct suggestions that financial gain, perhaps ill-gotten at that, may be at stake can be seen in this cross-examination excerpt:

> COUNSEL: Is there a rule in your University on consulting time?
>
> WITNESS: There is no rule in the University at the present time . . .
>
> COUNSEL: Your fees go directly to you and not to the University, I take it?
>
> WITNESS: That's true.
>
> COUNSEL: Have you been on the University payroll full time during the period when you have spent twenty-five working days on this case?
>
> WITNESS: I have.

Frequently, the questions to plaintiff and defense witnesses are even more specific, probing how much experts were paid, how many hours or days they worked on the case, and so forth.

A somewhat different line of attack focuses on the party affiliation of the witness and its potential impact on his or her interests, and, therefore, testimony. Consider the following questions:

> COUNSEL: And would this be a fair summary of the circumstances; that your colleague advised you that he was contacted by counsel in this case and that he wanted to put together, let's say a package of testimony, with several . . . of you putting together expert testimony, designed to show . . . [that] governmental discrimination was not a significant cause of the condition of residential racial segregation existing here?
>
> WITNESS: I was never asked to do a study that was designed to show anything. He approached me, asked me if I would be willing to do a study of the . . . black and white population of the city and what implications that might have for explaining desegregation.
>
> COUNSEL: But he made clear at the beginning that this would be as an expert witness on behalf of the school board.

WITNESS: Yes.

COUNSEL: And that was in the school board's interest to show that governmental discrimination was not a substantial cause of this?

WITNESS: I don't remember whether he said that or not.

COUNSEL: When he talked to you, as your testimony developed, as your research developed, is it fair to say that you knew what the others were doing, and they knew what you were doing?

WITNESS: I had less knowledge of what the others were doing, but generally my colleague and I discussed our studies as they went along.

In his response the witness makes it clear that he was not "out to prove" anything, but was conducting a study "to discover." The attorney did not make much further use of the alleged combination of witnesses. A somewhat similar approach was used in another cross-examination:

COUNSEL: I understand that you have testified in many cases involving the same examination of effects of residential movements in desegregation cases.

WITNESS: I have testified in many cases. The examination has varied from one to the other.

. . . .

COUNSEL: In any of these cases, have you testified on behalf of a board of education or other defendant wherein plaintiffs are seeking a desegregation order of some kind or another?

WITNESS: I cannot give a direct answer to that, because I do not follow that closely the legal status of who is challenging whom at the particular stage in which I appear. As I mentioned in the deposition, I have testified for a Board of Education when it was seeking the desegregation remedy that I believe was at stake at that particular stage of the trial.

The full meaning of this witness's answer remains somewhat unclear; perhaps deliberately so. It is unlikely that the witness really does not follow closely "the legal status of who is challenging whom," but clearly he does not wish to be made to appear to be an adversary by opposing counsel. Moreover, his insertion of the example where he did testify for the school board (which was the original defendant in a city suit and became aligned with the plaintiff in a metropolitan suit) indicates his sophisticated understanding of both the "legal status" issue and the attorney's intent in asking the question. This line of questioning was not followed further in cross-examination.

A variant of inquiry into witnesses' interests is the attempt to discover, or suggest, that the witness has personal views for or against desegregation that might impede his or her ability to act as an apparently neutral expert witness. As one attorney suggested of a witness:

> On a broad sort of basis he had just been committed to segregation. He has no real commitment to any sort of desegregation, he was really a racist and I wanted, through his writings and his previous testimony, to demonstrate that.

One example of this attempt is reflected in the following cross-examination:

> COUNSEL: Do you have any personal views on the desirability of school integration?
> WITNESS: I think the way to achieve school integration is through housing.

Not having received a direct (yes/no) answer to his second question, the attorney returned to it later in two different ways. First, he asked the witness about his views of his own city:

> COUNSEL: With regard to that type of busing, have you made a public position?
> WITNESS: What type of busing?
> COUNSEL: For school desegregation.
> WITNESS Have I made a public position on that?
> COUNSEL: Yes.
> WITNESS: No, I have not.

Apparently satisfied that the witness was not publicly and politically active (as other than a scholar) on desegregation issues, the attorney returned to the original question a second time.

> COUNSEL: At the outset of your direct examination, you were asked I believe, whether or not you thought school integration should be accomplished through desegregation of the schools I believe—and I'm not sure I can reconstruct it. I recall you saying something about how you thought school desegregation would best occur through the desegregation of housing, is that correct?
> WITNESS: I think that's a reasonable summary. The question was about—I think the first question was about—
> COUNSEL: Are you in favor of school desegregation?
> WITNESS: No, I think it was—the first question was about segregation in general. Then there was another question about

schools. I think the substance of what you're saying is correct, that I thought that the way to accomplish school desegregation was through some form of housing desegregation, that housing was the key.

Is the witness in favor of school desegregation? It is not yet clear, at least not from this testimony. Both the attorney and apparently the witness recognize that if the witness were to admit opposition to desegregation by any means, his credibility would be damaged. For the witness to be in favor of desegregation, but opposed to one or another way of accomplishing it, is quite another matter, and a legitimate one as far as the courts are concerned. This particular piece of testimony provides a feeling for the large segments of most cross-examinations which are sparring matches, and a sense of the inconclusiveness of most sets of questions and answers.

Search for Admissions of Legitimacy of Opposing Views

A fourth major strategy attorneys use is to try to get expert witnesses to admit that other scholars might reasonably come to a different conclusion about a situation or data set. If such an admission can be gained, the case truly becomes "one person's opinion versus another," rather than one person's views representing the bulk of scientific evidence. This effort is quite close to the "learned treatise" strategy of cross-examination described by Haddad (1979) and Poythress (1980). Here the attorney confronts the witness with a renowned article opposed to his view and asks if the witness is familiar with it. If the expert denies knowledge his qualifications may be cast into doubt; if he indicates knowledge he must argue against the learned treatise lest it and its fame cast doubt on his testimony.

Efforts to find admissions of reasonable doubt frequently require the attorney to use other witnesses' testimony or studies as a springboard. In this example, the witness first resists but then admits legitimate opposition.

> COUNSEL: So that it's fair to say that social scientists in good faith differ considerably as to what is the best way to study data.
> WITNESS: I think there is some debate about how to handle data. I think more debate comes on what the structure of the models are.
> COUNSEL: This is what I think I was getting at. Could different persons, using the same data—could they be using different models and thus come up with different predictions?
> WITNESS: Yes. I believe they would be using the wrong models.

COUNSEL: Right, but one could disagree on that?

WITNESS: Yes.

A similar tack on cross-examination also gets the following witness to admit to scholarly disagreement. However, when provided the opportunity by counsel, the witness indicates his continuing disagreement with alternative studies.

> COUNSEL: Isn't there a respectable body of sociological opinion that holds, no more than whites do, Negroes do not want to be a minority in their own neighborhood? They prefer, other things being equal, to live in an area where they are a majority group, at least a neighborhood where there is no clear majority group?
>
> WITNESS: No. I would disagree with that. There are two components. One is, are there sociologists that say that? And secondly, is there evidence that demonstrates that?
>
> COUNSEL: My question was somewhat different from either of those points. My question was whether there was a body of sociological opinion which holds to that point of view.
>
> WITNESS: Yes, there is a body of sociological opinion, opinion by sociologists to that effect.
>
> COUNSEL: Isn't there also a body of opinion that holds certain white ethnics will self-segregate voluntarily and without impact of restraints?
>
> WITNESS: Yes, there is some body of opinion to that effect.
>
> COUNSEL: Do you hold a view different from the body of opinion?
>
> WITNESS: I believe that the studies that I have seen on that have certain weaknesses. So that first, I am not sure that the kinds of voluntary self-segregation that are being talked about, for instance, the Polish community or Italian community or the Jewish community—I am not sure first that those are free of taint of historical discrimination to help determine the factors in the first place, and in some instances still continue to operate.

Most attorneys know that scientists have a tendency to "fairness" in evaluating other scholars' work, and so they often encourage their own witnesses to stick to their guns under fire. As one attorney commented:

> When you are on cross-examination, the other side is going to try to discredit you. So, how a person conducts himself on past cross-examination in one of these cases would be one of the factors we would look at in determining who we would want to call as an expert. Somebody that isn't easily shaken from his opinion, who doesn't hedge and backtrack from what he said on direct because

of a few pointed questions by the opposing counsel. So you want somebody who is firm on his opinions and can back them up because they are going to attack you. I think they have got to suggest, well, isn't it possible that other factors are the real reason why that happens and not the factors you listed? And he has got to be able to say no and this is why: because I have studied those other factors and this is why those factors are not the reason.

Exposures of Contradictions or Errors in Testimony

A final strategy attorneys use to challenge or impugn the credibility of opposing witnesses is to discover contradictions or errors in their testimony. Because experts are themselves adept and alert, attorneys can seldom extract damaging testimony or admissions directly; various subtle devices are more often used. Sometimes an attorney who is about to trap a witness has carefully thought out his approach well ahead of time, and has set up an intricate argument. At other times, the attorney just falls into it. One question leads to another and sooner or later the attorney discovers how he might be able to make an effective challenge. In the examples that follow we present several traps that were unsuccessful or avoided.

The first example of an attempted trap for error or contradiction comes from the cross-examination of an expert whose direct testimony linked housing and school segregation to governmental actions.

> COUNSEL: Is it true that it is your opinion that racial separation in housing occurs regardless of the character of local laws and policies, and regardless of the extent of other forms of segregation and administration?
>
> WITNESS: Would you check the last word? Yes, that is a sentence I wrote many years ago to which I still agree.

The witness has recognized that the attorney was reading to him from his own published works. Had he denied the comment, he would have been contradicting his own words. Now the attorney presses him to admit that this argument means that local systems cannot be held responsible for segregation, and the witness attempts to clarify (or extend) his meaning without letting local officials off the hook.

> COUNSEL: So that the phenomena of increasing separation or continuance of racial separation in housing can in fact occur regardless of local laws and policies of governmental agencies; is that not correct?
>
> WITNESS: It can indeed occur. This is not to say it has occurred,

but it can indeed occur despite the kinds of local efforts that have been made as of the earlier period. This quotation comes from a work written several years ago. The point that was being made was that every city in the United States had a high degree of racial residential segregation. There had been some feeling during that period of time, when civil rights legislation was just beginning; New York City has led the way with a fair housing law in 1958 and a few other cities had adopted such ordinances. My earlier conclusion was there was no evidence that those had a major impact and hence the residential segregation continues despite local laws which had not been in effect. It did not say residential segregation was not affected by federal laws, which is one of the forces that affect cities throughout the country.

In another failed trap, a witness openly discussed the role of *de jure* segregation in northern school systems. Given the legal history of *de jure–de facto* distinctions in southern and northern school systems, the attorney sensed that he had caught the witness in a critical error or a legal faux pas.

> COUNSEL: Oh, you have found a Northern city that does have a *de jure* segregated school system?
>
> WITNESS: By my understanding they all have it.
>
> COUNSEL: All Northern cities have a *de jure* segregated school system?
>
> WITNESS: By my understanding, yes.
>
> COUNSEL: If it should be determined that all Northern cities do not have *de jure* segregated school systems, then what would your conclusions be?
>
> WITNESS: Well, you are referring to a determination, using the particular determination within a court of law. I am referring to a scholarly definition with respect to the kinds of impact these laws and administrative uses, I have testified, effects residential patterns. I would not change my statement on the basis of what those Court determinations happen to be. This is referring to a legal rather than scholarly definition of the term.

The witness's response worked in this case. The cross-examining attorney persisted. The witness's own attorney intervened, and the judge finally halted the interaction by indicating that the witness did carefully distinguish between legal and sociological definitions, and that he had been clear enough.

Not all traps fail. In the following example, the cross-examining attorney spends a good deal of time asking the witness what materials he has read and how much time he spend on them:

> WITNESS: There were two huge boxes. I was a little dismayed when I sat down with all these documents. I did attempt to look at all of them but it was quite—it's quite obvious that I would not read what appeared to me to be about six thousand pages of housing documents. I looked at most of them and picked and selected, trying to get a feel for the housing documents. I looked at what other material was available and yesterday I spent some time with the bin of maps.
>
> COUNSEL: How much time?
>
> WITNESS: With the maps? I looked at all of the maps because I'm interested in maps.
>
> COUNSEL: How many maps and how much time?

The witness indicates that he worked hard and read a lot of material. This line of question and response continues. It is not yet clear what the attorney's intent is. Does he know where he's going or is he "fishing" for a vulnerability, an opening?

> COUNSEL: Can you tell me what depositions you read?
>
> WITNESS: If you would like me to consult my notes, I can. Just off the top of my head . . . I would have to look up the names because the names were all unfamiliar to me. Would you like me to do that?
>
> COUNSEL: Yes.
>
> . . . .
>
> WITNESS: It was a substantial document. It was perhaps—I'll give it by thickness. It was perhaps a half inch or three-quarters of an inch thick.
>
> COUNSEL: Did you read a quarter of an inch or a half inch or all of the inches?
>
> WITNESS: I thumbed through it. I don't think it's ever necessary to read every word in the volume to get an idea of what's in it. If we in academics had to do that, you would never get through all the stuff there is to read.
>
> COUNSEL: What other documents?
>
> WITNESS: As I said to you, I read and selected in that listing of housing documents, given the time constraints that I had, and I found many of them interesting and some of them I made a few notes on that I could add to my lectures. There were some interesting points made.

Counsel: What did you find interesting?

Witness: I found an interesting discussion of the public housing policies.

Counsel: Which aspect of the public housing, the fact that it was segregated?

Witness: No. I was more interested in the procedures for developing that and the way in which it had been effected in this city.

Suddenly, the questioning becomes more direct: a specific question is asked about a specific housing unit.

Counsel: Do you recall what it was you read about Perry Homes?

Witness: I think what I was interested in was that in some of the documents they indicated that the expansion—the growth of the black residential area to the west was affected by the location of Perry Homes, which was built by a black developer on vacant land and so influenced the growth in that direction.

Counsel: Was that private housing?

Witness: I believe Perry Homes was public housing but I would want to recheck that. I thought initially that Perry Homes was a private development and I was corrected in a conversation about that, so I would want to go back and check the document to be absolutely precise.

Counsel: Do you know how many units of housing are involved in Perry Homes?

Witness: No, I do not.

Counsel: Do you know its location—I'm sorry, strike that. Do you know the time it opened, the date that it opened?

Witness: The exact date?

Counsel: The approximate date.

Witness: In the twenties some time, I believe.

The Court: When?

Witness: I thought it was in the twenties some time.

Counsel: Do you know the surrounding area by race or by zoning, what was around Perry Homes site at the time that it opened?

Witness: I have not made a study of that specifically.

Counsel: Do you know if it was adjacent, immediately adjacent to the black expansion area?

Witness: I said I didn't make a specific study of that.

. . . .

Counsel: For your information, the Perry Homes housing project is the largest housing project in the metropolitan area. It was built and opened in 1952, all black.

WITNESS: That's an interesting piece of misinformation then in that document that I copied out. I have a note here that there's a comment about Perry Homes influencing the expansion west in the twenties and that is one of the housing documents. I would certainly like to look at that but I could be mistaken. As I said to you, I tried to look at as much of the housing information as I could, given the time, but I was writing rapidly and reading rapidly and errors do occur.

The trap is sprung. The witness does not remember key pieces of information about the "largest housing project in the metropolitan area," and a segregated project at that. The witness tries to double back by suggesting that there was "misinformation" in the record, talking about the work load, and admitting he might have been mistaken. One senses, however, that this witness overreached himself. Trying to overcome the general accusation that he did not have any local knowledge, he portrayed himself as knowledgeable about local history. A "good witness" would admit general weakness in this area. As one of the lawyers we quoted in chapter 5 pointed out, "A good witness will say 'I don't know' when he doesn't." By failing to do so, this witness allowed himself to be led into a trap.

Experts' Strategies in Countering Cross-Examination

The preceding excerpts illuminate various strategies of cross-examination and the challenges made by opposing attorneys, and provide some indication of why scientists experienced stress and conflict in the courtroom. However, they also indicate how scientists tried to cope with these challenges, and, in many cases, how they fought back. Scientists engaged in the struggle for power and control during courtroom testimony were not passive and dependent objects. They, too, developed procedures for deflecting or counterattacking attorneys' challenges. Their procedures were reactive, for the most part, because initiation of challenges lay in the attorneys' hands, but experts did have choices about how to respond.[5]

The exchanges in which experts successfully fend off attacks invariably contain elements of what makes a good expert witness. Among these elements are: (*a*) being "cool" or reasonable and cooperative; (*b*) giving direct answers, which are more persuasive than vague or frag-

5. As in the previous section, our discussion of "strategies" is a process of inference we make from observations of interaction. We cannot imply or impute deliberate intent to any specific attorney or expert in this regard. To a considerable extent, the general inferences we make about experts' strategies are supported by our interviews.

mented ones; (c) not exaggerating or going outside one's own field, which would weaken one's testimony; (d) not being extremely slow and therefore unconvincing while responding; (e) not qualifying an answer too much; and (f) following the lead of one's own attorney (Brodsky 1977; Loewen 1982; Pettigrew 1979; Poythress 1980; Taeuber 1979; Williams 1957; Wolfgang 1974). Experts follow these general suggestions in a number of ways during cross-examination, but often modify them when they feel they are under attack. We identify at least five ways in which experts thwart or counter attorney's attacks on their testimony. They are: (1) remaining cool and above the battle; (2) conceding minor points in order to appear "fair minded"; (3) parrying or reinterpreting the attorney's questions; (4) obfuscating a problematic question with jargon, circular reasoning, or technical doubletalk; and (5) attacking the attorney's logic or evidence directly.

Note that whereas (1) and (2) are cautious, reactive behaviors, (3), (4), and (5) are aggressive, proactive behaviors. They are tactics which an attorney is likely to tell his expert *not* to attempt while on the stand. In a sense, to adopt them is to go beyond being a "good witness" by trying to be a "good advocate."

As discussed in chapter 5, remaining in control of oneself is a central virtue of the good witness. One should try to stay cool, to be removed from and untouched by the battle insofar as possible, and to answer all questions as courteously and carefully as possible. In fact, as far as behavior is concerned, we would not know that the witness had been part of a contest at all. Examples of this strategy in pieces of testimony discussed earlier in this chapter include interactions that led to such comments as "I don't know," "If you give me an honest man's leeway," and "I do not follow that closely the legal status of who is challenging whom."

Experts often fight back for their point of view. Yet, a relentlessly adversary style of the part of the witness is, as we have noted, likely to hurt her credibility. The judge may conclude that the expert will agree only to points which support her party's case. If so, all points that the expert makes may be interpreted as partisan comments. Thus, a second strategy that experts used during cross-examination was to voluntarily concede minor errors or damaging admissions before they were introduced or emphasized by opposing counsel. This "fair-minded" behavior may have even gained extra credibility points, while at the same time defusing a potentially embarrassing contradiction or error. Examples of this strategy in the previous transcripts are remarks like "I would now soften what I said," "I think you dignify it to call it an investigation," and "I could be mistaken."

A third way in which experts attempted to hold their own during stressful cross-examination involved parrying the opposing counsel's questions. For instance, the expert may have asked the attorney to repeat or rephrase questions that the expert did not want to answer or may have wanted to think about. At the very least, such an approach stalled for time; at best, the attorney may have decided it was not worthwhile to pursue the issue. A related approach involved experts reinterpreting questions (often to themselves) and then answering the question they wished to answer, rather than the one that was asked. If the attorney asked a vague question to start with, this was an effective device. Even if the attorney asked a fairly direct question, this strategy permitted the expert to make the points he wished to make, or to avoid a direct response to an uncomfortable question. In order to counter this tack, the persistent attorney must interrupt, point out that his question has not been answered, and begin again. Examples of this strategy are comments like "I do not follow the question," "I did not understand the question," and "I think the way to achieve school integration is through housing," in response to a question about the desirability of school desegregation.

A fourth strategy included obfuscation, or the attempt to cloud a response with jargon, circular reasoning, or plain doubletalk. For example:

> COUNSEL: Thus you say, or might I conclude that desegregated schooling is a prime cause of increased [residential] segregation? Would that not follow, Doctor?
>
> WITNESS: No. It would not follow, in that it is my understanding that there is not a situation of desegregated schooling to the point at which the location, the residential location of the family, has no impact on the racial composition of the school which the children attend.

It is important to note that this answer was from a witness who could be very articulate when he chose to be. Of course, if such responses are used too frequently, they will damage the credibility of the witness. However, it is hard to challenge them directly, especially when the expert normally uses a heavy dose of typical scientific jargon in his answers.

A fifth way experts attempt to maintain control during cross-examination involves counterattacking when the attorney appears vulnerable. Gardner (1979) notes that expert witnesses may use this strategy when the attorney is ill-prepared—"if the witness realizes he is dealing with a new student in class" (18). Most lawyers recommend that their expert witnesses avoid this approach, because it does more than defend against attack; it opens up whole new avenues for challenge and response. As such, it might sacrifice the expert's credibility for minimal and momentary gain. Nevertheless, some experts used this approach, either deliberately or because they were provoked into it. Possible examples of interactions leading to such comments are "He has not studied this either" and "Has this article been published? . . . Where was it published?"

Moreover, no expert is "out there" by herself; the expert who remembers her preparation and her alliance with her own attorney has extra resources to rely on when the going gets tough (Philo and Atkinson 1978). For instance, several attorneys indicated their willingness to interrupt the cross-examination process to tip off their witness to a trap, to object to a line of questioning, or to otherwise prevent effective challenges to their expert's testimony. The first example of this tactic that we present occurred as the witness's own counsel was conducting direct testimony. The opposing counsel attempted to mount a challenge at an early stage of this testimony and was beaten back by the witness's counsel.

> COUNSEL: Doctor, in light of what you have just read and the testimony you have given previously, is it fair to say that if a white person is considering moving in an area—what does FHA say—with an incompatible racial element, that figuring up what he could pay or would pay for a mortgage, FHA is suggesting here that he include in the cost of a private school or transportation to a private school or another school which is more compatible racially?
>
> WITNESS: Yes. That's what this section suggests.
>
> COUNSEL: Is that the situation that prevails today as a practical matter?
>
> WITNESS: As a practical—
>
> OPPOSING COUNSEL: (Interposing) In this community?
>
> COUNSEL: In general, is my question.
>
> OPPOSING COUNSEL: I believe it would be better to limit it to this community.
>
> COUNSEL: My question is in general. If you want to ask questions, you wait until your turn.

We can expect that when the opposing counsel entered cross-examination this line of challenge occurred again.

Another example of attorney intervention in cross-examination occurred when the opposing counsel was questioning a witness's relationship to the case and whether he had demonstrated a potential "interest" (stake) in the case.

OPPOSING COUNSEL: I would like to establish a few facts with respect to your involvement in the events preceding this litigation directed to the litigation. As I understand it, you are the one who decided to make a contact with counsel for the Plaintiffs in this action; is that correct?

WITNESS: That is not correct.

OPPOSING COUNSEL: Would you tell us what the contact was then, or who made the first contact to your knowledge . . .
. . . .

COUNSEL: I think I am going to object to this line of questioning on a number of grounds. In the first place, I don't think it is relevant to anything. I also don't think it is proper cross-examination. I do not think it goes to any of the issues raised on direct.

THE COURT: It may and may not go to credibility. The Court fails to see the relevance.

OPPOSING COUNSEL: It goes to bias.

All of these response strategies by experts are part of the battle for power and control of testimony that occurs throughout the courtroom experience. The escalation of these issues during cross-examination highlights the underlying process of the adversary system. These responses indicate that there is an interaction occurring, and that experts are not simply passive and neutral agents acted upon by attorneys. Further, opposing counsel and expert are by no means the only actors in these situations. On several occasions, as we have indicated, judges have become active agents, either in making direct inquiry to the expert or in curbing one or another counsel.

Conclusions

The interactions presented above indicate some of the strategies used by attorneys and experts in courtroom cross-examination. The challenge to, and preservation of, certain roles and role behaviors involves scholars and attorneys in a series of delicate interaction sequences. In many cases it is difficult for experts experiencing such challenges to present the kinds of testimony they wish to present, in the manner in which they wish to present it. It is even more difficult for scholars to exercise the same control over their presentations during cross-examination that they do during preparation and direct examination, or in their publications and classrooms.

As plaintiff and defense attorneys try to present and interpret social reality in ways that make the best case for their side, experts appearing on behalf of those parties are inevitably drawn into the adversary contest. Then the contest for experts' resources, and for interpretations of their offerings, involves them directly. Cross-examination represents the clearest, but by no means the sole, challenge to expert control in the adversary arena of the courtroom.

8 The Effect of Testifying on Experts
Political Conflict in Applied
Social Science

The last several chapters have focused on the skill and role problems faced by scientists. In this chapter we focus on political and career problems, both of which create political conflict for witnesses (see Chapter 4 for a definition of these problems). Political conflict stems from disparities between scholars' political stance and that of the party for whom they testify, or of their professional community. Witnesses encountered both personal and professional political conflict.

Examples of personal political conflict include conflicts among a scholar's own values or between the scholar's values and those of his clients or constituencies. These conflicts can lead to difficult decisions such as whether to publish controversial research findings or to testify in ways contrary to one's own values or allies' interests.

Professional political conflict arises when substantial disagreement exists between an individual and his colleagues or his institution, and when the individual believes that his activity may be sanctioned. Such conflict can influence the choice of a research topic, or, in the case of an expert witness, the decision to testify in ways contrary to colleagues' norms (see Sagarin 1980). These conflicts are broadly characteristic of applied social science, but they are escalated when scientists adopt the role of expert witness, particularly in the midst of social controversy involving a well-organized social movement.

Political Conflicts of Expert Witnesses
The expectation that a party witness will give testimony favorable to the party that calls him makes partisan affiliation and loyalty more explicit for scholars acting as expert witnesses than for scholars in other applied roles. Such a clear-cut party affiliation may conflict with experts' own political beliefs. Where the litigation is part of a social move-

ment, the pressures for loyalty and commitment are even greater, one's position is likely to be widely known, and colleagues are also likely to have a personal position concerning the issues in question.

Examples of the personal and professional political conflict associated with the role of expert witness comes from several diverse areas. For instance, anthropologists testifying for the government in Indian land-claim cases often experienced conflict about their party affiliation because they generally sympathized with the Indian cause. Moreover, these experts were often stigmatized within the academic community for testifying against the Indians (Fritz 1963; Jones 1955; Manners 1956).

Scholars who were criticized by their colleagues also include those who challenged the value of testimony by social psychologists questioning the accuracy of eyewitness identifications in criminal cases. For example, Loftus (1983a, 1983b) responded as follows to an article by McCloskey and Egeth (1983a, 1983b) that was critical of such testimony:

> At the same time that psychologists are reading the McCloskey and Egeth articles that are so deeply critical of experimental psychologists offering testimony as an interesting intellectual exercise, prosecuting attorneys across the land are using them for an entirely different purpose: Judges are being told that the articles are proof that the psychological testimony does not even pass the "Frye test"[1]. . . . Even as we speak, prosecutors are using the McCloskey and Egeth articles to argue that there is no general acceptance in the field. (Loftus 1983b, 576)

Ultimately, many social psychologists involved in eyewitness testimony contributed to a special issue of *Law and Human Behavior* devoted to the ethics of expert testimony (McCloskey, Egeth, and McKenna 1986).

A third example of professional political conflict arising from expert testimony occurred when a feminist historian testified on behalf of Sears, Roebuck and Co., the defendant in an employment discrimination case.[2] Professor Rosalind Rosenberg testified that the relatively smaller percentage of women in higher-paying, high-ticket, commission sales jobs (e.g., television sales) might be explained by male and

---

1. *Frye v. United States*, 293 F. 1013 (D.C. Cir. 1923), which, in a case involving a precursor of the lie detector, held that a scientific principle or disovery must have general acceptance in its particular field before a witness can base an expert opinion on it. Contrary to the implication in the quoted passage, however, the *Frye* test is in general decline as a restriction upon the admissibility of expert opinion (McCormick 1984, 606).

2. *Equal Employment Opportunity Commission v. Sears, Roebuck and Co.*, 628 F. Supp. 1264 (1986).

female differences in job preference.[3] This testimony created strong reaction among other feminist historians. Her testimony was called an
"immoral act" in a widely circulated letter. The Conference Group on
Women's History passed a resolution stating: "We believe as feminist
scholars we have a responsibility not to allow our scholarship to be used
against the interests of women struggling for equity in our society"
(Sternhell 1986, 87). Some of the attacks were *ad hominem*. For example:

> Most people are quite appalled that Rosalind Rosenberg put her
> skills in the service of a company when we mostly identify with the
> position of women workers and the Women's Movement. Some
> people think she was misguided, that she made a mistake. Others
> think it was more than that, that she was stupid or evil. Personally,
> I can't believe anyone could be so stupid. I'm more inclined to be-
> lieve she was defending a class interest as she understood it. (Ren-
> ate Bridenthal, quoted in Sternhell 1986, 49)

The Equal Employment Opportunity Commission (EEOC) had its own
expert witness, Professor Kessler-Harris, who testified that discrimination is a significant reason for gender differences in these jobs. In her
article in Ms. magazine, Sternhell reports that "no one was willing to
publicly criticize Kessler-Harris's testimony, although a few historians
said privately they had found it weak" (1986, 87).[4]

The Political Context of School Desegregation Cases

The school desegregation cases created, for many people, extreme political conflict. The issue was at the center of public life, especially in
those cities where litigation was under way, and, at least during most
of the twenty-five years of litigation, there was a clear, dominant liberal
position within the academy. As Orfield noted, "From World War II

3. The court summarized her testimony as follows: The results . . . were supported by
the testimony of Sears' expert, Dr. Rosalind Rosenberg who testified that women generally prefer to sell soft-line products, such as apparel, housewares or accessories sold
on a noncommission basis, are less interested in selling products such as fencing, refrig-
eration equipment and tires. Women tend to be more interested than men in the social
and cooperative aspects of the workplace. Women tend to see themselves as less competitive. They often view noncommission sales as more attractive than commission sales,
because they can enter and leave the job more easily, and because there is more social
contact and friendship, and less stress in noncommission selling. (628 F. Supp. at 1308)

4. In an interesting sidelight, the attorney for Sears was Charles Morgan, a former civil
rights attorney and former head of the Washington, D. C., office of the ACLU. It is a
measure of the norms of proper lawyer conduct that Morgan's "changing sides" does not
produce a great sense of moral outrage, even among lawyers committed to civil rights..

until the mid-sixties . . . no leading scholar attacked the goal of integration" (1978b, 153). Those who participated in the school desegregation cases on the side of the school boards were, like plaintiff experts in eyewitness cases and government witnesses in Indian cases, in a distinct minority (Orfield, 1978b).

Brown supported two core liberal values: racial equality and educational opportunity. In terms of the former, Brown endorses the notion of the equality of all people before the law. As to the second, education has historically been viewed as the grand equalizer of societal inequities. In the tradition of a liberal consensus, education provides tools for all students to fulfill their potential and to make career choices unencumbered by constraints due to their background. Liberal reaction to Brown cast the plaintiffs as right and the defendants as wrong. Plaintiffs, in attempting to desegrate schools, were seen as representing the core values of American society. Defendants, in supporting state-mandated segregation, were seen as representing racism.[5]

It is difficult to be certain how pervasive this liberal framework of desegregation was within the academy, but since World War II, surveys of the faculties of U.S. colleges and universities show them generally holding liberal political attitudes (Ladd and Lipset 1975; Noll and Rossi 1966). Particularly relevant to our concerns is the finding that faculty were more supportive of busing to achieve racial integration of public schools than was the general public (Ladd and Lipset 1975, 33). In addition to being more liberal than the general public, social scientists tend to be more liberal than scientists in other academic fields.

Personal Political Conflict

Personal political conflict was coded as present when experts spontaneously volunteered statements of ambivalence, discomfort, or conflict related to perceived disparities between their political views and those of the party they represented. These comments were most frequently volunteered in response to the interview question, "Did the decision

5. For a more detailed presentation of the liberal view of school desegregation, see Kluger (1975), Sanders (1980), and Yudof (1978). For the "conservative" framework of school desegregation, which emphasizes states' rights, individual rights, judicial restraint, and the sanctity of the neighborhood school, see Glazer (1972), Graglia (1976), Gregor (1963), and Van den Haag (1960). There has long been a group comprised mostly of black scholars who opposed school desegregation because it concentrated on racial balancing rather than on community control and improving black schools (Bell 1976, 1980b; Edmonds 1974; Hamilton 1968; Willie 1984). Because scholars adopting this "radical" frame do not endorse desegregation, they typically do not appear in court, and thus none of these social scientists are represented in our sample.

Table 8.1. The Relationship between Party Affiliation and Personal Political Conflict

	Party Affiliation		
Personal Conflict	Defense	Plaintiff	Total
Present	68% (15)	13% (4)	37% (19)
Absent	32% (7)	87% (26)	63% (33)
Total	100% (22)	100% (30)	100% (52)

Notes: $\chi^2 = 16.47$; $p < .001$; df $= 1$; $N = 52$.

about whether to testify generate any conflict for you?" Personal conflict was much more prevalent among defense experts, as indicated in table 8.1: 68% of them, as opposed to only 13% of the plaintiff experts, reported experiencing personal conflict. The following statements from defense experts are examples of this kind of conflict:

> There was some sense of ideological conflict because I had always identified myself as a liberal and I was testifying on behalf of school boards who were generally pointed to as the culprits in these things.

> I was in conflict because the party on the other side was the NAACP and I had been a member of that organization. I felt there but for the grace of the evidence go I, on the other side. And it was disconcerting. . . . I approached it with trepidation because of my liberal leanings.

> At some levels I understood that I was entering the case on the side of the school district, who was regarded by many liberal and black organizations as foot-dragging, basically racist, had committed greater crimes against black children. It began to hit me how ironic I should land up on this side rather than on the other side.

As these remarks indicate, many defense experts appear to have adopted the liberal framework of school desegregation. Some even identified with the civil rights movement and with the NAACP as the leading movement organization. They described their own political stance as similar to that of liberal plaintiff groups, and also labeled school boards as conservative and perhaps racist. Yet, they testified for these school boards and against the party representing their broader political views.

Many defense witnesses testify for the defense in spite of, rather than because of, their personal political position. The perceived disparity between their personal political orientation and the one they ascribe to the side they represent is the source of their conflict.

We gain further insight into the relationship between personal conflict and party affiliation by examining the political positions of the four plaintiff experts who did experience personal political conflict and the seven defense experts who did not. Qualitative analysis of the interviews with the four plaintiff experts who experienced party conflict indicates that they were all ambivalent about the liberal framework of desegregation. They were more cautious or negative about it than most other plaintiff witnesses.

> School desegration is from my perspective extraordinarily complex and fraught with ambiguities. Whether it's beneficial, the conditions under which it can be beneficial, whether these conditions can be realized, in simple terms, whether it's a good or bad thing and I can't answer that. The school board isn't the side I generally favor in school desegregation cases. But the government side isn't something I can enthusiastically support either.

> [When I first got involved with school desegregation] I had a very naive belief in the power of public schools to change children. I also had a rather naive view of the public school system. I regarded it as a monolithic evil and didn't really think too much beyond that. When I began, I didn't understand the terrible dilemmas that were involved for black parents and kids and for white parents and kids in something like desegregation.

These plaintiff experts had come to view the desegregation movement in increasingly complex terms. They no longer viewed it and its proponents as unconditionally positive, as the liberal solution to the problems of race and education. As such, they experienced some ambivalence about testifying for plaintiff groups who continued to view desegregation as unconditionally positive and the legal contest in terms of good and evil.

Three of the seven defense experts who did not experience party conflict also questioned the liberal background of desegregation. Rather than producing mere ambivalence, however, their doubts tended to produce a stronger rejection of the liberal framework.

> I had decided that busing wasn't working and that it was on balance far more negative than positive. I thought that the pro-busing advocates had issues to deal with in court. The prospect of some modest gains for blacks was real enough, but the bulk of the difference in achievement was not going to go away because of the busing. And this needed to be said. I also had decided that the manner of

> support of busing adopted by some had become quite insulting to blacks.

> I testified for one side because it so happened that I'd written and come to a position which it turned out helped them. . . . I'd felt that the remedies designed in these cases were not good remedies and therefore it was pointless to prove liability of this type. Then they would start moving everybody around and one third of the whites would leave and it would be a big mess. That was their [the plaintiff's] position. I thought they were wrong.

If, as we have argued, party conflict for defense experts is rooted in ambivalence about rejecting the liberal view of desegregation, these defense experts, who unambiguously rejected that view, had no basis for conflict.

The other four school board experts who reported no party conflict neither explicitly rejected nor endorsed the liberal framework of desegregation. They expressed no reaction whatsoever to their party affiliation. Instead, they contended that their feelings about desegregation or the party for whom they testified were made irrelevant by their professional responsibility to disseminate data to any requesting party. Their views are represented below.

> I regard it as a duty of anyone who has some sort of expertise in the field if he's asked to appear before a court to do so. You become an expert ultimately to make your expertise or knowledge available.

> My personal beliefs and how they relate to the position of the people asking me to testify is not a relevant factor in my decision.

> I viewed myself as providing technical scientific information to people who would have to make political decisions. I was an impartial advisor and my personal beliefs were irrelevant to my testifying.

These respondents experienced no party conflict because they did not perceive the fit between personal and party beliefs as a relevant issue in deciding whether to testify.

A final indicator of the differential relationship between party affiliation and party conflict for both plaintiff and defense experts was their response to the interview question, "Would you testify for the other side if asked?" Individuals with a political view similar to that of their party should have been less willing to testify for the other side. The liberal framework of desegregation positively evaluates the plaintiffs

Table 8.2. The Relationship between Party Affiliation and Willingness to Testify for the Other Side

Testify for Other Side?	Party Affiliation		Total
	Defense	Plaintiff	
Yes	100% (22)	60% (18)	77% (40)
No	0% (0)	40% (12)	23% (12)
Total	100% (22)	100% (30)	100% (52)

Notes: χ^2 = 11.44; p < .001; df = 1; N = 52.

and negatively evaluates the defendants, and for plaintiff experts who viewed themselves as liberal, changing sides would represent moving from the "right" to the "wrong" side. Their basic comfort with their party affiliation, combined with their negative feelings about school board defendants, should have made them relatively more reluctant to answer "yes" to the above question. Our data indicate that this was the case.

All of the defense experts, but only 60% of the plaintiff experts, stated that they were willing to testify for the other side.[6] The reluctance of some plaintiff witnesses to change sides is illustrated by the following statements:

> I have not lost my sense about how American society is lined up. The defendant groups are on the other side.

> I don't think that [testifying for the defense] would be a very constructive thing to do. . . . I just wouldn't put aside everything else I had to do and go to work for somebody who was trying to make the cities segregated.

> I testify because I believe in the cause of equal educational opportunity. I believe that testifying on the other side would retard that cause. I don't want to have any part of that.

These results are consistent with the fact that a substantial portion of plaintiff experts viewed themselves as part of a social movement and therefore committed to one party in a two-party conflict.

Given the prevailing political climate of the time, it is not surprising

---

6. We are reporting attitudes, not behaviors. It appears that in fact more plaintiff experts have testified for defendants than the other way around. From the interviews we cannot assess whether there is an attitude-behavior gap or whether these defense experts simply have not been asked to testify for plaintiff groups.

that we did not encounter any defense experts who expressed reservations about testifying for the plaintiffs. In fact, some defense experts noted that for them to move to the plaintiff's side would be to move from the "wrong" to the "right" side of the case. One respondent commented,

> The fact that the NAACP happens to be on the other side of this makes it easy for me to say that I'd be willing to testify for the other side.

Even those defense experts who expressly espoused the conservative view of school desegregation did not rule out testifying for plaintiffs under all circumstances.

The willingness to change sides is also related to the decision to select social scientific norms to govern one's own behavior in court. Only 44% of the plaintiff experts adopting a legal-adversary stance stated that they would testify for the other side, whereas 75% of the plaintiff experts adopting a social science normative stance and 83% of those with a mixed normative stance said that they would testify for the defense.[7] Experts adhering to legal-adversary norms were less willing to act neutrally and to change sides; experts adhering to scientific norms were more willing to disseminate their knowledge to any and all parties.

Professional Political Conflict

Professional conflict arises from the expectation or experience of negative professional consequences associated with one's party affiliation. Material consequences may include nonpromotion and reduced employment, funding, or publishing opportunities. Status consequences include negative labels associated with one's party affiliation and diminished prestige within the professional community. Such sanctioning, or even the perception that sanctioning may exist, reflects the degree to which the social movement's contest for resources has penetrated the walls of the academy.

Two of our interview questions asked about professional conflict: "Have you had any disagreements with or criticisms from professional colleagues about the propriety or wisdom of testifying?" and "Has testifying had any effect on your professional career, positive or negative?"[8]

---

7. $\chi^2 = 3.87$, $p < .14$, df $= 2$, $N = 30$. The unanimous willingness of defense experts to report that they would switch sides makes this analysis moot for them.

8. For a response to be coded as reflecting professional conflict, it had to contain at least one of the following: (1) the anticipation or perception of being negatively labeled by one's colleagues or generally having lost status in one's professional community be-

Some statements indicating professional conflict are the following:

> You know there's a sense in which it's a motherhood, apple pie, American flag issue among most social scientists. I think it's professionally very difficult to take a position that could be seen to be less than perfectly liberal.

> There have been professional conflicts in the sense of colleagues being aghast at the fact that I would testify against what was at one time regarded as the only wise and true position. This has been a very strong conflict.

> I would be willing to bet that in terms of politics of funding, I would be looked at with less favor than someone who testified on the other side.

As these comments suggest, defense experts were more likely than plaintiff experts to report experiencing professional political conflict.[9]

---

cause of one's party affiliation; (2) the anticipation or perception of diminished employment, funding, or publication opportunities due to one's party affiliation; and (3) the perception that other experts who testified on one's side had been labeled, lost status, or suffered material sanctions because of their party affiliation. Informants who did not mention any of the above consequences of party affiliation were coded as reporting no professional conflict.

9. Our measure of professional political conflict is based on scholars' perceptions rather than on the actual occurrence of negative career sanctions. We can document that many social scientists testifying for the defense experienced conflict due to anticipation or perceptions of such professional sanctions. However, we do not have objective data indicating whether such sanctions actually occurred. It may be argued that scholars' reports of negative professional sanctions are examples of perceptual distortions. Nonetheless, some plaintiff and defense attorneys also reported that such sanctions did occur, and that there was a general scholarly unwillingness to testify for defense groups because of the professional costs that some scholars felt they might have to pay. We quoted two defense attorneys and one plaintiff attorney on this point in chapter 4. Still another defense lawyer commented:

> We would find people who, because of peer pressure, did not want to testify for the defendants regardless of what the facts were or anything else. . . . We were told, off the record, that if they did work for our side their access to grants, to promotions, and to new relationships in their profession would be greatly jeopardized.

And a plaintiff attorney observed the same process.

> I've certainly picked up, just talking to experts at various universities, that there's a certain distaste for people who will help a school board out. I'm

Table 8.3. The Relationship between Party Affiliation and Professional Political Conflict

| | Party Affiliation | | |
Professional Conflict	Defense	Plaintiff	Total
Present	68% (15)	13% (4)	37% (19)
Absent	32% (7)	87% (26)	63% (33)
Total	100% (22)	100% (30)	100% (52)

Notes: $\chi^2 = 16.47$; $p < .001$; df $= 1$; $N = 52$.

Our data support this expectation (see table 8.3).[10]

This result can be substantially explained by the aggregate leaning toward liberal political attitudes in the academy, which sometimes induced sanctions against scholarly activities which did not support the majority view. In addition, as we noted above and in chapter 6, scientists who deviate from traditional academic norms to conduct applied social science, or, more important, applied scientists who depart too far from acceptable notions of applied work, are likely to be sanctioned by their colleagues because of professional politics within the scientific community. A combination of the professional politics of science and a liberal ideology concerning public affairs makes it particularly likely that defense experts will meet with some type of sanction.

The impact of both these factors together may be seen when we compare social science experts with educational science experts. General survey data which show substantial variation in the aggregate political stances of different academic disciplines indicate that social science tends to be more liberal, whereas education may lean more toward conservatism.[11]

sure it goes back to this whole claim of constitutional rights and that these are discriminators you are helping.

Moreover, several plaintiff scholars admitted knowledge of career sanctions encountered by defense scholars. On the basis of this evidence, and on our own observations of various actors, we are convinced that there is more than "smoke" here, and that professional sanctioning of some scholars has occurred.

10. Although the distribution of respondents is identical in this table and in table 8.1, this is a coincidence. The cell counts do not represent the same individuals. The two variables (personal political conflict and professional political conflict) are, as one might expect, related ($\chi^2 = 5.89$, $p < .02$, df $= 1$, $N = 52$). And, again as one might expect, plaintiff experts are less likely to experience both types of conflict than are defense experts ($\chi^2 = 24.79$, $p < .001$, df $= 2$, $N = 52$, Gamma $= -0.91$).

11. This scale, as reported in Ladd and Lipset (1975), combined attitudes toward four major social issues (the Vietnam War, legalization of marijuana, causes of Negro riots, and busing to achieve school integration) with faculty members' self-categorization of their political ideology.

Because educational science experts come from a more applied discipline, they should be sanctioned less often by their colleagues for their applied role. In addition, given the slight conservative thrust of the discipline, any sanctioning that does occur against educational scientists might occur against both plaintiff experts and defense experts. This is reflected in the following statements by educational scientists who testified for plaintiffs:

> The negative consequences of testifying for the plaintiff were collegial rejection and written reprimands from university administrators.

> After I had testified for the plaintiffs against the school board and administration, I called a former faculty colleague who is now part of the school administration. She refused to acknowledge that she knew me, failed to return phone calls, and let it be known that no research proposals I had anything to do with would be welcome in the school system.

The data in table 8.4 lend support to these reports, although any conclusion is suspect given the small numbers of informants in many of the cells. There is a weak, nonsignificant relationship between professional conflict and professional affiliation.[12] Twenty-one percent of the educational scientists reported such conflict, compared to 45% of the social scientists. Among the educational scientists, there is no significant difference in reporting conflict based on whether the expert testified for the defense (27%) or for the plaintiff (23%). For social scientists there is a strong relationship between the experience of professional political conflict and party affiliation. Eighty-eight percent of the defendant social scientists experienced professional conflict, as opposed to only 6% of the plaintiff social scientists. Thus, party affiliation affects the experience of professional political conflict only if the expert is based in a social science department.[13]

12. $\chi^2 = 3.09$, $p < .08$, df $= 1$, $N = 52$.

13. Below are the results of a saturated log linear model with professional political conflict as the response variable and professional affiliation and party affiliation as independent variables:

Analysis of Variance Table

Source	DF	Chi-Square	Probability
Intercept	1	4.06	0.044
Professional Affiliation	1	1.21	0.271
Party Affiliation	1	5.69	0.017
Prof. Affl. × Party Affl.	1	8.04	0.006
Residual	0	0.00	0.000

Table 8.4. The Relationship between Party Affiliation, Professional Affiliation, and Professional Political Conflict

Professional Political Conflict	Professional Affiliation			
	Social Scientists		Educational Scientists	
	Defense	Plaintiff	Defense	Plaintiff
Present	88% (14)	6% (1)	17% (1)	23% (3)
Absent	12% (2)	94% (16)	83% (5)	77% (10)
Total (N = 52)	100% (16)	100% (17)	100% (6)	100% (13)

The professional political conflict experienced by the defense experts was intensified by the heat of the external social struggle. For instance, experts testifying on the "wrong" side of the eyewitness identification issue might have met with criticism, but not with the extremes of verbal abuse and attempted sanctions experienced by some defense experts in the desegregation cases. The difference seems to be that the effort to desegregate schools was part of a social movement, a movement which, like all such movements, felt that the stakes were high and the cause was important; as a result, its supporters were sometimes intolerant of dissent. As one defense expert put it:

> This testimony made me a controversial person and probably deprived me of a number of [professional] opportunities. The other side makes it quite clear that they regard any testimony contrary to their views not just as scientific disagreement, but as a form of disloyalty.[14]

Testimony in the Face of Political Conflict: Defense Expert Strategies for Reducing Conflict

The conflicts experienced by defense experts were sufficient to cause some individuals not to testify at all.[15] The comments of two social sci-

---

As is obvious from examining table 8.4, there is a significant interaction between professional affiliation and party affiliation.

14. As one might expect, given this analysis, the level of criticism and the experience of political conflict should have receded as desegregation moved off the national agenda and the desegregation movement became relatively inactive. Brief interviews in the past year with some of our original respondents have reflected decreased acrimony and conflict in peer relationships.

15. Unfortunately, we have no way to measure the number of people who refused to testify for either plaintiffs or defendants, or why they did so.

entists who declined to testify for the defendants illustrate the link between political conflict and decisions about professional activities.

> I was tempted to testify when asked. I concluded that even though
> I agreed with a number of the arguments of the group asking me
> to testify, if I did testify I would be rendering support against the
> black community and the NAACP, of which I was an active sup-
> porter. [I decided not to testify] but it wasn't a simple or clear-cut
> decision for me.

> I think that a great deal of the reluctance of social scientists to testify
> when asked to by school boards is not entirely due to a reasoned
> conclusion that the goal of racial reassignment is valuable. I think
> this because there's so much social disapproval from one's col-
> leagues [for testifying for school boards].

Yet, a considerable number of individuals did testify for the defense. If
defense experts were uncomfortable with, or anticipated, personal and
professional consequences due to their particular party affiliations,
how did they deal with these political conflicts? Why did they testify
in the face of these apparent pressures?

An examination of how defense experts dealt with these conflicts
revealed two major coping strategies or justifications for these actions.
The first involved arguments in support of party affiliation which the
expert believed to be more important than the personal discomfort or
professional consequences associated with testifying for the defense.
We termed these *higher-order justifications*. The second involved distinguishing the plaintiff and defense groups in their particular case(s) from
the larger categories of liberal plaintiffs and conservative defendants.
We called these *differentiations*.

The higher-order justifications employed by defense experts added
purpose and meaning to their party affiliations, and thus potentially
eased party conflict. In particular, these experts raised two critical
professional obligations: disseminating data neutrally and using data
to inform public policy.

Neutral dissemination refers to the transmission of any data generated according to the established canons of scientific research, whether
or not they support the researcher's (or the research community's)
value preferences. Therefore, experts' feelings about defendant school
boards should not deter them from testifying. Similarly, anticipation of
negative professional consequences should not override their responsibility to respond affirmatively to school board or other requests for
testimony. In a more general context, Merton (1957) argues that adopt-

ing the role of disinterested technician permits intellectuals to retain their personal and professional integrity while participating in public programs and policy that are contrary to their values. Although such actions may not be neutral in their outcomes, given the legitimacy of policymakers, they may feel neutral to the scholar.

Of the defense respondents, 48% described their party affiliation in terms of the scientific ideal of neutral dissemination. The following statements are illustrative of this trend:

> As a scientist I feel obligated to tell anybody what the facts are. . . . If you're asked to testify and you're an expert on a certain question you should testify for anybody.

> If my work indicated that desegregation was a bad social policy, I would present that, even though I am supportive of desegregation. I think that the basis of a social science expert in court is their application of scientific techniques to understanding the phenomena and not their ideology to understanding phenomena.

> I do not think that it is for me (as a scholar) to say that this will have harmful social consequences, therefore even though it is true I will withhold it. If we proceed in that way, the scholar would be a political manipulator instead of a witness.

Some defense experts explicitly contended that they were professionally bound to disseminate data to school boards, even if such a party affiliation was negatively sanctioned by their colleagues.

> Ideologically, there is no question in my mind that if I have some data, I ought to report it. I'd feel pressured to do that no matter what the professional costs were.

> I think it's an obligation of a scientist to testify to the truth whatever the career consequences.

A related justification used by defense experts was the professional obligation to inform public policymakers about their findings. If intelligent policy can evolve only from consideration of all of the facts, scientists are required to present any and all relevant data to policymakers. Even if the data do not support the researcher's (or her professional community's) immediate policy preferences, over time they can be expected to help yield sensible public policy. For example:

> However the data turn out, they should be used to guide policy intelligently.

> I had a professional responsibility to get involved once I concluded [the plaintiff's desegregation] plan was educationally unsound.

> The data indicated that there were certain mistakes about the desegregation of schools and I wanted to apprise the court, nation, whatever level I found.

These views concerning a scientist's duty to neutrally disseminate information and to aid public policy formation are, of course, compatible with the defense witnesses' adoption of a social science normative stance in court. Adoption of a social science stance does not reduce the likelihood that a defense expert would experience role conflict. It does, however, provide a context within which the higher-order justifications are possible (these particular higher-order justifications are meaningless within the context of a legal-adversary normative stance). Thus, a social science normative stance indirectly helps a defense expert deal with personal and professional political conflict.

Differentiation processes exemplify another strategy used by some defense experts to ease political conflict (particularly personal conflict). The particular school boards for which they testified were distinguished from the assumed category of conservative and racist defendants, and/or the plaintiffs were seen as other than liberal, progressive, and pro-civil rights.

Some respondents began this differentiation process before deciding whether to testify in a particular case. They made inquiries into different facets of the litigants and the cases as they developed, including the attorneys, the legal theories, the administrators' desegregation plans, and other actors' positions on school desegregation. These inquiries were designed to provide scholars with information on whether they could testify for a particular party "in good conscience." For defense experts dealing with potential political conflict, this generally meant that they could support the defendant's position in a particular case, but not an antidesegregation position in general. Over half the defense experts (52%) reported making inquiries into the litigants and/or the case before agreeing to testify, whereas only 14% of plaintiff experts reported doing so. The following statements by defense experts illustrate the nature of their inquiries.

> I really needed to know where these people actually were because I'm an old-fashioned liberal. School administrators in the past have

frequently opposed busing for either their own convenience or for motives that are somewhat racist or political. And I needed to know for sure whether the school administrators had a reasonable plan, that they were acting in good faith. I got a copy of the plan and talked extensively with other experts who had testified on their behalf and whom I respected.

Before I agreed to testify I wanted to get a feel for what the litigation was about and get some view of the actors in the trial. I made a trip to the city to talk to the lawyers. I wanted to see who I'd be working for. . . . I agreed to testify because my investigation convinced me that the plaintiffs' (desegregation) plan was so unfeasible that I felt comfortable being on the side opposing it.

By particularizing a situation, a differentiation process breaks down the centralized ideological (as well as geographic) structure of the social movement. It allows individuals to reduce or avoid the overall ideological meaning of their action. Presumably, any time one particularizes a movement's generalities, one humanizes opponents, rationalizes mythology, and questions unquestionables, thus attenuating the force of the movement's claims.

Although most of the defense experts (86%) reported using one of these strategies, very few indicated using both.[16] After all, they are incompatible with one another. On the one hand, the differentiation strategy implies that scholars will testify only for parties whose beliefs are similar to their own. Thus, those liberal defense experts who anticipated discrepancies between their own positions and those of school boards gathered information to ascertain whether defendants requesting their testimony shared their views about the case and about desegregation. On the other hand, the strategy of neutral dissemination implies the professional obligation to disseminate data to any requesting party. From this viewpoint, it is inappropriate to testify only for parties whose political views mirror one's own. As such, experts should not limit their defense testimony to those school boards that upon investigation have been found to be "exceptional cases."

Summary of Political Conflict

The concept of personal political conflict illustrates the complex relationship of scholars' values and their applied efforts to the communities

---

16. Three defense experts reported using both differentiation and neutral dissemination justifications, sixteen reported using one justification, and three reported using neither.

in which they live and work. To successfully manage bias, scholars are encouraged to collect and analyze data in a manner that permits rejection as well as acceptance of their relevant beliefs and values. Many scholars we interviewed did in fact manage their biases by generating data that challenged their beliefs about desegregation and by presenting evidence for parties whose beliefs were inconsistent with their own. However, many of these same scholars still faced personal political conflict due to a disparity between their courtroom affiliation and their political views.

The notion of professional political conflict adds to our understanding of applied social science. Clearly, all experts did not face the same courtroom or collegial environments. The perceived professional costs of engaging in applied efforts are determined in part by the degree to which one's discipline encourages application (e.g., education or social work vs. sociology or political science). However, at least in the area of school desegregation, perceived professional costs are fundamentally related to the compatibility of one's efforts with the general political orientation of one's discipline. Those social scientists who testified for the defense experienced the courtroom and the role of expert witness differently from those who testified for the plaintiff. Defense scholars appear to have faced a set of political conflicts, related to their party affiliation, that were relatively nonexistent for plaintiff experts, partly because testifying for a party would have been looked on with political disfavor by a majority of the members of their discipline.

The differences in the experience of plaintiff and defense witnesses must be understood as something more than being on the political majority or political minority side of the case. Many plaintiff experts were part of a social movement. Some were fully committed to the movement, and some only moderately so; but even those who were not committed were shielded by the legitimacy of the social movement from some personal political doubts and from sanctions for their involvement. Most defense experts did not have the same institutional resources. They had neither the ideology and vision of a movement to shield them from personal doubts nor its political influence to act as a buffer between them and those who would sanction them for their activity. Confronted with such an uncomfortable situation, many constructed a vision of their activity and a style of expert witnessing which could be more easily justified and defended by reliance on the traditional academic virtues of neutrality and autonomy.

Consequences for Social Science

This chapter has focused on the consequences of testifying for individual social scientists. We have said relatively little about the effects of the school cases on the social sciences themselves. At this level the threads of cause and effect are tenuous. Nevertheless, a few observations are in order.

The school desegregation cases, and the other areas of civil rights litigation which followed, opened up an era of much wider involvement by social scientists in the courtroom. As a consequence of this involvement, some subdisciplines grew more than they otherwise might have, such as the psychology of prejudice and discrimination, the factors affecting educational achievement, the nature of classroom dynamics, and the sociology of educational change. Equally important, these areas had an applied flavor, a product of the policy involvement of scholars working in them. Social scientists did not restrict themselves to studying the relationship between desegregation and achievement; they studied the courts' efforts to change the schools, the effects of various implementation schemes, and the relative advantages of using courts, administrative agencies, and legislatures to promote social change. Many of the citations in this book are part of this literature.

A substantial portion of this literature, including the research underlying this book, is a part of the desegregation movement in a direct way. It is the product of federal grants and grants from private foundations aimed at increasing knowledge about race relations, school desegregation, and the structure of schools in the United States. The Coleman Report was called for in the 1964 Civil Rights Act partly to provide the background data on school inequality that would justify desegregation efforts and other changes. Studies examining the impact of desegregation on racial attitudes and minority achievement (Weinberg 1983), on the effectiveness of desegregation plans in various cities (Rist 1979), on the impact of metropolitan segregation (Green 1985), and on general topics concerning legal and social science aspects of school desegregation (Levin and Hawley 1978) were part of a concerted effort to generate social science resources in the movement for school desegregation.

As a reflection of countermovement activity, one of the early efforts of the first Reagan administration was to have the then Department of Education stop funding research on school desegregation.[17] The impact

17. A highly critical commentary on Department of Education funding procedures for unsolicited proposals during the 1982 funding cycle was made by disgruntled staff members of the National Institute of Education. It was published anonymously in the American Sociological Association newsletter, *Footnotes* (Anonymous 1983). The thrust of the article is that the Institute was not following normal methods of peer review funding in certain areas, including school desegregation. Specifically, the Institute was using pro-

of diminished federal efforts with respect to school desegregation is reflected today in the relative difficulty of acquiring data on changing levels of segregation in American schools. This is far different from the late sixties when federal funds were used to create the Coleman Report data and to fund desegregation centers under Title IV of the 1964 Civil Rights Act. As each administration has understood, an important element in the social movement to desegregate schools has been the production and mobilization of one of its key resources: social science knowledge.

The acrimony and politicization of social science which some feared might be the result of active involvement did, to some extent, occur (see chapter 6 for a discussion of these controversies). Some academics who supported or opposed the movement to desegregate schools were not simply participants in the serious debate which is a routine part of the academy. For them, each piece of evidence which appeared to argue against their view of desegregation was apostasy. The movement, by mobilizing social science evidence, helped create acrimony and adversary relations within the academy. Some expert witnesses felt that this harmed the social science disciplines.

> When you get a lot of conflict like that it looks like we don't know what we are doing. Either that or we don't know anything or that it is an unreliable discipline. It's not really a science at all and you might as well just forget about it.

> What happens when laymen listen to a bunch of sociologists disagree on an issue? They usually draw the conclusion that nothing is known, and these guys don't know what they're talking about.

Others, however, saw a more positive side to this involvement with desegregation litigation.

> I think it is good for social science to be involved in desegregation issues in terms of clearing up some of the research and recognizing some of the inherent problems with generalizing from data. It provides us with a good sense of the limitations of [the evidence].

---

posal reviewers who were not, according to the authors, properly qualified as "experts," but who were chosen in part because of their political positions. Even when desegregation proposals did well in peer review, they were not funded. The director's comment was simply: "During this round of unsolicited proposals, the Institute is not funding any individual desegregation projects" (11).

I think in the long run it's got to have a good effect. It's an impetus for the discipline to answer questions, to try and resolve things. It seems to me that the white-flight stuff is a good case in point. We are beginning to learn something about the sources of discrepancies in data. Initially you just have people saying this and people over there saying that and it sounds like they are both nincompoops, but they cause each other to go out and analyze new data and try and find out what the differences are between what the data is that they analyzed and what I'm analyzing and where it's coming out differently.

As this last remark suggests, those who tried to turn social science to their purpose often found that they had mounted an unruly horse. Even partial adherence to core values of neutrality and autonomy often creates data and interpretations contrary to the values of those who produce them.[18] These core scientific values also provide the justificatory armor for some defense experts who withstood personal and professional political conflict to produce research results or to testify in ways that were critical of prevailing trends in the academy.[19]

18. See, for example, St. John's (1975) preface to her book on school desegregation outcomes for children.

19. See, for example, Wolf's (1981) preface to her book on the Detroit desegregation case.

9 The Panel Alternative

Throughout the history of school desegregation litigation, there has been disagreement about the proper role of social science and the social science expert. Often the debate is not about whether social science evidence should be introduced into the decision-making process but about how it should be introduced. Not surprisingly, individuals uncomfortable with party witnessing have argued for alternatives (Buckhout 1986; Kantrowitz 1977; Loewen 1982; Martin 1977; McGurk 1959/60; Nyhart 1981; Sperlich 1980; Weinberg 1978).

One alternative recommended by some involved in the school desegregation litigation is an expert panel (Orfield 1978b; Pettigrew 1979; Wolf 1976). A panel would allow experts to meet in a noncourtroom context and exchange views and data with one another. They would participate in litigation in a way more consistent with their scholarly and academic roles, and should therefore experience fewer of the role and skill problems typically associated with party witnessing. Thus, according to Orfield,

> a more useful approach for a court or other agency dealing with a large city school district would be to create an independent group of experts to respond to questions formulated by the judge or agency. This group could assess the existing research on various issues, initiate short-term research where needed, and report on conclusions. The contending parties should also have access to the data, and the right to question the experts when they submit their report. (1978b, 171)

As Pettigrew (1979) views the issue, the panel role is "far closer to the role that academic social scientists are accustomed to playing—researchers and writers rather than disputants in an argument" (28).

Supporters of panels believe that if experts were freed from the adversary process, they would be better able to collect the data they deem relevant and to present it in a more neutral and objective way, filled with traditional scholarly detail, complexity, and qualification (Sperlich 1980).[1] Should the courts follow this advice and employ panels in school desegregation cases?[2] This alternative is available. At least since the Middle Ages, judges have had a common law power to call experts (McCormick 1984, 43). The Federal Rules of Evidence formalize this power. Rule 706 gives the trial judge wide discretion.

> (a) Appointment. The court may on its own motion or on the motion of any party enter an order to show cause why expert witnesses should not be appointed, and may request the parties to submit nominations. The court may appoint any expert witnesses agreed upon by the parties and may appoint expert witnesses of its own selection. An expert witness shall not be appointed by the court unless he consents to act. A witness so appointed shall be informed of his duties by the court in writing; a copy of which shall be filed with the clerk, or at a conference in which the parties shall have opportunity to participate. A witness so appointed shall advise the parties of his findings, if any; his deposition may be taken by any party; and he may be called to testify by the court or any party. He shall be subject to cross-examination by each party, including a party calling him as a witness.
>
> (b) Parties' experts of own selection. Nothing in this rule limits the parties in calling expert witnesses of their own selection.[3]

1. Some support for this argument can be found in a laboratory experiment by Vidmar and Laird (1983).

2. Panels are not the only alternative to party witnessing. One widely discussed alternative suggestion has been a "science court" assembled under the aegis of some respected organization such as the National Academy of Sciences. Under a version of the science court proposed by a Presidential Advisory Group, a panel of judges (some of whom could be scientists) would be created and case managers would present the case for and against some principle or technique at issue. The science court finding would create a rebuttable presumption for trial courts to use in specific cases (Saks and Van Duizend 1983, 95; see also Kantrowitz 1977; Martin 1977). Note that the science court, at least in this form, is itself an adversary institution. The objective of the court is to get the best possible evidence before judges with substantive expertise.

Recently, Monahan and Walker (1986) have argued that social science evidence resembles legal authority more than empirical fact. Therefore, they propose that such evidence, which is normally introduced by the oral testimony of expert witnesses, should, like legal arguments, be introduced through the use of written briefs instead.

3. Rule 706 does not specifically mention panels, but the judge does have the power to

Table 9.1. Scientists' and Attorneys' Views of an Expert Panel at Remedy

Views of an Expert Panel	Social Scientists	Attorneys
Approve	55% (27)	44% (20)
Undecided[a]	20% (10)	9% (4)
Disapprove	25% (12)	47% (21)
Total	100% (49)[b]	100% (45)

Note: $\chi^2 = 5.9$; df $= 2$; $p < .05$.

[a]The "undecided" category includes informants who explicitly said they could not make up their minds, as well as those who said they favored both or an equal combination. While some of the "undecideds" were no doubt due to intellectual ambivalence, some are a reflection of the abstract and largely untested notion of a panel in these cases.

[b]The N for social scientists in this chapter is only 49 because three of the respondents were not asked about their panel preference.

Because lawyers are steeped in the adversary tradition, whereas social scientists are trained in a model of scientific neutrality, we might expect that attorneys would support party witnessing and that social scientists would support a panel (Sperlich 1980).[4]

Our data confirm the expectation that a significantly greater percentage of social scientists than lawyers would support a panel. But neither lawyers nor experts are unanimous on this issue (see table 9.1).

Although social scientists and lawyers were asked the same general question, lawyers made a key distinction that was disregarded by social scientists. Almost all school cases are conducted in two parts: first, a hearing on violation, to determine whether the school board unconstitutionally discriminated against minorities, and second, a remedy hearing, to decide upon a desegregation plan to remedy the violation. Social scientists rarely made a distinction between these two aspects of a trial. Even when the distinction was brought to their attention, their preference for panels versus party witnessing was relatively unaffected by the stage of the trial. In all cases, it was clear that lawyers rejected the panel at the violation stage, but almost 50% were willing to approve it at the remedy stage.

---

appoint several experts who could file a joint report. Note, however, that the parties would have a right to examine and cross-examine each expert in court. Thus, there is no way to isolate experts entirely from the adversary procedures of the courtroom.

4. Experts and attorneys were asked whether a panel should be used in the school desegregation cases. Both groups were asked to respond to the following general question: "Some people have argued that social scientific testimony can be most effective when presented as part of a consultant panel to a judge, personally, rather than as open testimony in a courtroom. What do you think of this approach?"

Analysis of the interviews with scientists and attorneys suggest that the choice between panels and party witnessing involves basic judgments about issues such as control of experts and the trial process, the proper style of dispute settlement, and the nature and role of social science and of the social science experts involved in litigation. Thus, to prefer panels or party witnessing is to some extent to take a position on a set of fundamental issues concerning the relationship between law and social science.

Control of the Courtroom Relationship

Because of social science commitments to neutrality and autonomy, and because social science findings may change over time, the social science expert is sometimes an unreliable resource in the midst of heated controversy. Even strong supporters can become disappointed when findings cause some scientists to alter their once favorable position (Clark 1977). The parties to litigation may buffer themselves from changing and conflicting views within the social sciences by trying to control the expert and the evidence he places before the judge. The party attorney, as the agent in control, selects, prepares, and examines witnesses and retains final control over the arguments to be presented. Reports one expert:

> I think that the lawyers on both sides like to have somebody they can predict with very high certainty what they will say when asked a certain question by opposing lawyers. They work with them a couple of days before the trial and get all the ducks in a row.

This very control by the parties, according to those who oppose party witnessing, corrupts the presentations of experts by driving them to advocacy positions (Horowitz 1977; Pettigrew 1979; Wolf 1981). A number of our expert informants share this view.

> There is an enormous attempt [by the attorney] to shape this [the expert's] testimony so that it will push as hard as possible on one side of the issue. In the lawyer's view, at least, the expert is not supposed to express the truth as he sees it. He is supposed to express evidence which will push as much to this side as possible, with the notion that on the other side there will be evidence produced and somehow out of this will arise truth.

Some scholars support a panel precisely because it removes them from these stresses. They feel that under less pressure, and with more opportunity for self-control, the quality of their testimony may improve.

> You're not in a'stressful situation [on a panel]. . . . you can easily forget certain facts and details when you're sitting on the damn stand, unless you're prodded. Whereas on a panel you have time to collect your thoughts.

Of course, most scholars agree that the personal comfort of witnesses is not the issue; the issue is the quality of the testimony itself. Who is to exercise control over the entire form and content of the evidence? Within the adversary system, most interactions between judge and witness are restricted to responses to questions formulated by attorneys for the parties. If it is in nobody's interest to ask certain questions or to cover certain issues, they are set aside. Rebuttal to a point made by the plaintiff's witness does not come immediately, but only later, during cross-examination, or even later still when the defendant puts on his own case (Wolf 1981, 261). Some scholars expressed support for a panel especially because it would alter the expert-judge relationship and the judge's relationship to the entire body of social science evidence.

> The panel is a good idea because it makes social scientists responsible to the court [judges] rather than the parties [lawyers]. That is how it should be.

> The panel is superior. Adversarial encounters do not avail themselves to a full discussion of either the issues or the implications of the issues. In court the interaction is tightly circumscribed within the rules of evidence. Experts can't expand on their answers.

> I would strongly support a return to some sort of neutral presentation to simply provide the judge with whatever the available information on the point is.

Freed from the attorney-controlled confines of the adversary process, scientists may not be limited to the parties' definitions of relevant issues, and the judge may be exposed to new and additional information which may broaden his perspective on the case and the issues. Scientists' views on these matters cut across party affiliations; there were no significant differences or trends distinguishing plaintiff and defendant experts' views of panels.

By way of contrast, lawyers emphasize the power and responsibility they carry in the traditional witnessing process. Some are concerned about the potential for a panel to dilute this control. They feel that the issues to be considered should remain those defined by them as the legal representatives of their parties.

> Sure if the guy [expert] doesn't come down right I can fire him, but the court's panel, I don't know, hell they might go in any direction.

> When the expert is on the witness stand you can confine him much more than when he is on a panel of experts in which he is free to bring his own personal predilections to bear on the problem.

As noted above, however, the attitude of many of the attorneys in our sample was contingent upon whether the panel was convened at the merit stage or at the remedy stage of trial. At the merit stage they adopted a traditional, private law view. Their position stems from a general desire to view desegregation cases as the adjudication of matters of constitutional right and the plaintiff as either having or not having a right. This is not a matter for compromise or for experiments with lessening attorney control.[5] Although several attorneys recognize that in this area, as in many others, the law has been pushed past the traditional scope of what is justiciable, they nevertheless remain opposed to panels during the violation stage of hearings. The following comment sums up this view:

> I think most such panels are eunuchs. You end up with a political compromise solution to what is a constitutional issue.

Yet, when we turn to remedy, half the attorneys interviewed supported the expert panel. Their reasons are similar to those of the experts: first, party witnessing causes legal relevance rather than the contours of science to define the scope of admissibility, and second, important issues may not be represented by the parties to the litigation and may therefore go unexamined. In the Los Angeles case, for example, several of the experts on that particular panel filed reports to the court discussing the desirability of a metropolitan plan for school desegregation. They argued that the demographic composition of the city prohibited a substantial mixing of children of different races in the same school unless the pool of predominantly white children living in the suburbs became involved. The legal issues in the case did not include metropolitan desegregation; no attorney for either party had advocated it; and if all expert evidence had been introduced by way of

---

5. Some early critiques of *Brown* were along similar lines, that the Supreme Court's adoption of the "all deliberate speed" standard for desegregation was an impermissible compromise with a constitutional right. If the plaintiffs had a right to a desegregated education, they had the right immediately, not some years later as the political problems of white resistance were worked out.

party witnesses the discussion would probably not have surfaced. That was the assessment of at least one lawyer in the case, who noted:

> The nice thing about the experts was [that] they were very refreshing. Nobody in the case wanted to talk about metropolitan. I think everybody had a different reason. I think one reason is that a lot of the lawyers are just exhausted by the case and the judge is exhausted and the thought of another ten years of litigation, nobody just wanted to deal with it. The experts didn't have that view, and they said there is only really one way to desegregate this area and that is through a metropolitan plan. Now whether it was practical or reasonable or feasible . . . I saw a simulation of costs for the busing of 800,000 kids a day. But I guess if you are talking about the ascertainment of truth, there is a definite and distinct advantage in this case by having those experts. They pointed to something that no one else would have pointed to, and that was that you should have a metropolitan plan and you shouldn't implement any of these other plans because that is what you need. And if these witnesses had testified for a party it is likely they would not have come out with that.

Because loss of control of the witness and of the evidentiary process is equally possible at both the merit and the remedy stages, it is clearly not the only consideration for lawyers.

Styles of Dispute Settlement

Abram Chayes' distinction between private law and public law models of adjudication, discussed in chapter 2, helps explain lawyers' doubts regarding traditional adjudication procedures in a public law type of case. As one attorney noted:

> Well, the basic question is whether or not this kind of case is justiciable at all . . . is really subject to courtroom determination.

This doubt intensifies at the remedy stage, where individual legal rights appear to become less relevant and where the court-ordered plan is going to reach far beyond the restoration of the status quo ante.

Within the private law model of adjudication, a limited set of issues is defined and contested between two clearly defined parties. The parties' interests are coequal with all relevant interests in the case. The outcome of the contest is expected to be a clear legal victory for one party. The remedy will be an effort to restore aggrieved individuals to the position they would have occupied without the legal wrongdoing. In this respect, the private law model is reasonably well served by what we call an *issue decision* type of procedure, in which the dispute remains focused on narrow legal issues and the law declares one side the winner (Lempert and Sanders 1986).

The public law model, as described by Chayes, does not focus on narrow individual legal rights. The remedy is directed toward constructing a comprehensive plan, which, in the case of school desegregation, is aimed at the structural integration of two (or more) groups. The ideal "root and branch" remedy must look to the future, and must reintegrate the contending parties into complex, ongoing relationships. Because the parties must continue to interact and live together, the aim is to settle the dispute by some agreed-upon, or at least consented-to, solution, rather than to declare a winner and a loser; and many things pertaining to the relationship of the parties are relevant in the determination of that compromise. Disputes between such parties tend to be polycentric in nature, involving many cross-cutting conflicts, the resolution of any one of which influences the other conflicts (Fuller 1971, 1978; Yellin 1981). The goal of such a dispute-settlement process is to settle relationships rather than to decide (legal) issues (Griffiths 1984).

When lawyers suggest that school desegregation cases are not justiciable, they are implicitly arguing that such disputes are difficult to resolve with traditional (issue decision) procedures.[6] Consider the following comments:

> It is not every problem that can be solved by courts. Courts are ill-equipped to solve this kind of problem. The courts are not by and large institutions that remediate situations. They just say you are right, you are wrong.

> In this type of case we are getting far beyond the use of courts as a method of resolving disputes. Desegregating whole school systems is not the type of things courts traditionally get into. You are having courts make decisions based upon their own sociological (i.e., extralegal) concepts. . . .

Settling who is legally right and who is legally wrong is not enough, in these attorneys' view. At a local level, the parties are in a complex and enduring relationship. The school board and administration must continue to interact with parents and children who bring litigation. The

---

6. A preference for a public law model of violation or remedy does not inevitably push parties to a preference for a relationship-settlement procedure. Other objectives of the parties (e.g., playing for long-term legal rules) and their underlying relationship to one another (e.g., outsiders who are involved in the community only for the duration of litigation) also influence the choice of a style of dispute settlement.

school is also a central element of community identification and solidarity, and parents and students are an important part of the school.[7]

At a more macro level, the character of the entire community, including its business and residential climate, is affected by the nature and quality of its schools. Relations between the plaintiffs and defendants in school cases create a broad public controversy, and there are often numerous interveners in school desegregation suits. For example, in St. Louis, in addition to the school board and the original private plaintiffs, lawyers also represented the United States Department of Justice, the NAACP (which sued to intervene in the suit over the original plaintiff's objection because it opposed a potential settlement of the case),[8] the city of St. Louis and the state of Missouri (concerned with who would pay for any court order), and one "white parents group" (resisting the alteration of neighborhood schools). When metropolitan desegregation became an issue, numerous surrounding communities became additional parties to the litigation. Even with this plethora of parties, interveners, and *amici*, the parties to the litigation do not always represent every interest affected by the litigation. For instance, since no organization such as the Mexican-American Legal Defense Education Fund (MALDEF) was a party in St. Louis, other minorities were not represented in the case.[9]

What alternatives do parties and courts have when confronted with this situation? Macaulay (1963) notes that businessmen who engage in contractual relationships with one another over long periods of time often avoid the courts. Out-of-court settlements allow parties to consider any issues they deem relevant, regardless of their legal significance. And such settlements allow the parties to reach compromises which may involve a number of issues at once. Some lawyers in the desegregation cases might have preferred a compromise.

> I would much rather have sat down with the plaintiffs . . . and try to negotiate outside the [legal] system.

7. The Second Circuit captured the nature of the problem with the following passage:

> The precise remedy does not follow logically from the determination of liability, but rather reflects a careful reconciliation of the interests of many affected members of the community and a choice among a wide range of possibilities. The nature of litigation does not lend itself to complete success by one side or the other. (*United States v. Bd. of Educ. of Waterbury*, 605 F.2d 573, 567–77 (2d Cir. 1979))

8. *Liddell v. Crawford*, 546 F.2d 768 (8th Cir. 1976).

9. In other cases filed by the NAACP lawyers, the interests of Hispanics produced later retrials or appeals.

However, during the period we studied, out-of-court settlements were remarkably rare in school desegregation cases. For the defendant school board, any attempted compromise may have had serious political consequences. In a number of communities, board members opposing desegregation plans had been elected as part of a reaction against previous school boards which moved toward desegregation. Even if the board were of a more liberal bent, it may have preferred that the court, not the board, bear the brunt of community anger regarding a desegregation plan (Kalodner and Fishman 1978). Where some local plaintiffs attempted to settle cases (Atlanta, St. Louis), national plaintiffs (the national NAACP) have attempted to prevent this outcome. The national plaintiffs' refusal to agree to these settlements was apparently based upon a desire to play for rules in the legal process (see Galanter 1974; Orfield 1978a, 400–402) and upon their concern that a compromise in one city would make victory in other cases more difficult. The impossibility of reaching an out-of-court settlement has caused attorneys as well as experts to be open to dispute-settlement procedures which are compatible with a public law model of remedy.

Panels of experts may help produce a *relationship settlement* type of resolution. Scientists who are not tied to parties may be better able to alter or broaden the range of issues, and therefore the nature of the possible remedies. Panels can introduce new evidence or issues which increase the possibility of compromise (see Lempert and Sanders 1986; Menkel-Meadow 1984). By doing so, they move the parties away from the win-lose emphasis of private law adjudication. In the words of one attorney:

> The evolution of the law is such that it is not altogether clear whether or not you're dealing with some social injustice or a constitutional violation. I think that a panel of experts is really essentially an accommodation of the political process. I think to some extent it involves the court mimicking or setting up sort of a mini-legislature to deal with an issue that probably ought to be dealt with in the real legislature to begin with. Really, I have a feeling that those panels really perform a function more suggestive of what the community will accept, rather than giving any better idea of what's right and what's wrong.

At the remedy stage, a workable plan must be developed and implemented. It must recognize and respond to the complex and enduring relationship between parties, and must gain the more or less willing support of opposing parties. Once the trial is over, minority groups,

Table 9.2. Attorneys' Views of Expert Panel at Remedy, by Party Affiliation

Views of an Expert Panel	Plaintiff (N = 21)	Defense (N = 24)	Total (N = 45)
Approve	62% (13)	29% (7)	44% (20)
Undecided	9% (2)	8% (2)	9% (4)
Disapprove	29% (6)	63% (15)	47% (21)

Notes: χ^2 = 5.92; df = 2; $p <$ .10 (without Undecided, χ^2 = 5.37; $p <$ .05).

white groups, parents, students, and educators must be reintegrated and be able to work together.

We noted in chapter 2 that defendants are more likely to view the school desegregation cases from a private law perspective. If the willingness to consider a panel is tied to one's view of the adequacy of a private law model in school desegregation cases, we might expect plaintiff attorneys to be more accepting of the idea (see table 9.2).

Defense attorneys may be less receptive to panels because they represent the professional staff of school employees who already have control of the school system. Many judges believe that these staff members have the experience, expertise, and moral authority that entitle them to a leading role in creating and managing a desegregation plan.[10] If the plaintiffs wish to have much control over the eventual plan, to introduce expertise of their own, they stand a better chance of doing it during the trial, while the remedy options are still before the judge. Thus, to the extent that a scientific panel helps take the remedy out of the hands of school people, and places it in the hands of experts operating within the judge's purview, it may be more attractive to plaintiff attorneys. Finally, many defense attorneys assume that a liberal bias exists in the social science community, and they oppose panels partly because they doubt the ability of the scholars on the panel to present a complete and balanced account of existing evidence.

The Nature and Role of Social Science and the Social Science Expert

Social Science experts disagreed considerably with regard to the panel: 55% approved, 25% disapproved, and 20% were undecided (table 9.1). Nearly 75% of the experts who adopted a social science stance supported a panel, whereas only one-third of those who adopted a legal-

10. Whether they actually have such expertise, or are willing to use it in the service of desegregation, is a good question. The record is quite mixed on this point, and we discuss some of the relevant issues in chapters 1 and 11.

Table 9.3. Scientists' Views of an Expert Panel at Remedy, by Normative Stance

Position on Panel	Normative Stance Social Scientific	Mixed	Legal - Adversary	Total
Approve	74% (17)	57% (4)	32% (6)	55% (27)
Undecided	13% (3)	0% (0)	36% (7)	20% (10)
Disapprove	13% (3)	43% (3)	32% (6)	25% (12)
Total	100% (23)	100% (7)	100% (19)	100% (49)

Notes: χ^2 = 10.53; df = 4; $p < .03$.

adversary stance did (table 9.3). Experts adopting the social science stance support a method of introducing evidence which they believe will further limit partisan pressure, whether that pressure comes from themselves, from their profession, or from courtroom procedures. Experts who adopt the adversary norms of the courtroom do not prefer a panel.

Both the choice of normative stance and courtroom structure appear to be related to fundamental opinions about the proper role of the expert. These opinions are in turn influenced by what scholars believe to be the social science evidence in this area. In fact, experts' comments concerning why they prefer party witnessing or panels reveal the basic viewpoints that propel them to social science or adversary stances in court. Moreover, these considerations are not restricted solely to experts; attorneys, too, prefer panels or party witnessing based in part on their judgments about social science and experts.

Most of the experts whose opinions we have quoted so far believe that the problems encountered in presenting social science evidence in court are caused by either the way in which experts are selected or the way in which they are forced to present their evidence in court.[11] Some attorneys and scientists who resist the panel alternative simply do not

11. This perception is not new. Over a century ago, one English judge described his view of the process as follows:

> [T]he mode in which expert evidence is obtained is such as not to give the fair result of scientific opinion to the Court. A man may go, and does sometimes, to half-a-dozen experts. . . . He takes their honest opinions, he finds three in his favor and three against him; and he says to the three in his favor, 'will you be kind enough to give evidence?' and he pays the three against him their fees and leaves them alone; the other side does the same. . . . I am sorry to say the result is that the Court does not get that assistance from the experts which, if they were unbiased and fairly chosen, it would have a right to expect. (Jessel, M.R., in *Thorn v. Worthington Skating Rink Co.*, L.R. 6 Ch.D. 415, 416 (1876), quoted in McCormick 1984, 42)

believe that adversary procedures are the main source of difficulty with expert testimony. In fact, their view of social science leads them to prefer an adversary procedure for witnesses. Many of the lawyers believe that the social sciences are generally "soft," and do not lend themselves to the kinds of precise statements possible in the natural sciences.[12] Panel opponents believe that especially in the desegregation cases, many of the questions raised led to soft answers.

Some findings in this area do seem to be inherently fragile. Much of the debate concerning the effects of segregated schooling on attitudes and achievement appears to have turned on how the data was collected or analyzed. For example, with respect to the "doll studies," when Greenwald and Oppenheim (1968) used three dolls (dark, medium, and light) and interviewed white children as well as black, more white children than black children "misidentified" with their race (Rosenberg 1986, 196). Ideas about black self-esteem have also been contradicted:

> The results of the numerous studies by Rosenberg and those he has discussed sharply challenge and to a large degree contradict the earlier studies. Black self-esteem is not lower and is sometimes higher than white self-esteem. When the question of segregation is introduced as a variable, it has usually proved to increase, not decrease, black self-esteem. (See, e.g., Drury, 1980; Goering, 1972; Heiss and Owens, 1972; Katz, 1976, Chap. 4; McCarthy and Yancey, 1971; Taylor and Walsh, 1979. For general reviews and commentaries and some confirmation of earlier findings, see Adam, 1978; Asher and Allen, 1969; Porter, 1971; Porter and Washington, 1979; Williams and Morland, 1976). (Yinger 1986, 237)[13]

The Coleman Report was also subjected to methodological and substantive challenge. The earliest critiques of the findings of the report were by economists, who disapproved of using standardized beta weights in multiple regression analysis; they preferred unstandardized coefficients (see Cohen and Weiss 1977). Others critiqued the work because it used easily collected "objective" variables to the exclusion of "softer" variables such as student-teacher interactions, which may be of equal or greater importance.

In areas like the effect of school desegregation on academic achievement, there seem to be nearly as many conclusions as there are studies.

12. As Strong (1970) notes, similar critiques have been made against "harder" sciences.

13. Whether Clark's original studies would have produced similar results with similar methods is, of course, impossible to know. What is clear is that theories about self-esteem and its causes have changed over the years.

Arguments turn not only on questions of methodology but also on differing interpretations of the same data. The result is a body of literature with often unclear and contradictory policy implications.[14]

Cohen and Weiss (1977) offer two reasons why there is relatively little consensus in the area of desegregation. They note that it is generally the normal business of science to raise more questions than it answers.

> The progress of research on social problems tends to move backward, from relatively simple ideas about problems and their solutions to ever more basic questions about both. The net result is a more varied picture of reality. (89)

With particular reference to the school desegregation research, they provide a second reason:

> The research has grown, and grown more sophisticated, but the findings have not been cumulative. A good part of the reason is that there is no strong theory that suggested what influences should be observed, or what outcome variables are most important. Given this situation, social science tends to proliferate under the influence of empirical ideas, weak theories, intuitions from practical experience, suggestions from other fields, or the analytic possibilities suggested by new methodologies. Under such conditions, scientific improvement is a term with a somewhat special—and often purely technical—meaning. The fruit of such scientific developments is sometimes rich and always varied, but not necessarily very coherent. (88)

Some scholars have attributed the lack of a theoretical foundation in desegregation research to the fact that much of the work was driven by the controversy itself, done to assist one side or the other in the desegregation conflict. Prager, Longshore, and Seeman argue as follows in their 1986 collection of articles designed to "rethink" several desegregation issues:

> It is our view that desegregation research could well benefit from reconsideration precisely because the topic is increasingly removed from the public spotlight. Once the press of events no longer pro-

---

14. For example, see Robert Crain's remarks concerning Nancy St. John's conclusions about the relationship between desegregation and standardized test scores (Crain 1976, 40–41). After discussing what he sees to be the faults of St. John's analysis and interpretation, Crain concludes: "St. John recommends against compulsory desegregation, but the achievement data which she has compiled do not support her in this view" (41).

pels research willy-nilly in different directions (often with different conclusions), serving different purposes, and speaking to different masters, it now becomes possible to take stock more calmly of what we know and what we still need to find out. Such stocktaking is seldom possible when academic research is closely monitored by involved and competing publics. . . . Researchers have been defining their questions in terms of the interested parties, not in terms of scientifically derived criteria for evaluation. Scientific inquiry, in short, has sacrificed its autonomy and lacks a distinctive agenda of its own. (4, 5)[15]

If this point of view about social science in general, and the evidence presented in court in particular, is correct, it undermines a major argument of experts who expressed support for a panel. For instance, some scientists believed that the panel would provide a more neutral and autonomous environment in which experts could agree on many aspects of the evidence.

I think there are a lot of factual points that the witnesses from both sides of these cases could agree upon. There are a lot of things that Armor and Orfield would agree on.

I think that the responsibility of social scientists in the role of expert witness, the basis of their expertise, is the application of scientific techniques to understand social phenomena. . . . You can only speak where there is clear support in your data for it.

However, if a large number of the questions about desegregation concern data generated directly or indirectly by the parties and open to alternative interpretations, then the area of agreement is either relatively small or exists only at a very general level.

Some scholars who oppose the panel argue, in fact, that the essence of being an expert does not lie in a particular fact or knowledge base, or in the willingness to share that base with public figures. Rather, the essence of being an expert is sharing a general viewpoint, which, in the marketplace of ideas within social science, is pitted against other viewpoints in a dialectical (adversary) relationship. The task is to present a view shaped by an understanding of scientific research as well as of other experiences.

15. One can read into this passage some devaluation of applied research, at least when it is done outside of the academy. It is presumably this type of criticism that our social scientists are referring to when they report the price of doing applied work.

To quote one expert:

> More and more I feel that I am presenting a perspective on how to interpret reality rather than a set of hard and fast proofs . . . and the other side knows that it is coming. They have a chance to challenge this perspective.[16]

Cohen and Weiss (1977), in their essay on the role of social science in areas like school desegregation, ultimately adopt a similar view. They conclude that at its best, social science presents alternative visions of, rather than specific solutions to, a problem.

> We expect that courts, like most other customers at the social science supermarket, can expect no relief. Most litigants in school cases will be able to find some scientific support for their views, and many judges will try valiantly to decide which is right. . . . At its best, social research provides a reasonable sense of the various ways a problem can be understood, and a reasonable account of how solutions might be approached. Such general advice about controversial and problematic issues is a useful contribution of social knowledge, even if it is not crisply relevant to particular decisions. (89)[17]

In addition to questions concerning the data, those who oppose a panel have questions concerning the autonomy and neutrality of the experts themselves. Autonomy and neutrality are, of course, matters of degree. There are no totally value-free scientists (Weber 1946). Panel opponents argue, however, that the study of race relations and school desegregation by American academics is an area where personal neutrality is an especially rare commodity. In chapters 6 and 8 we noted occasions where academic work in the area is laden with *ad hominem*

---

16. In chapter 10 we consider in greater detail the idea that the primary thing social science has to offer to the court is a perspective, rather than specific information (see Sanders et al. 1981/82).

17. Such views find a sympathetic ear in philosopher Francis Sparshott, who notes that complex issues such as desegregation are not easily settled by an appeal to the facts.

> This compound problem of the nature of man and of his world, is not a factual one but a deliberative one to be settled, that is not by finding things out but by making up one's mind. There are, of course, hard facts that determine what answers to the question are admissible but it is not these facts which are in question. There are many ways in which, many aspects under which, we can think about ourselves and about the world considered as our environment without committing detectable errors of fact. (Sparshott 1972, 110–11)

attacks among scholars and implicit or explicit assaults upon the politics and integrity of the work of others. As those interactions indicate, many social scientists who work in this area have points of view and can be expected to prosecute them. The following two comments, the first by a lawyer and the second by a social scientist, reflect this expectation:

> We seek to imbue any professional with the idea that they are non-human philosopher kings who have made an intuitive leap to the knowledge of the good. That itself contains a fallacy. When you get into subjects like race, obscenity, things that have an emotional overload in this society, the perception of either side of expertise does tend to get skewed. What the reality is, is a very difficult thing to say.

> Particularly in the area of a volatile social issue, such as race relations, the potential exists for the involvement of ideological positions in the findings of social scientists.

Thus, panels that remove scholars from the adversary pressures of the courtroom will not necessarily yield consensus on key points. In the words of two scholars:

> I think there is a fundamental political perspective on the nature of current reality, and the issues have become so entwined with strong feelings about current policies that only some of the issues can be resolved by genuine scholarly debate. Some of it is just differences of opinion and perspective.

> I think it is unrealistic to think that you are going to get unanimity of opinion with a panel. We do not have consensus in our field. Somehow when it comes to policy implications, we want to present a united front. Why? There isn't a united front, why should there be one in court?

This second comment warns that although panels cannot create actual consensus among scholars, they may be used to create the veneer of such consensus, legitimating particular policy decisions with the stamp of scientific approval.

> The panel will be biased and therefore offer a polemic for one side.

> The panel sounds a little odd to me because it sounds like an effort at dispassionate social science. But I know those people and I know that they are not dispassionate.

> You tend to make them [experts on a panel] appear to be something they are not if you say they are paid by the court rather than by the plaintiffs. They are still going to have their own preconceived notions about a particular solution.

Concerns about the illusion of neutrality in a panel are increased by the potential for bias in the selection process. Federal Rule of Evidence 706 allows the judge to appoint experts on his own motion or after nominations by the parties. Safeguards built into the rule (the right of parties to call their own experts and to examine and cross-examine the court's experts) may not overcome the effect of an adverse report by court-appointed experts. Although there are no federal court examples to point to in this area, the Los Angeles experience (a state-court case) does not alleviate concern. The court asked both the plaintiffs and the school board for their recommendations. None of the first choices of the defendant were chosen. Most who have examined the makeup of the panel would agree that it represented a range of opinion which leaned toward the plaintiffs.[18] Said one of our respondents:

> And in the case of the L.A. panel, there is no question that the judge did not make an attempt to get a representative cross section of opinion. In fact, not only that, he got a panel from among the most activist prodesegregation people in the field.

The question of bias goes beyond the individual bias of the witness or the trial judge. There is also a serious question regarding the influence of a collective liberal bias in the social science profession. The pressure and attacks on experts who have testified for school boards, or who have challenged the liberal desegregation agenda from the right or the left, are indications of this bias.[19]

---

18. The panel members were: Professor Beatriz Arias, School of Education, University of California at Los Angeles; Dr. Robert Crain, Rand Corporation; Professor Reynolds Farley, Department of Sociology and Population Studies Center, University of Michigan; Dr. Bernard R. Gifford, Russell Sage Foundation; Dean Elwood Hain, San Diego Law School; Professor Gary Orfield, Political Science Department, University of Illinois at Urbana; Professor Thomas Pettigrew, Department of Psychology and Social Relations, Harvard University; Professor Francine Rabinovitz, University of Southern California.

19. This type of pressure and attacks on experts is a reason some legal scholars have given *for* court-appointed experts. They argue that court-appointed experts might ensure the presentation of unpopular positions (McGurk 1959/60). One of the justifications advanced for Federal Rule of Evidence 706 was that it would allow the judge to assist parties who were unable to procure the assistance of an expert "because either they cannot afford

Those who are opposed to panels believe that it is incapable of accomplishing the objectives its supporters wish to achieve, both because the data do not lend themselves to clear policy mandates and because the ideal of autonomous and neutral social science is rare in the school desegregation area.

> It [the panel] always struck me as a simple response to Eleanor Wolf et al.'s criticism of the adversarial pattern being inappropriate. I don't know what you would accomplish by putting Armor, Coleman, Orfield and Taeuber in the same room and saying you guys come up with a [desegregation] plan. They don't start from the same premise. It basically is an adversarial process where there are different views.

This expert, and several others, do not view party witnessing as a necessary evil of litigation. They have adopted a legal-adversary stance in court and have concluded that party witnessing is a positive aspect of the system.

> I understood the partisan nature of the courtroom and I realized that I would be on the stand arguing for a position without also presenting evidence that might be contrary to my case or side. But you see, that didn't bother me, because I knew that the other side was also doing that.

> I don't think there is a substitute for advocacy law. Let ours be presented and let theirs be presented and let the attorneys do the cross-examination under the rules of law and evidence.

> I am most concerned about personal opinions and personal desires creeping into the situation and somehow being presented in a panel situation where they can't be pulled out or rebutted. One

one or they cannot convince one to help" (Saltzburg 1978, 75). According to this argument, parties may not be able to detect defects in other expert testimony without the help of experts. Nor will errors in one-sided testimony be deterred by ordinary methods of academic scrutiny (e.g., refereed journals, rebuttal articles). As Wolf (1981) notes, "The expert testimony given during a trial is virtually a secret as far as the 'scientific forum' is concerned" (274). Of course, a court-appointed expert is not the same thing as an expert panel. Neither attorneys nor social scientists discussed the possibility that a court-appointed expert might be an adversary tool. At a more behavioral level, as far as we could determine no lawyers in the school cases ever requested a judge to call court-appointed witnesses, something they have a right to do under Rule 706: "Appointment. The court may on its own motion or *on the motion of any party* [emphasis added] enter an order. . . ."

of the things about the adversary situation in a courtroom is that it permits careful examination of information through cross-examination.[20]

These comments reflect an acceptance of the logic and theory of the adversary system as a method of using and controlling bias, and of the role of a party witness in such a system. Saks and Hastie (1978) present the logic of the adversary system in the following terms:

> The venerated Anglo-Saxon–American system is deliberately dialectical. . . . Justice comes not from the wisdom and good will of dedicated and sincere people; it comes from a system intended to work with or without wisdom, good will, and sincerity. Truth comes from a system that balances competing views of truth, not from well-intentioned seekers of truth. This is typical of our system of "laws, not men"—structures are to be trusted, not people. Hopelessly flawed and biased humans are organized into a structure that, through its dialectic, converts systematically biased inputs into correct and fair outputs. (206)

Table 9.4 suggests that experts who have testified most frequently prefer party witnessing. The critical break in opinion occurs when an expert has testified three or more times. Only 33% of the experts who have testified in three or more cases prefer panels, whereas over two-thirds of those who have testified in fewer than three cases prefer panels.

Unlike most "peripheral experts," who appear in only one or two cases to "fill in the gaps" (e.g., local experts who present local data or experts who can present data on some novel or idiosyncratic aspect of a particular case), the core experts have testified repeatedly in school

---

20. As this last remark indicates, most experts had an exaggerated view of the practical differences between a court expert panel and party witnesses. In our interviews we did little to disabuse them of these views. Federal Rule 706 allows for examination and cross-examination of court witnesses. In fact, in some respects these experts are more open to examination than are party witnesses, for whom cross-examination is generally restricted to the scope of direct examination. And, from our own interviews and studies such as that of Eleanor Wolf, it is fair to say that quite often lack of experience and expert assistance has caused defense lawyers to fail to enter rebuttal testimony or conduct cross-examinations which reveal inadequacies in the plaintiff witness's testimony (Wolf 1981, 262–264). Within the interviews, we did not introduce all of these complexities before soliciting an opinion from experts as to their preference for panels. All of the aggregate findings in this chapter should be read with the understanding that both supporters and opponents of panels probably overestimate the differences between testimonial procedures.

Table 9.4. Scientists' Views of an Expert Panel at Remedy, by Experience

	Experience[a]		
Position on Panel	Less than three times	Three times or more	Total
Approve	68% (21)	33% (6)	55% (27)
Undecided	16% (5)	28% (5)	20% (10)
Disapprove	16% (5)	38% (7)	25% (12)
Total	100% (31)	100% (18)	100% (49)

Notes: χ^2 = 5.61; df = 2; $p < .06$.
[a]If the break on testimony is one time versus more than once, there is no trend in the data.

cases. Many of them have come to adopt an adversary stance, either by initial inclination or later socialization and commitment.[21] Sixty-one percent of the experts who have testified in fewer than three cases adopt a social science normative stance, whereas 22% of the experts who testified three or more times adopt this stance.[22]

These inner-circle experts are also more likely to have strong and enduring ties to the social movement itself. Experts who are themselves caught up in the adversary process, and who see social scientists as advocates (partisan, nonobjective) on desegregation-related issues, are more likely to prefer the party witness procedure. In addition, these experts usually have only loose or episodic ties to the community in which they are appearing as witnesses, and they may therefore have less incentive to search out dispute-settlement techniques, such as the panel, which produce relationship settlement solutions. Plaintiff lawyers who represent national groups like the NAACP, the MALDEF, or the ACLU are also relatively loosely tied to the community involved in the litigation. Although the numbers within each group of plaintiff lawyers are not sufficient to support firm conclusions, the national organization lawyers, like the core experts, are the least accepting of panels.

Summary

Our interviews with scholars and attorneys suggest that the choice of panel versus party witnessing involves the consideration of several is-

21. Because our data are essentially cross-sectional, we cannot measure the degree to which repeated testifying causes one to adopt a legal-adversary stance as compared to the stance causing one to be an expert in several cases (do lawyers prefer such witnesses and ask them to testify in new cases, or are such witnesses self-selected because they enjoy testifying?). Presumably, both processes are at work.
22. χ^2 = 8.2, df = 2, $p < .02$, N = 49.

sues, such as the division of power and control in courtroom interactions, dispute-settlement procedures, and bias in courtroom testimony. Social scientists generally favored panels as a reaction to the constraints and adversary pressures of party witnessing. Lawyers preferred party witnessing because of the control that it gave them, although some were willing to try panels as a dispute-settlement procedure at the remedy stage of litigation. Scholars and attorneys held varied opinions on how panels affected testimony. The interaction of preferences for an adversary or integrative style of litigation, along with an adversary or consensual model of social science, help explain experts' and attorneys' views of a panel of scientific experts.

10 The Effect of the Social Science Evidence on the Trial of the Cases

Much of the theoretical battle in the school cases has been over the question, What kind of a problem is racial inequality? According to some, it is a problem of individual prejudice, created by intentional acts of specific persons. According to others, inequality is a problem of social structure, created by historic and socially determined patterns that overshadow individual intentions or specific acts. Within the context of legal theory, an important part of this contest between litigants is the attempt to define the scope of the lawsuit, to make it conform to a public law model or a private law model. Unlike what happens in many "private" suits, in these and similar "public" cases the question of the nature of the dispute and the choice of adjudicative model is nearly always contentious (Zemans 1983). Competition over these models in turn leads to competition over the relevance and admissibility of the social science evidence. The evidentiary contest is not only over what facts are true but also over what facts are relevant at all. The contest is over a point of view.

Plaintiffs (and occasionally defendants) tried to use social science to convert judges to their point of view. This chapter explores how these efforts altered judges' general understanding of the causes of school segregation and how this altered understanding affected (*a*) the way judges interpreted evidence of violation, (*b*) the nature and scope of the remedy, and (*c*) the procedures used by the judges to construct a remedy.

Changing Judicial Views of Race Relations in Education

Attempts to change a judge's view of local race relations and education generally relied on processes of both cognitive and emotional change occurring as a result of education or persuasion. New conceptions of factual matters (e.g., the explanation of psychological harm, white flight, differential achievement) or new notions of cause and effect relations in complex social situations (e.g., the reciprocal effects of schooling on housing or the existence of a "web of discrimination") could be offered.

Plaintiffs consistently believed that one of the primary purposes of their social science testimony was to present to the judge new notions of cause and effect, and new contexts within which he should understand school desegregation. The following comment by a plaintiff attorney reflects this general objective:

> We use social science evidence because it is not possible to talk about or deal with racial discrimination or racial segregation in a societal vacuum. . . . We figure it is important for a judge to understand the context within which the individual actions produced the segregation, and to characterize the discrimination that took place. Whether this is testimony having to do with the impact of school segregation on black children's learning ability, or anything else, doesn't make a difference. The effort is to present the full context within which the public officials who created segregation carried out their game plan.

And from the witness side, this is how one of the plaintiff's core experts who testified on segregated housing explained his testimony:

> I think maybe I played a part in kind of an overall impression that the judges get that virtually every level of society, from the federal government to the local school board, conspires wittingly or unwittingly to cause this awful situation we're in right now. But they haven't been able to see, so far as I can determine, legal relevance to my testimony. To the extent it's helpful at all, it is so by adding to the panoramic picture of a society in which for years everything led to segregation.

Several attorneys we interviewed noted that conversion efforts were an important part of their legal strategy.

> Their [plaintiff attorneys'] experience in other communities has been that they've had to train the judge, teach the judge, educate the judge. I think some of that had to happen here.

> The strategy we used was to educate or re-educate the judge. Most judges come from conservative traditional backgrounds. They have sort of a "gut" reaction about uprooting and busing and that kind

of thing. So you have a problem of convincing and educating a judge to do something which goes against his gut. In order to really be able to do this, you can argue the law—but the law is not going to get to that visceral part—it takes the crafting of a lot of different kinds of information; also you have got to deal with the emotional aspect.

This was a situation where a judge started off with every preconceived idea about education: why kids learn, why races are separate, so forth and so on, every Sunday supplement-type belief. A case like this is a mosaic and the first thing that you work on is the built-in attitudes that you perceive the court has. So it is a teaching experience. The best kind of expert witness that you can have is somebody who suffered sometime. What you do with a [Judge X] is put on a guy like [Expert X]; one who he knows is very bright, very articulate, tremendous educational background, extremely knowledgeable about education and usually gifted in its expression. I asked [Expert X] three or four questions after I got his background. The rest of the time he and the judge talked to each other. It was just a full exchange; when it was over the judge has some idea what it might be like to be a minority person in this society.

Judges we interviewed agreed with these attorneys' assessment of some members of the judiciary, and the appropriateness of an educative legal strategy.

I think it's true that part of their job is educating the judge. Of course blacks have suffered some systematic and institutionalized racial animus. If you had someone on the bench who doesn't have this kind of knowledge, I suppose if I were a plaintiff's counsel, I would want to make sure in an important case like this that the judge is thoroughly familiar with racial problems in a large city and all the demographics that go with it.

Not all attempts to educate judges via social science occur in the courtroom. One social scientist reports his role in changing the trial judge's view:

After I was his consultant, the judge and I went to visit a minority neighborhood. It was a slum neighborhood, it was an awful slum. There was a superhighway around behind them and they were locked into this neighborhhood, and it was just a very inferior neighborhood with very inferior housing. And the judge said, "These kids never get to know what a beautiful city they live in.

They never see what a lovely place my city is. You get those kids out of here."

This report of conversion is supported by the judge.[1] Although this interaction occurred outside the courtroom, it did occur within the context of the case.

Other efforts occur outside the boundaries of ongoing litigation. Although the norms in support of judicial neutrality and against *ex parte* communication with litigants are designed to control extracourtroom contact, district court judges do not live outside society. They are often part of the prevailing elite of their local community and are influenced by their participation in various organizations and associations.[2]

Both sides of the school desegregation controversy attempted to engage judges in meetings, conferences, and other forums in which the participants exchanged ideas, planned strategy, and discussed ways to influence certain members of the bench. At times, these conferences were advertised as efforts to review new technical developments in the law or social sciences. At other times, they were rather explicit efforts to share strategic information and to collaborate on manufacturing a new consensus on policy and programs.[3]

---

1. Why some social scientists are effective in personally affecting a conversion of select judges is unclear. A critical factor is the judge's openness to the kind of information being transmitted. Lawyers for both plaintiffs and defendants agreed that some judges did not have their views altered by any testimony:

> The judge was extremely powerful, aggressive, intelligent, competent and very activist on segregation. He felt very strongly that segregation is wrong.

> The judge has his predisposition already. He was going to rule against the school board no matter what.

> He had formed his opinion already.

Both prodesegregation and antidesegregation judges fell within this category.

A second factor is the scholar's ability to deliver the material in a useful manner. In chapter 5, we delineate the characteristics of a good witness as perceived by experts and lawyers. Judges generally confirm the criteria discussed there. With respect to qualities of "persuasiveness" the judges stressed "sincerity," "a balanced approach," "witnesses who weigh their knowledge," "demeanor and appearance," "relationship to the parties or the subject matter," "interest in the outcome," and "common sense."

2. In extreme cases, judges report meeting with litigants outside the courtroom and advising them as to effective tactics. The meetings we are aware of were efforts by the judge to advise school boards, at their behest, on how to best proceed so as to avoid litigation or limit the probability of a suit.

3. We use the term *collaboration* to describe meetings where there is no one present

One example of a prodesegregation collaboration was a conference on the sociology of school desegregation, held in December 1975. In attendance were two federal judges with a prodesegregation record, five attorneys generally operating as counsel for one or another civil rights agency, and a number of social scientists who had appeared or would in the near future appear for the civil rights plaintiffs in court. Another such conference, held in May 1980, concerned school desegregation research. The attendees were two federal judges with a prodesegregation record, seven attorneys generally operating as counsel for civil rights agencies or groups, and several social scientists who either had a history of testimony for plaintiff groups or of conducting research used to support such groups.

Not present at these conferences were school board lawyers, judges who were "known" to oppose desegregation as a national policy, and social scientists who regularly appeared as experts for defendants.[4] However, interviews with judges indicate that defendants also conducted conferences and informal meetings, although civil rights groups and their various collaborators were better organized at the regional and national level. The existence of such meetings indicates that when a body of litigation is part of a social movement, the judiciary, like other groups, will find it difficult to remain completely detached.

Several judges attended these public conferences or more private gatherings, sometimes held for the judiciary alone. Their comments downplay the "collaborative" aspects of these sessions.

> I did go to a two-day session of judges in Washington. It wasn't at all publicized, and it shouldn't have been publicized. Some of the judges were under serious possibility of physical attack. I think there were twenty-five to thirty district court judges who attended this meeting, but no conclusion was reached. No record was made, but I think the discussions and conversations were very important.

> There are foundation seminars where we generally have a case study. . . . At one conference we used Denver. We used it as a starting point, and we have big city educators and we have federal

---

whose mind needs to be changed. Where such individuals are present, the meeting is an effort at conversion.

4. As we noted in earlier chapters, most expert witnesses become identified as a plaintiff witness or as a defense witness. A few switch sides, and, of those who do, even fewer ever switch back. None of the experts we encountered routinely worked both sides of the street.

judges. We also talk not only about matters of school desegregation, but other areas where federal judges are involved in schools.
A lot of ideas are traded around.

You have to assure them [the judges] there's nothing irregular, so
they're sure they can talk freely. Once that happens, federal judges
are very eager to talk, because we don't get to go anywhere and do
this. It's a great opportunity to sit around with some great people
who you've heard about early on in the history of school desegregation . . . Skelly Wright, Constance Motley, etc.

Some judges recognize, however, that many meetings and conferences are more than attempts to dispense information. As one of the
judges we interviewed noted:

The lawyers still perceive the fact-finder, whoever he is, as someone
who must be persuaded. And he is sensitive to extraneous things.
It's not a pristine system and I think that's what lawyers have in
mind.

The social science evidence presented at these conferences, like that
presented in the courtroom, is designed to influence the judge's view
of social reality, altering his sense of the appropriate legal model, his
interpretation of evidence introduced at violation, and his conception
of the remedy to be ordered if there is a violation. What influence did
such testimony have?

The General Effect of Social Science Evidence on Judges
Some trial judges have stated that they found little use in social science
testimony, especially at the violation stage (Doyle 1977). And as one of
the judges we interviewed put it:

I told him [the expert] that when he got things straightened out in
Boston he could come here and tell me how to do things. I don't
need social science evidence. I only need to decide a constitutional
right, not the social aspect of these cases.

From our interviews and other sources, however, it is fair to say that
the social science evidence introduced during trial did give a number
of trial and appellate judges some new information and insights about
the general situation of minorities, and that this information influenced
their opinion (Wisdom 1975).

Several judges explicitly reported that the evidence in the case did
play a role in changing their views on racial inequality.

You asked how you get educated and I suppose it's absorption of some kind of everything you hear and see and experience over a long period of time.

In observing my own children, it's obviously broadened them. In their lives to be lived, I'm certain they will get along with their fellow men better than my generation, because they were required to associate with one another.

I thought segregation was an incidental question until I began to learn something about it from the testimony. In fact, the schools were still badly, well almost completely segregated. It was these facts, not opinions, that were important. It took several months of studying to recognize that, as far as race was concerned, all things took place with the action of the state, county, city school board and federal authorities.

Richardson and Vines (1970) report a similar such conversion of Judge Waring of South Carolina's Eastern District, a member of the three-judge panel in *Briggs v. Elliott*.[5] In this judge's words:

I'd never thought about the race problem, most of my life. . . . I'd never met any Negroes, except as laborers. Then in the courtroom I began to see the realities and inequalities. It gives one a sense of futility at times. . . . I began to see illogicalities, and suddenly the whole segregation system appeared absurd. (99)

Judge McMillan, writing of his experience in *Swann*, noted:

In *Swann v. Charlotte-Mecklenberg Board of Education*, before reaching any conclusions, the district court went to considerable pains to review thousands of pages of sociological evidence, most of it from official school board and other government files, and found as a fact that segregation in Charlotte was caused and required by numerous discriminatory governmental actions.

It was the view of the district court at that time, and now, that no answer to the question of discrimination could be given without a serious and careful study of that information. (McMillan 1977, 162–163)

5. Judge Waring wrote a twenty-five-page dissent to the majority opinion upholding the constitutionality of South Carolina's separate-but-equal statute. He wrote in his dissent, "Segregation is per se inequality" (98 F. Supp. 529, 548 (1951)).

The most dramatic change of a viewpoint occurred in the case of Steven Roth, the trial judge in the original Detroit litigation. In the plaintiffs' view, Judge Roth began the trial hostile to their position. They began the social science part of their case with the Sloan-Taeuber-Green group of experts, who testified tó the effect of governmental policies on housing segregation, the relationship between school segregation and housing segregation, and the harmful effects of segregation on black children. None of this evidence was legally relevant in a narrow, private law model: it did not prove school board intention. Yet, near the end of this testimony, before the plaintiffs had introduced most of their evidence on school board violations per se, a lawyer for a white-parents group told the school board attorney that he thought the case was lost. An attorney for the plaintiff describes Judge Roth's change of view in somewhat dramatic terms:

> Judge Roth is a classical example of where an educational process was required. Judges are often people who have lived in a largely white cocoon, all their lives, because of segregation—white prep school, white colleges, white downtown club, white offices in many instances. And the whole notion of the significance of racial experience in this country has to be presented in some guise at some point to sensitize them to get their attention to what the case is all about. Consequently, there is a strong argument to be made for: "Look your honor. Let me set the stage for what the rest of the play is to follow. I will explain to you in a way that you probably do not know first hand the role of race in our history in this country."

Evidently, the testimony helped convert Judge Roth to a belief that the courts should adopt a public law model of violation. Wolf (1976) quotes the judge as saying later that

> it is unfortunate that we cannot deal with public school segregation on a no-fault basis, for if racial segregation is an evil, it should make no difference whether we classify it *de jure* or *de facto*. Our objective should be to remedy a condition which we believe needs correction. (109)

Roth came as close as any judge to being persuaded to adopt a public law view of violation which would not require proof of specific, intentional segregative acts on the part of the school board. Roth's ultimate attempt to stretch the law to allow for a metropolitan remedy in Detroit without proof of intentional segregation with interdistrict effects was overturned by the Supreme Court in *Milliken v. Bradley*, 418 U.S. 717 (1974). But even though the plaintiffs' social science evidence did not lead to new substantive law concerning violation, it did affect the interpretation of other facts, and it did affect both the remedy and the methods used by the judge in constructing it.

The Interpretation of Other Evidence at Violation

Evidence on factors such as the relationship between school and housing segregation often provided a context within which judges could understand other, specific evidence. Plaintiffs, of course, have the burden of proving their claim by the preponderance of the evidence, and must put their case on first. In some ways this offers the defendants an advantage, because they are able to judge the strength of various aspects of the plaintiff's case and adjust the defense accordingly,[6] but going first allows the plaintiff to anticipate the defense and attack it before it is presented. Part of the social science testimony put on by the plaintiffs in the violation stage of the school cases served this objective.

Normally, the plaintiffs could anticipate a neighborhood-school defense by the school board. The defendant would argue that its actions were in pursuit of a racially neutral plan of student assignment to the nearest school, and were therefore not motivated by a segregative purpose. However, testimony about segregation in housing, jobs, and so forth could undermine the defendant's case in two ways. First, it could establish the context within which apparently neutral acts led to further racial isolation. Second, by indicating how other individuals and organizations had acted in segregative ways, it could suggest that the school board must have acted this way as well.

The use of expert testimony to influence the impact of the defense's arguments was an explicitly stated strategy of plaintiff groups. To quote plaintiff lawyers:

> Part of putting on a housing case is as a means of countering a pat defense that the school board uses. Their pat defense is that all they did was build the school where the kids were.

> You show the whole housing phenomenon, the whole business. Because when the school board comes on with their proof about the neutral reasons, the non-racial reasons, why they did all these things—by the time you have finished setting the scene in which those things happened, the real world, then the judge, in order to

6. This advantage should not be overstated. With modern discovery rules there is relatively little surprise at trial. Still, depositions cannot always reveal the impression that various pieces of evidence may have.

believe that race was not a factor in those decisions, has to believe that there was a magic door in the schoolhouse.

Part of the reason we need to use these people is to anticipate the defense. The defense generally has very little to say other than "We haven't done it." So part of what we present with social science testimony is "The board of realtors has done it, the governor's office has done it, and if everybody is doing it, how can it be reasonable that in the same time frame the educational institution wasn't doing it?" It is a tactic, part of what we're presenting. Beat them before they can even come in and say it. Make them look silly.

The courts have not been receptive to a neighborhood-school defense and have been willing to accept a limited set of incidents as proof of segregative purpose, placing upon the defendants the burden of showing that these incidents were not undertaken with any racial animus (*Brinkman v. Gilligan*, 583 F.2d 243 (6th Cir. 1978)). The Columbus and Dayton cases reinforce this line of argument, which apparently established an affirmative duty to desegregate in nearly every school system which contained *de jure* segregated black students in 1954 (*Columbus Board of Education v. Penick*, 443 U.S. 887 (1979); *Dayton Board of Education v. Brinkman II*, 443 U.S. 526 (1979)). At least with respect to intradistrict cases, it has become difficult for defendants to justify any act which has the effect of segregating students.

Although critics argued that the plaintiff experts made misleading and erroneous statements concerning the causes of school and housing segregation in cities, the plaintiff social science witnesses went largely unchallenged until quite late in the school cases (Wolf 1981). Finally, in some of the incremental segregative effect hearings in cities such as Omaha, and in the metropolitan suit in Atlanta, the defendants began to challenge plaintiff views with witnesses of their own. These experts argued that housing segregation had other causes in addition to (and perhaps more important than) the segregative purpose of institutions, and that school decisions, however motivated, had little incremental segregative effect. By way of example, the following is an excerpt from the testimony of a defense expert on the issue of housing segregation:

> COUNSEL: Dr. [X], again, in your opinion and given these preferences [of whites and blacks for neighborhoods of different racial mix] are stable integrated neighborhoods likely?
> WITNESS: No, . . . we have an interesting phenomena whereby both groups, both whites and blacks, endorse in principle the concept of integrated neighborhoods. Very few blacks . . . express a

preference for all black neighborhoods. Very few whites would object to integrated neighborhoods but their definition of integration is quite different.

What we see in the case of blacks is a definition of integration that is something on the order of pointing toward a fifty-fifty neighborhood, possibly leaning more toward majority black. We see in the case of white preferences, in terms of that ratio that would lead to stability, that integration would be possibly an eighty-twenty or ninety-ten neighborhood or at most a seventy-thirty neighborhood.

The result of this differing definition of integration—in effect I guess I could say that they can't get together. The kinds of neighborhoods that blacks would choose are the kind of neighborhoods that whites would leave. The result of this situation based upon these attitudes which have held fairly constant in the past ten years, in effect is an explanation for the racial transition that we see going on in many cities and in fact has gone on in [City Y].[7]

If nothing else, the witness has provided an alternative explanation for housing patterns in cities, one which explains the existence of segregated housing on the basis of individual preferences of white and black residents, not on the basis of governmental action. If the state is not primarily responsible for segregated housing, the implication is that it may not be primarily responsible for school segregation either. It is worth noting, however, that this counterattack on the plaintiff's explanation of residential segregation is not an attempt to persuade the judge to adopt a private law model; rather it is another attempt within a public law model to provide a different structural (tipping point) mechanism for segregated housing.[8] One can only speculate on the extent to which such public law-oriented testimony, had it been presented in earlier cases, could have neutralized plaintiff expert testimony on the causes of housing and school segregation.

Influencing the Scope of the Remedy
The influence of a public law model on the school desegregation cases has been more direct at the remedy stage. In fact, "root and branch"

7. Of course, this transcript is a matter of public record, as are the remarks of the witness. Nevertheless, as we promised all of our subjects anonymity, we have chosen not to disclose the witness or the city when we quote from transcript material.

8. For a general discussion of the process described in this testimony, including the general outlines of a plaintiff rebuttal, see Granovetter (1986, 104) and Schelling (1978, 93–94).

desegregation can be understood only if we adopt the perspective that there is more at stake than correcting the individual acts of school officials (Fiss 1971). A public law model calls upon the school system to take affirmative acts to overcome the segregation and inequality caused by the social, organizational, and demographic factors which separate white and black children. Such a model focuses on future dealings rather than on the past wrongdoing of the parties, and it considers a wide range of issues necessary to construct a comprehensive remedy aimed at structural integration, rather than a narrow set of "legal" facts needed to adjudicate responsibility.

The social science evidence that plaintiffs presented at the violation stage appears to be one of the factors which moved the judiciary, often with considerable reluctance, toward such remedies, remedies which were more legislative than adjudicative. Early in the process of litigation, such evidence may have begun to sensitize the judge as to what would be necessary if the remedy were to be "just and viable" from the plaintiff's perspective. It reflected an understanding on the part of plaintiff counsel that

> judges who were asked to decide questions of social and economic policy ought to be educated about the social and economic "facts of life", since their decisions necessarily would reflect their attitudes toward these matters. (Schubert 1964, 2)

Of course, it hardly needs saying that this movement toward a public law view of remedy in school desegregation cases is the product of many factors beyond the social science evidence, but the evidence has played a role in widening some trial judges' vision and in altering their perceptions. To quote one judge:

> To me social science is the study of people and how they got where they are and how they act vis-à-vis other people. It is the history, politics, economics, legislation, court decisions, the traditions, money and everything being done by the legislature and other people to get where you are. I'd say social science has been an integral part of considering the constitutional question.

The social science evidence slowly moved the courts toward a consideration of other, more micro issues, in their desegregation plans. Plaintiff groups began to introduce social science evidence designed to influence the judge's order with respect to "second-generation problems" of desegregation, including suspension policies, interracial fighting, and minority achievement.[9] For example, one of the social scientists we interviewed reported the following events:

> The focus in testimony was on tracking at the junior high school level. I brought in the whole concept of the common school, the school as a place where you get common learning for everybody in contrast to differentiated objectives/goals for different kids. The judge said—"You wouldn't recommend such a thing?"—and I said: "Yes, I would." Then he kept pressing me and arguing with me. So I was talking about remedy for the differentiated and unequal tracking operation. I might not have had all the evidence to back it up, but I was pretty sure of what I was saying. The judge had announced at the beginning that his decision was going to be to uphold the tracking system, but they could make a case for appeal. When the trial was over he ordered the tracking system stopped—which was a complete surprise.

Procedures Used to Construct a Remedy

As social science helped the courts move toward a public law model of remedy, trial judges were pushed toward an unaccustomed, activist role in formulating and selling a remedy plan.[10] As one of the judges we interviewed commented:

> From the calm sit-back judges of adversarial interactions, we had to become activists, we had to become innovative, we had to look for practical solutions rather than legalistic rulings.

9. In *Milliken v. Bradley II*, 433 U.S. 276 (1977), the Supreme Court held that a variety of such issues were appropriate subjects of Judge DiMascio's remedy order. These included the following: (*a*) remedial reading and communication skills programs; (*b*) the creation of five vocational education centers in areas such as construction trades, transportation, and health services; (*c*) two technical high schools focusing on a business curriculum; (*d*) a uniform code of conduct; (*e*) a community relations program; (*f*) an in-service training program for the instructional staff; (*g*) a testing program to ensure nondiscriminatory testing procedures; (*h*) a counseling and career guidance program; (*i*) inclusion of multiethnic studies in the curriculum; and (*j*) plans for cocurricular activities with other artistic and educational institutions (Levin 1978). Even after this approval of remedies which address "second generation problems," most observers would agree that both party evidence and remedies ordered by courts remained focused on racial balancing as the first priority.

10. For comments, both positive and negative, on the more activist role that judges often play in institutional litigation, see Fiss (1983), Merritt (1983), Resnick (1983), and Wald (1983). In chapter 11 we argue that despite their relatively more active roles, it is difficult for federal district court judges to adopt a long-term managerial relationship with institutional defendants, and that this limits the nature of remedies.

This active role involved pushing parties to a relationship–settlement style of dispute resolution, and it involved using social science to educate various segments of the community about the meaning and resolution of the case.[11]

Pushing parties toward settlement. The parties to a dispute are more likely to discover mutually beneficial solutions through a procedure which brings into the settlement process other issues about which there is less conflict (Menkel-Meadow 1984; Raffia 1982). Moreover, a narrow focus on issues of individual responsibility and school board wrongdoing further poisons the realtionship among parties who are going to have to live together in the future. A formal resolution to a conflict is of little use if the parties cannot be reintegrated into society after the resolution is achieved (Bohannan 1965; Lempert and Sanders 1986).[12] Judges who adopted a public law view of remedy, and who were concerned about more than the ceasing of discriminatory school board practices, often indicated that traditional adversary procedures were not particularly useful in these widespread community controversies. They took steps to push the parties toward achieving a compromise.[13]

> I had hoped we could settle the matter in some way or at least remove the advocacy aspect of it, move the bitterness out of it, and so I suggested the use of monitors.[14]

11. Kirp (1981, 1982) has described a range of possible judicial positions. At one extreme is the traditional model of the "legalistic judge" who is passive and limits his role to stating and deciding the law of the case. Next is the "mediator judge" who looks for agreement between the parties. Finally, there is the "political activist judge" who tries to shape political relationships.

12. These consequences of unrelenting adversariness are part of the difficulties Chayes (1976) sees with the use of a private law model to settle institutional reform litigation.

13. As the following quotations indicate, the judges usually describe these as "mediative procedures," that being the most prevalent term at the time. Today they would probably talk about alternative dispute resolution (ADR) procedures. Insofar as the judges are trying to employ procedures which widen the scope of relevant issues ("freedom from the rules of evidence"), and which look for compromise solutions ("remove the advocacy aspect of it"), their objective is to encourage a relationship-settlement process.

14. Given these comments, it is perhaps surprising that the judges were not more open to the panel form of witnessing. As the last remark suggests, those judges who wished to retreat from adversary processes apparently preferred working through monitors, special masters, and other devices (see Aranow 1980; Diver 1979; Kirp and Babcock 1981). One explanation for this preference may be that the judge could keep tight control over a master whereas a panel of experts might prove to be as much of a loose cannon for the judge as it would be for lawyers in the case. In hindsight, one of the shortcomings of our judicial interviews is that we did not pursue this issue.

Social problems sometimes don't fit into the rhetoric or procedures of courts. Mediation was a good way to handle these cases, it provided more flexibility and freedom from the rules of evidence.

One judge consciously used the social science evidence to force the parties into getting a wider, more complex vision of the case.

The social science evidence did exactly what I expected it to do. What it did was to educate the parties from the very simplistic approach that both sides had taken in the first hearing. The people represented in the first hearing dropped out because they saw this wasn't the lawsuit that they knew. This was a very complicated lawsuit, and the younger people came in and accepted the social science implications.

Some judges have described the fairly active roles that they played in gathering informal power to assist them in their effort. They tried conferences and other informal sessions to try to generate a plan that school system officials and community members could "own on their own."

Black board members came up with a plan, too, a minority plan. And I got the administration's plan, the majority plan. I sort of picked and chose, and told them that I sort of liked some things in both plans. The last thing I was going to do was to take the minority plan. I liked it better, but I wanted it to be the majority's plan . . . I wanted them to own it.

We used pretty much of a conference type of thing. We would set the case down and then we issued orders, and school systems that had problems with these orders would come back to court. We'd go to a library . . . the school board and the government and the interveners, the Legal Defense Fund, the NAACP and all of that. We'd just sit around the table and look at the statistics, at the maps, at the enrollments, all on an informal sort of basis. We really ruled as to each school system's problem in the library, and then backed off and issued an order to confirm what we had decided in conference. It was unusual in that respect, but I think it moved the thing along instead of having all the inhibitions of a courtroom context when lawyers have to show off a little bit with the formalities and legalities of it. It was designed to sort of break down the animosity between the two sides.

Occasionally, judges used their political savvy to ensure that a remedy worked out by the litigators and negotiators would not be summarily rejected by the parties or the community.

> There had been a serious division in the school board, and one reason I kept jurisdiction was that I wanted to forestall a reversal in the majority of the school board. I kind of guessed what would happen the next time around in the school board election. The two who were very much opposed to me were making public statements all the time about how they would rather be in contempt of court than have the order or decree complied with. If those two had added another two, which they tried to do, they would have had four, and they would have voted to scrap the whole plan, and I would have had more serious problems.

Educating the community. In addition to generating a remedy, some judges became actively involved in selling the remedy to the public. They attempted to inform the public about what was going on and to explain the complexity of the issues involved, hoping to produce a remedy which could be accepted by a substantial portion of the community.

> The first thing I wanted to do was to make sure that everybody knew as much in the community as I could possibly arrange. That's why we had all kinds of crazy arrangements for the press and I did everything that I could to make sure to get the newspapers to print the decision. Anybody who wants a copy of it, I have tons of them here and I can send them. And I tried to write it in the style that, if somebody with an 11th grade education wanted to read it, they could, with perhaps a few terms thrown in for the lawyers. And hopefully, if somebody was going to be dead set against this thing, at least they would have some idea of what they were against.

> The courtroom is not necessarily the forum in which an integration case is fought. The public arena is where it is fought. The courtroom doesn't mean anything. The judge can come out with all the decrees he wants to but unless there is some understanding in the community of what the problem is, of what the possible solutions are, unless the community understands that, the judge's decree doesn't amount to a tinker's damn. Experts were extremely important in informing the community of what the case is about. It never knew what the case was about, either from listening to the

board's side or from listening to the plaintiff's side. As far as they were concerned all it had to do with was busing.

I want people to come to court. It's sort of a full disclosure thing. Many federal judges are rather private. Today, when a federal judge can issue orders of broad social concern, you've got to do everything you can to make those orders somewhat acceptable to the citizenry. I don't think you ought to compromise your ethical concepts, but, within your role, whatever you can do, you've got to do. I just don't believe in stuffing things down folks' throats unless you have to. People will just say, "To hell with a federal judge, you're not elected."

These comments reflect judges' appreciation of the limited ability of the traditional model of adjudication. They obviously adopted and justified a much more active role for themselves in the resolution of this community controversy, and were concerned with the ways in which ongoing parties related with one another and with the judicial decision. Moreover, they did not assume a community consensus on the issue of desegregation; many of these comments reflect an understanding of elite and grass roots conflict in the community, and of the need to work with and perhaps overcome these conflicts in order to improve the school system. Most of the judges demonstrated an astuteness about local political considerations and a good deal of skill and diplomacy in fashioning a remedy which achieved at least public acceptance by most parties to the litigation.[15]

Partly as a result of the rise of this type of remedy, the judges in school cases abandoned the traditional passive judicial role for a more active role which pushed the parties toward a relationship-settlement procedure and which attempted to educate the public about the case and the remedy.

However, contrary to some images of judicial involvement in institutional-reform litigation, the judges did not eagerly pursue this activist role. Several expressed trepidation concerning their ability to carry it out.

The system just wasn't fitted to the problem, because a true adversarial situation would just inflame from both sides if you let it

15. This view of judicial skill in fashioning and selling their decrees is similar to that found in Rebell and Block's (1982) study of sixty-five educational policy cases.

get out of hand. We effectively became administrators . . . and I'm not sure judges are very good administrators.

At some point many judges resisted agendas which they felt to be beyond their abilities or their constitutional mandate. Such is the import of this judge's comment:

> The function of an integration case is to make certain, I think, that the district treats its children equally, period. That is all of them. And whether they fail academically or whether they don't is something that I am not to be concerned about.

These remarks indicate that there still are limits, self-imposed and otherwise, to the ability of the courts to implement effective long-term changes in schools.

11 Implementation
Limits of Social Science Testimony, Courts, and Social Movement Organizations in Altering Local School Systems

The underlying problem prompting the movement for school desegregation was racial inequality in America. The NAACP's choice to pursue school desegregation as a challenge to racial inequality was based upon several factors. Because *de jure* segregation raised constitutional questions, desegregation could be pursued through litigation. Litigation could be undertaken without grass roots political and economic support, and a national movement could therefore pursue its objective with minimal support from local communities and the public at large. Successful litigation mobilized the power of the state behind the movement, hopefully countering the influence of entrenched local opposition.

Added to these tactical reasons was a belief that in a relatively meritocratic society such as the United States, education was an essential prerequisite to long-term economic and social equality. In several respects this was a remarkably successful strategy. With very few exceptions, the plaintiffs won; that is, the court agreed with the plaintiffs' claim that the school district had been unconstitutionally segregated.[1] In the process, the plaintiffs were able to mobilize some of the political power of the federal government to their cause.

Balanced against the advantages of school desegregation litigation are its limitations. There are questions regarding the degrees of correlation among desegregation, improved schooling, economic and social gains, and racial equality in general. This book's focus on the school desegregation movement should not obscure the fact that the NAACP and other organizations involved in school desegregation efforts were

---

1. But see *Alexander v. Youngstown Board of Education*, 675 F.2d 787 (6th Cir. 1982).

also involved in many other efforts to lessen racial inequality, including voting rights legislation, the 1964 Civil Rights Act, open housing legislation, and local community problem-solving and change. Of course, organizations sometimes disagreed about the relative importance of different efforts,[2] and over time there developed a certain division of labor. But if the NAACP Special Contribution Fund concentrated a substantial portion of its resources on school desegregation, it was not because it felt that other goals were unimportant.

Constitutional litigation as a method of social change ties the movement, inevitably, to the limits of the courts, including the willingness of the judiciary to place plaintiff interests in school desegregation above other interests. In retrospect, it is clear that a crucial imitation has been the 5–4 decision in *Milliken I*, which ruled against a metropolitan plan in Detroit. The relative inaccessibility of metropolitan remedies has made it virtually impossible to formulate plans in central cities which could substantially desegregate the schools as well as overcome the long-term segregative effect of white withdrawal from central city districts.[3] Ironically, under such circumstances the racial isolation of minority children in large cities increases as their schools become desegregated. As Farley (1984) notes:

> Thirty years ago, schools were segregated in the South because of state laws and in the North because of neighborhood segregation. But most school districts enrolled both whites and blacks, so some integration could be accomplished by transferring white and black students. Today public schools are segregated because blacks and whites live in separate school districts. (32)

Under these conditions, minorities inhabit and inherit control of relatively poor school districts in which few whites have a stake. Many people therefore argue that desegregation plans should not devote all their energy toward districtwide desegregation but should concentrate on within-school and within-classroom changes which will promote educational quality as well as desegregation. However, desegregation

2. For example, the Legal Defense Fund turned away from school desegregation efforts after the Charlotte and Denver cases to concentrate on other efforts they felt were more important. At a more fundamental level, some organizations such as the Student Non-violent Coordinating Committee (SNCC) rejected the strategy of working for legal changes which dominated the activities of the older civil rights organizations.

3. By most assessments, the withdrawal is not primarily attributable to white flight as a function of school desegregation efforts, but is a result of broader demographic trends (Farley 1984).

plans have made only minimal efforts in this direction, and have usually been limited to the establishment of policy rather than involved with its implementation.

The following sections discuss the limited ability of the school desegregation effort to reach inside communities, school districts, and schools to implement changes in local education. We examine the limits of three interrelated parts of the resources mobilized: (1) the social science evidence and testimony, (2) the legal system embodied in the federal courts, and (3) the national movement organizations themselves.

Limits of the Social Science Evidence and Testimony

In a recent article, Yinger (1986, 250) notes that the art of successful school desegregation involves an understanding of problems and processes at a number of different levels. He offers the following list:[4]

Levels of Analysis	Variables to Consider
1. Society as a whole	Demography
	Major technical and economic changes
	Housing policies
2. Relationships among school districts	All of the above, plus—
	Laws bearing on desegregation
	Court decisions
	Media attention
3. Relationships within school districts	All of the above, plus—
	School board policies with regard to: school locations, busing, teacher selection and training,
	Ratios of different groups
	Sorting processes
4. Relationships within a school	All of the above, plus—
	Methods of discipline
	Peer groups, youth cultures
	Language variation
	Processes affecting weak ties
	Teaching methods
	Effects on self-esteem

4. Even this extensive list is not exhaustive. For example, one could add a level discussing the relationship of the school system to the community, to the business or minority community, and so forth.

5. Relationships within a class-room, or other specific activity	All of the above, plus— Age of the students Range of socioeconomic status Criteria for participating in activities
6. The Individual	All of the above, plus— Racial or ethnic group Socioeconomic status Attitudes concerning desegregation Levels of competence Ambition, distinguishing plans (aspirations) from motivation (expenditure of effort)

Factors at each of these levels may affect the success of a desegregation plan. More important, the likelihood of a plan being successful depends upon the attitudes and actions of school officials at each level.

The public stance of the school board influences the reception that any desegregation plan will have in a community (Rodgers and Bullock 1972). So can the opposition of the school district leadership (House 1974) and individual school principals. Berman and McLaughlin (1980) have discussed the importance of moral leadership on the part of the principal in implementing any school change.

> The principal's unique contribution to implementation lies not in "how to do it" advice . . ., but in giving moral support to the staff and in creating an organizational climate that gives the project legitimacy. (677)

The role of the principal as mediator, organizer, and planner is central to success (Crain, Mahard, and Narot 1982; Noblit and Johnston 1982). But even with the support of all these officials,

> the classroom, however, can be an almost impenetrable barrier, and persistent demands for innovation seem to be among the circumstances that are moving teachers to build a second wall around the classroom. (Suttles 1986, 60)

Judges received relatively little information on such issues. Most of the efforts of plan writers were devoted to level 3 on Yinger's (1986) list, relationships within school districts. Thus, for example, a how-to book by Hughes, Gordon, and Hillman (1980), three plan writers in these cases, devotes five chapters to level-3 problems of between-school desegregation, two chapters to other, districtwide issues (e.g., educational programs such as bilingual education, community monitoring agencies, and staff in-service training), and one concluding chapter to second-generation desegregation problems which may arise after pupils of different races attend the same school.

Some courts did devote energies to engaging the local community in the plan (e.g., citizen monitoring groups), and, especially in the years after *Milliken v. Bradley II*, 433 U.S. 276 (1977), they began to write plans which dealt with second-generation issues such as in-service training for the staff, a remedial reading and communication skills program, multiethnic studies in the curriculum, a uniform code of conduct, and so forth. Even here, however, most of these efforts reached no deeper into the school than level 4 (within-building factors).[5]

Why did most social science evidence at remedy focus upon between-building desegregation and fail to specify conditions promoting maximum organizational change? Part of the reason has to do with the limits of the social science used in the school desegregation cases.

Social science that studies harm and social demographics is not necessarily the same social science that can explain how to engineer the changes suggested by these studies. Science that is noninterventionist, that does not examine the tactics of facilitating change in local schools and school systems, is not especially effective in aiding implementation.

Nor was an active or interventionist form of applied social science commissioned or even encouraged by the social movements[6] or by defendant school districts. Scientists were infrequently called upon to testify to the long-term practical goals of desegregation beyond mere racial mixing. And without a commitment to creating and using applied studies and theories regarding the integrated school building or classroom (issues at levels 4 and 5), scientists could not assist courts and school systems in their efforts to implement local plans in buildings and classrooms.

One reason social science evidence was not particularly helpful at the

---

5. Research which specified some of the conditions under which local school building desegregation might work best was slow in developing, and much of it was published only after the trials of our cases (Aronson 1978; Chesler 1971; Crowfoot and Chesler, 1981; Forehand and Ragosta 1976; Hawley 1981; Slavin 1980, 1983; Von Euler 1977; Weinberg 1977).

6. By way of contrast, as we have noted earlier in this book, achievement gains due to desegregation, the effect of segregation on self-image and self-esteem, and the relationship between school segregation and housing segregation were research topics encouraged by movement groups.

point of implementation is that many experts, especially plaintiff experts, had little local knowledge and little expertise in studying or altering local districts. Local data and knowledge are crucial to practitioners seeking to alter local events and organizations. Many scholars did not seem to be greatly interested in these issues. This may in part be because, as noted in chapter 3, in later years fewer and fewer of the experts who appeared in school desegregation cases had their formal training in psychology or social psychology—the disciplines most directly interested in the dynamics of classroom interaction. It may also be because many of these experts were "national experts," chosen partly for their national scholarly reputation and background in comparative study against which they could assess a district's dynamics. Many witnesses had little prior experience in applied work; coming from academic backgrounds, their appearance as expert witnesses was often their first applied venture. Few had been deeply involved in implementing or studying actual practices in local schools or had served as consultants/planners in processes of local school change.

Limits of the Courts

A good deal has been written about both the legitimacy of judicial efforts at institutional reform (Glazer 1975) and the capacity of the courts to implement reforms (Cavanaugh and Sarat 1980; Horowitz 1977; Rebell and Block 1982). The more plans move beyond racial mixing, the more they require the court to become concerned with the deployment of human resources, the power arrangements, and the financial assets of the local school system and community. In all of these activities the court must step further and further outside the traditional judicial role. As it does so, the legitimacy of the court's actions diminish. As a judge we quoted in the last chapter said, "People will just say, 'To hell with a federal judge, you're not elected.' " Then the judiciary's capacity to implement these broad changes also becomes more problematical.

Judges' visions of the goals of desegregation, and thus of the role of the courts in adjudicating these disputes, differed considerably. Some moved well beyond racial balancing, and were quite concerned with the overall quality of education offered to all students. As one judge commented:

> There could have been another direction of the law in terms of equal protection, and that would be to make damn sure that schools work. I've had on the stand black witnesses who testify, "Judge, don't worry about the percentages, just make our schools good ones." That was really what I was there for at that point in time.

Still other judges adopted an even more ambitious agenda, setting the issue of desegregation within a larger vision of changes in school resources and practices:

> I also felt that I would be able to make this an opportunity to make some changes in the way we do things. I wanted to try and get some money and do things that will help the kids.

Judicial involvement may vary regarding the degree to which the judge becomes and remains actively involved in the implementation of a desegregation plan, and the degree of detail and specificity in it. Judges and their plans have varied substantially on these dimensions.

Nakamura and Smallwood (1980) compare, for example, the level of involvement with implementation reflected in the orders of Judge Weigel in San Francisco and Judge Garrity in Boston. According to Kirp's (1982) analysis, Weigel "left implementation in the hands of those formally charged with the responsibility for running the school system" (99). Garrity, by way of contrast, dealt with overt resistance by creating a special Department of Implementation in the Boston school system, and made that department directly accountable to the court. "In effect, Judge Garrity and his appointees became both the desegregation policy-makers and the implementers for the Boston schools" (100). Although Garrity himself did not become the implementer, appointing social scientists Robert Dentler and Marvin Scott as experts and monitors to represent and supervise his orders (Dentler and Scott 1981), he did specify implementation roles and programs. He emphasized his concern that the programs be carried out, and announced his intention to monitor these processes over time.

The Boston and San Francisco plans also varied with respect to their detail and specificity. The San Francisco plan, like the majority of plans, leaves considerable discretion in the hands of the school board, making very little effort to alter the school system's organizational environment.[7]

Willingness to act. Most observers would agree that the potential for successful implementation increases if the court becomes and remains actively involved. As we saw in the last chapter, many judges are willing

---

7. In addition to the voluminous literature on organizational change in schools (e.g., Milstein 1980; Schmuck and Miles 1971), there is a growing literature on the implementation of public policy decisions (see Crain, Mahard, and Narot 1982; Gardiner 1977; Sabatier and Mazmanian 1979; van Horn and van Meter 1977).

to step outside a passive role and not only design a specific plan but also create an ongoing relationship with the school system in order to increase the likelihood of reforms being carried out. Nevertheless, there are limits to their willingness and capacity to move in this direction.

Several judges noted that desegregation was a judicial issue by default, and that they often felt a sense of isolation when deciding these cases.[8]

> I think there are limits to what any court can do in solving all the social problems. I think that any of us involved can take pride in the fact that in essence there was a constitutional revolution and the courts made it possible without it being a violent revolution. My own theory is that the executive and legislative branches, both federal and state, absolutely failed. Somebody had to do something, and this is what pulled us out of our traditional role.

> If the Congress or state legislature, or if governors or the president had stepped out in front and done something, the courts might not have gotten all chopped up like this.

Some judges, in fact, felt that in the absence of legislative action the courts should not have become involved in the first instance.

> The Congress could have passed laws desegregating schools. The Congress has the right to pass civil rights laws, but the courts should not have moved into these areas on their own, based upon some social theory of experts.

Even when they did have some local support, the choices that judges faced were not easy to resolve. On the one hand, most judges have a commitment to dismantling what they see as unconstitutional racial segregation in schools. On the other hand, they are committed to maintaining separation among the various branches of government, and to behaving in accordance with the knowledge that the judiciary are not elected representatives of the people. There is a tension between commitment to popular democracy and majoritarianism on the one hand, and to constitutionally guaranteed civil rights on the other. The isolation and self-imposed limitations of the judicial role define the context within which judges craft desegregation plans.

---

8. This argument, of course, must acknowledge that the movement organizations would probably have made less headway in achieving school desegregation by working through the legislature; that is one reason movement strategists selected a litigation approach (see chapter 2).

Thus, although some observers have argued that leaving school officials primarily responsible for altering the segregated school system is like "putting the foxes back in charge of the chicken coop" (Monti 1980, 1985), most federal district court judges felt there were definite limits to using judicial authority to challenge professional expertise and prerogatives, and felt that primary responsibility for plan development and implementation should remain in the hands of school system professionals.

Limits of judicial capacity. Even when judges are prepared to act, there are limits to what they can do. Much of what a judge can accomplish depends on the response of the local school board. In the San Francisco case, Judge Weigel faced a basically friendly school board which put up only a token defense in the litigation (Kirp 1982, 95). In fact, later in the case, interveners representing the Chinese community challenged the original litigation as indicating collusion between the plaintiff and the defense parties (104). The situation in Boston was, of course, very different. There Judge Garrity confronted a hostile school board from the start. The point is that Garrity had little choice but to intervene vigorously, and that Weigel did not have much of a choice but to allow the school board and school administration wide discretion.

Yet, although a "hostile" school system may provide a judge with an opportunity to become and remain active in a case, a board's continued opposition is usually sufficient to thwart any initiative that the court might take. Stinchcombe and Taylor (1980) have noted with regard to the Boston case:

> The problem with governing stably once the issue has escalated to this proportion is that the judiciary is badly set up for administering a school system, and in many ways badly set up even to make policy for a school system. Further, the fundamental illegitimacy of non-democratic administration of a central function of government prevents the judiciary from taking over the function of running the school system. (1980:81).

Glazer (1975) also comments on the actions of judges in the desegregation cases, arguing that active and continued intervention by the federal judiciary "serves to reduce the influence of people over their own lives and their own fates" (105). He, too, questions the legitimacy of local school-system "governance" by a nondemocratically elected and accountable court.

Many judges observed the difficulties experienced by their colleagues such as Judge Garrity in Boston, and did not wish to find themselves in the position of trying to run a school system in the face of a hostile school board and administration.

> My commitment, within the confines of this office, is to make the least intrusion into the affairs of the board of education. It is their obligation to run the school system, even mis-run the school system, as long as the Constitution of the United States is complied with. So I didn't want to get into their areas, even in some areas where I thought they were dead wrong.

Capacity is limited not only by the judge's intent and the school board's (or superintendent's) response but also by the social organization of school systems themselves. Schools have been called "loosely coupled organizations," in which goals and means are not well integrated, lines of authority are blurred, and the enforcement of any behavior on the part of the teacher in the classroom is problematical (Weick 1976). The deeper a desegregation plan attempts to reach into a school system, the more difficult implementation problems become. To find their way into practice, court orders must pass through multiple layers of the local educational bureaucracy, from the board to the superintendent, central office staffs, principals, and teachers, and finally to parents and students. At each step the decision may be misheard, misunderstood, or reinterpreted and modified. The sheer number of steps in the complex structure may blur the responsibility for carrying out the court's orders. According to Nakamura and Smallwood (1980):

> When the court decisions should affect the behavior of large numbers of people who are not direct parties to a case, there still can be uncertainty about which other actors should obey the decisions. Since the court's communication with these parties is not direct, there are opportunities for these parties to misperceive or selectively perceive their newly formulated legal obligations. (93)

Schofield and Sagar (1979) have reported on such limitations in one school. The student population was approximately 60% white and 40% black. The faculty was 25% black. There was no tracking system, and the principal stressed the importance of the social outcomes of schooling and discouraged situations conducive to competition. Yet, most of his teachers rejected the idea that their primary mission was anything other than teaching academic skills, a view shared by a number of parents and children.

These difficulties are compounded by two factors built into the timing of parties' involvement in litigation. First, most of the parties to the litigation—and most of the actors—withdraw from the scene when the lawsuit is settled. The national plaintiffs and their attorneys move on to other cases, and the local school board defendant is happy to have things return as much to "normal" as possible. Second, the judge has other cases to try and other interests to pursue. Even special masters, appointed by the judge to formulate a plan and see that it is implemented, are likely to withdraw from active participation in the case within a few months.

Limits of the National Social Movement Organizations

The limits imposed by the social movement are related to the fact that the plaintiff organizations were, at least with respect to most school desegregation efforts, nationally based, "funded social movement organizations."[9] School desegregation is a minority agenda, and an agenda which usually does not appear to whites to be imperative to the political and economic health of the community.[10] The combination of desegregation being a minority social movement and one that relied on white support meant that the agenda was bound to be limited by the political flexibility that (white) elites felt at any particular time or place. This, of course, is precisely why movement strategists elected to pursue their goals in court—to overcome the minimal power accruing to a minority movement, and to play for legal rules that would overcome the flexible or even arbitrary responses of people in positions of local power. Because the courts are not completely independent of the body politic, and certainly not at the implementation stages of adjudication, the change that could occur on this basis was limited.

In the actual trial of cases, the fact that plaintiff groups were national organizations, litigating case after case, gave them a substantial advantage over their opponents. As Galanter (1974) notes, one of the advantages "repeat players" have over "one shot players" is that they can play for rules; that is, they can direct their litigation strategy toward the objective of building a body of favorable case law. These movement or-

9. See chapter 2, page 9, and McCarthy and Zald (1973; 1977) for a fuller discussion of this term.

10. Of course, many scholars and some public figures of both races argue that educational inequality, on racial, class, or other grounds, does indeed harm the community, economically and otherwise. Plaintiff groups may try to persuade leaders that desegregation is in their interest. Crain (1968) indicated that white elites were more likely to support desegregation efforts when they saw desegregation as essential for the realization of other objectives such as peace in the community, a sense of charity or altruism for deprived groups, maintenance of a stable economy, and maintenance of an image of a progressive community.

ganizations were rule-oriented: they viewed most cases partly as an opportunity to build a favorable corpus of desegregation law.

From another perspective, however, the fact that the movement organizations were repeat players sometimes trapped them into playing for rules to the exclusion of other approaches. One of the remarkable things about the school cases is how infrequently they were settled out of court. This appears to be partly due to the unwillingness of plaintiff attorneys to compromise a case in any way which might adversely reflect upon other cases. Plaintiff attorneys seem to have devoted relatively little energy to searching for a compromise.[11] As noted in chapters 8 and 9, national plaintiff attorneys (and national plaintiff experts who testified in three or more cases) were more oriented to a legal-adversary position than were other attorneys and other experts.

A desegregation plan which seemed to go easy on one city (e.g., magnet schools rather than substantial transfers) would make it more difficult to argue for sterner measures in the next case. The plaintiff groups were especially unlikely to trade between-school segregation for other objectives. Thus, there was little opportunity to find an accommodation in which the school system would feel bound to work for within-school or within-classroom change as part of an overall bargain. When a plan was constructed in an adversary atmosphere, organizations focusing on a national agenda were at a disadvantage with respect to particular changes within local communities. Not only were experts concerned primarily with generalizable knowledge and attorneys with multicase rules, but they also did not often have access to local resources to implement and monitor changes in local communities.

The national objectives of the movement organizations sometimes caused an estrangement between the movement and local minority groups which did not share the larger agenda.[12] In a few cases, the

11. An adversary posture may have even made it relatively more difficult to gain extraeducational community elite support for some desegregation. Of course, there must have been limits to what plaintiff groups could be willing to trade for such support, and presumably only capitulation could have won elite support in some communities. As we have noted, compromise settlements have become more commonplace in recent years. In part this may be attributable to the willingness of plaintiff groups to settle for less than mandatory transportation of large numbers of students as a method of desegregation.

12. Similar conflicts of interest arise in other areas. Thus, programs organized to provide legal assistance to the poor must balance the objective of resolving a conflict according to the wishes of the client against the objective of attempting to get the client to sacrifice some of his particular interest to the larger goal of playing for a change in legal rules in some general area such as tenant rights. In institutional reform litigation, the attorneys are relieved from some of the moral dilemmas posed by this conflict because

conflict of objectives developed into public controversy. The most note-worthy case occurred in Atlanta, where the local chapter of the NAACP settled the desegregation case in return for putting more black admin-istrators in the school system. An angry national NAACP suspended the entire Atlanta leadership (Orfield 1978a, 400–401). The continuing pursuit of national objectives, including the primacy of between-school desegregation on the part of the national organizations, also caused some black lawyers and educators to publicly withdraw their support from the desegregation effort (Bell 1976; Edmonds 1974).

The national movement thrust, led and somewhat loosely coordi-nated by the NAACP, sometimes encountered difficulty establishing working coalitions with representatives of other minority groups in-volved in school desegregation. Although the NAACP-LDF has been instrumental in supporting the creation of the Mexican-American Legal Defense and Education Fund, cooperation at the local level was not al-ways effective. As one attorney representing Hispanic interests reported:

> In one city, the NAACP and MALDEF wanted two different kinds of plans. Since they could not accommodate the difference between themselves, we had to go into court with two separate requests.

The splintering of the civil rights movement in the 1970s—between whites and blacks and Hispanics and between black power advocates and more moderate black interests—also made it difficult to maintain a coherent national thrust on school desegregation objectives.

The problem of mobilizing local resources is especially critical after the parties agree upon a desegregation plan and active attorneys, ex-perts, and organizational representatives withdraw from the local scene. Plaintiffs were aware of this, and tried to ensure that plans had built-in monitoring efforts such as mandatory school system reports to the court, special masters, state or local monitoring agencies, or some combination of all three (Hughes, Gordon, and Hillman 1980, 132–134; Laue and Monti 1980). These efforts, however cannot fully replace an active grass roots organizing effort that continues to draw attention to implementing desegregation. Such organizing is not easy: as Orfield

---

they have no particular client (or the titular plaintiff does in fact support the larger, na-tional agenda). When we asked some plaintiff lawyers about this problem, and how they would proceed in the face of surveys which indicated that the majority of the local mi-nority community did not support their agenda, some responded that this would not alter their behavior. Their task was to secure the constitutional right to a desegregated education for their plaintiffs.

has pointed out, "ideological mobilization over a long time for an improbable end is extraordinarily difficult" (1978a, 156).

Conclusion

One should not assign too much responsibility for school desegregation outcomes to either the social scientists or the national plaintiffs. Regardless of the evidence, and regardless of plaintiffs' national orientation, the courts strongly felt the limits of their power and were cautious about intervening in school board affairs.[13] Even courts which adopt a public law model of institutional litigation do not become radical, activist organizations.

Various observers agree that the Supreme Court decision in *Brown* was a central part of "a social revolution in race relations" (Wasby, D'Amato, and Metrallier 1977, 5). Gains have gone far beyond the racial mixture of youngsters in schools. There have also been losses, temporary setbacks, and the discovery of unanticipated barriers to the effective implementation of desegregation. As one of the architects of the NAACP's civil rights strategy has argued, "we are faced with the sobering reality that litigation may be just the beginning of a long and difficult process to enable people to fight for their own rights" (Taylor 1986, 9). Each of the vital resources involved (the movement, the courts, and the scientific academy) was partly successful in the effort for racial equality in schools, but also experienced limits in winning major victories. Racial inequality in American society and in its schools has proven very resistant to change.

13. Such caution is not unusual in such cases. Rebell and Block (1982), in their study of sixty-five trial court proceedings between 1970 and 1977, found that the courts operated in a fundamentally conservative manner. As Clune (1984) notes in a review of the Rebell and Block book: "The book sees courts as extremely cautious institutions. They do not stand in the vanguard of social change, but rather wait until social movements have achieved a high degree of legitimacy" (778).

Appendices

Table of Cases

Bibliography

Index

Appendix A
Methods and Analytical Approaches

Scholarly concern with social science testimony and evidence in the school de-segregation cases certainly does not begin with this study. Various researchers, with different concerns and using a variety of methods, have explored these issues. For instance, one approach has been to conduct original social science research on matters relevant to desegregation, or to gather and analyze research that others have done in this area. The most popular foci of research appear to have been those reviewed in chapters 2 and 3: the extent and causes of residential segregation; the relationship between residential segregation and school attendance areas/boundaries; the relationship between desegregation and residential patterns (white flight); the analysis of social factors associated with learning; the relationship between desegregation and achievement scores; the relationship between busing and achievement scores; and the existence of school practices dysfunctional to desegregation. This list could be lengthened, as different scholars had different notions of relevant issues and evidence.

A second approach to the general question of social science evidence in the desegregation cases has involved the review of case records to assess what evidence has been presented, and the review of the quality or relevance of this evidence. For the most part, such research has been conducted by legal schol-ars, and their emphasis has been on the existence and use of evidence, rather than on its evaluation (Levin and Moise 1975). One notable exception is Wolf (1976; 1981), who has extensively studied one case and has analyzed the quality of the social science evidence presented there in some detail. Because the case involved, *Milliken v. Bradley*, is a central one in the history of school desegre-gation litigation, her work is a helpful step forward. The summaries of a con-ference wherein several social scientists commented on the issues in *Milliken v. Bradley* is another example of this type of approach (USCCR 1974).

A third approach to this general problem has been to investigate the probable or actual impact of social science evidence on the court. Typically, this has been done second-hand, by reading and analyzing court transcripts or written opin-ions. In some cases, judges writing these opinions have commented directly on the quality or utility of the evidence they heard. Judge Craven (1975) went further, and commented in a public journal on the impact that social science evidence had on him in the Richmond case. In this article, Craven lauded the precision with which Karl Taeuber was able to analyze the role of discrimination in creating segregated housing patterns, and noted that "the testimony of other social scientists—Dr. Thomas Pettigrew, Dr. Martin Sloane, and Dr. Jeanne Biggar—were [sic] not so precise" (155). It is not clear exactly what Craven meant by "not so precise," and how it came to impress him less, but even this kind of public judicial comment is rare.

A fourth major approach has been for scholars—of law or social science—to consider and elaborate on the problems that social scientists can expect to encounter in the courtroom. For the most part, these efforts have been conceptual rather than empirical in orientation, drawing on a long tradition in the sociology of knowledge to warn social scientists of certain pitfalls. For instance, Levin argued that "legal proceedings are endeavors in advocacy with each side seeking that evidence which will support its own position" (1975, 233). In this advocacy arena of the courtroom, Judge McMillan concluded that "social science weapons are therefore legitimate" (1977, 163). This comment suggests an adversary view of the social science enterprise sure to cause dismay within the profession, and Wolf summarized this dismay in noting that "the adversary mode in the presentation of evidence always tends to offend our most basic notions of scientific inquiry" (1976, 114).

Levin (1975), in presenting his own view on these matters, appeared less sanguine about the history of truth-seeking in social science, and less surprised about scientists' adversary role in the courts. He reviewed some themes in the social background and training of social scientists that constrain their objectivity, and asserted that in the attempt to be influential on the courts, social scientists were likely to: present evidence that stresses complex statistical methodologies that are beyond lay competence to interpret, so to mystify their findings and create reliance on their own interpretations; shun ambiguity and alternative explanations which might be detrimental to the adversary position at stake (in Wolf's terms, simple causal chains); avoid interpretive frameworks that may be ideologically or politically confusing or illegitimate to the court, so that Marxist perspectives on the origins of class differences or racial labor market dynamics under capitalism are avoided; and avoid remedies that might go beyond the political feasibilities considered by the court.

Each of these four prior approaches raises some very important and interesting issues. However, they have not been addressed definitively, nor do we have much sound empirical evidence on what actually occurs in the minds and actions of major actors in these relationships between social scientists and lawyers and the judiciary. In this study, we attempt to look at some of these issues in a different way, by studying actors' reports of their own experiences with social science testimony in the courtroom, and of their own interactions with others in this endeavor. The primary database for this research project is in-depth interviews with expert witnesses, judges, and attorneys who participated in a sample of school desegregation cases. In addition, we reviewed case records, briefs, judges' opinions, and transcripts of court testimony in some of these cases. In the following sections of this appendix we describe how we conducted this study (see also Chesler, Sanders, and Kalmuss 1981).

Sample of Cases

In order to study expert testimony as the actors experienced it, we wanted to set the problem within a specific set of cases, and with a somewhat delimited set of individuals who actually encountered one another. Thus, we defined our sample (at least in part) in terms of court cases in which scholars, attorneys, and judges dealt with one another face to face. We drew a sample of seventeen school desegregation cases through a two-stage sampling process.

First, we established a pool of cases to be included in a sample. Individual cases had to meet the following criteria: (1) they had to be active as of 1970, (2) they had to have been tried in a federal district court, and (3) they had to have employed academic social science or educational experts as witnesses. We limited choices to cases active after 1970, in order to minimize loss of information due to death and the increasing haziness of the memories of key actors. We focused on the trial (federal district court) level because it was there that systematic social scientific testimony was presented. It is also the place where debates about federal intervention in local school affairs, and concerns about "outsider" attorneys and scientists (both issues of considerable interest to us), most often occur. Because the focus of our study involves interaction among social scientists, lawyers, and judges, it made sense to limit our choice of cases to ones in which actual testimony and court appearance occurred. Thus, if no social science evidence was presented, or if expert depositions were taken but no actual appearance was made, the case was omitted from the pool.

We compiled a list of all school desegregation cases that met these three criteria, using a directory of federal school desegregation cases published by the Center for Civil Rights at the University of Notre Dame Law School (Wise 1977). Of the sixty-nine federal student desegregation cases involving social science evidence that were active after 1970, thirty-nine were from southern (and border-southern) states, whereas thirty were from northern and western states; thirty-seven were from relatively large urban areas, and thirty-two were from small cities or rural areas.

In the second stage of the process, we chose a sample of seventeen cases from this larger pool. We purposely included the Detroit, Richmond, and Los Angeles cases. The first two were selected because they represented a northern and near-southern version of a metropolitan suit. Metropolitan desegregation is a key legal issue involving the inclusion of neighboring (predominantly white) school districts in the desegregation of a large (high proportion minority) city district. It also raises interesting evidentiary problems, and we wanted to ensure representation from this class of cases in the final sample. Los Angeles was included because it employed a novel use of academic experts, a panel of scholars responsible to the judge during remedy proceedings.

The remaining fourteen cases were selected by constructing a four-fold matrix of larger and smaller school districts and northern and southern (pre-*Brown*, state-imposed segregation) cases. We wanted a mix of cases from the North and the South and from large and small cities. Region captured the key legal distinction between *de facto* and *de jure* segregation. In addition to being legally important, the *de jure–de facto* distinction represents different challenges for experts. Size of city was important because we expected the legal, political, and educational issues (and therefore the scientific evidence) involved in desegregating a large city to be different from those involved in desegregating a small city. From each of these four (region × size) categories we chose cases which were legally and/or politically significant, which had various types of expert testimony, which had judges of varying political reputation, and which together seemed to provide a reasonable sample of school desegregation cases across the nation. The fourteen cases selected in this procedure occurred in: Atlanta, Austin, Baton Rouge, Charlotte, Columbus, Corpus Christi, Dayton, Denver, Indianapolis, Minneapolis, Kalamazoo, Montgomery, St. Louis, and Omaha. Of the total of seventeen cases, then, nine are "northern" and eight "southern" (in the sense of a *de jure* dual school system at the time of *Brown*). City size ranges from Los Angeles and Detroit at one extreme to Kalamazoo and Baton Rouge at the other. Wilmington was originally part of this sample, but our time and energy limits, and difficulty in gaining access to attorneys and judges in that case, caused us to drop it. These procedures are part of the creation of a purposive or "theoretical sampling" design, in which our theoretical concerns, rather than a priority on statistical representativeness or randomness, drive the sample definition (Glaser and Strauss 1967).

Sample of Actors

We generated a list of experts involved in these seventeen cases by noting the names mentioned in judges' opinions and in other written materials. Moreover, as we began speaking with attorneys, we asked them for the names of experts they had employed. In addition to experts involved in these cases, we used a snowball identification technique to identify other scholars testifying in any desegregation case. We also placed notices in the newsletters of the professional organizations associated with sociology, psychology, political science, and education, asking individuals who had testified in school desegregation cases to contact us.

The sample size of academic-based experts was eighty-five. Of these, two refused to be interviewed, and our sample size was, therefore, eighty-three. Not all of those interviewed were used at each stage of the analysis, for various reasons. As table A.1 indicates, not all of these interviews were full and complete; some were not taped or were otherwise too scanty to permit full analysis (fifteen). Moreover, during the interviews we discovered that several informants had not actually testified (but had perhaps given a deposition), and that several others had appeared in court, but as consultants or panelists, not as expert witnesses (sixteen). Thus, among our experts we had fifty-two full and complete interviews. Of the eighty-three experts we interviewed, fifty-one were social scientists and thirty-two were educational scientists. Of those who actually testified, forty-two testified for the plaintiffs and twenty-six for the defense; four experts testified for both parties in different cases. Thirty-one experts testified in more than one case. These frequent testifiers illustrate that the use of experts in these cases is more prevalent than indicated by the sample size itself: the total number of person-appearances is well over two hundred.

The disparity between the number of social and educational scientists and the number of plaintiff and defense experts is explained by discussions in various chapers. Some of the issues relating to attorneys' selection and use of scholars, and scholars' decisions to testify, are explored in later chapers. However, there are also some potential artifacts of the sample that we should note. With regard to scientific experts, we were interested in investigating conflicts between the roles of scholar and witness; therefore, we decided to interview primarily academically oriented experts. Scholars employed in settings aligned with one of the parties to the case were eliminated; for example, educators employed by the school system who testified for the defense. Thus, by focusing on academic scholars, our sample probably underestimated the number of local educators and defense experts utilized in these cases.

Overall, the sampling process appears to have been successful. Currently, we know of only ten academic experts active after 1970 who were not included in the sample. We assume that the list of experts in the seventeen cases was relatively complete, having been generated from judges' opinions and interviews with lawyers. Moreover, the snowball sample began circling back on itself, so that after several months in the field we virtually ceased generating the names of new experts. Rather, informants would volunteer names we already had on our list.

Because many cases contained multiple parties, and the parties themselves sometimes used several attorneys, we could not interview all the lawyers who worked on each case. In choosing which attorneys to interview, we always included at least one from each of the major parties to the litigation: at least one school board (defendant) attorney and one plaintiff (civil rights group or government) attorney. Where there was more than one plaintiff or defense group in the litigation (e.g., both the Justice Department and the NAACP, or the school board and a white parents' group), we interviewed at least one from each group. The choice of which particular attorney to interview was partly guided by a desire to include those lawyers who had played a critical role in litigation at the trial level, and who had worked with the scientific experts in preparing the cases. As time and circumstances allowed, we also interviewed additional attorneys from the major parties and from other parties to the suit (e.g., neighborhood groups and state boards of education).

We attempted to interview seventy-five attorneys. Six refused, and seventeen other conversations were too brief or too adversary to be considered full and complete interviews. Of the sixty-nine interviews, thirty-eight were with plaintiff attorneys and thirty-one with defense attorneys. Moreover, fifty-two were

Table A.1. Sample Pools and Samples of Social Scientists, Attorneys, and Judges

	Social Scientists	Attorneys	Judges
Interviews requested	85	75	20
Refusals	2	6	10
Interviews done	83	69	10
Did not testify	16	—	—
Not full/complete interviews	15	17	3 .
Full and complete interviews	52	52	7

locally based attorneys and seventeen were based in national or regional organizations of agencies (LDF, Department of Justice, and so forth).

Judges

We wrote to the federal district court judges who had heard each of these cases, describing the project and asking for permission to speak with them. We were successful in gaining access to roughly half the judges (in a few cases a three-judge panel heard the case, so the sample pool is larger than 17), but not all those interviews are full and complete either (see table A.l). Although the data on judges is less complete, by reputation and self-report the judges we did interview ranged across the "liberal-conservative" and "traditional-activist" spectrums. Therefore, they provide at least an indication of judicial reactions to these cases and the use of social scientific evidence in court.

We were and are sympathetic with any person's decisions not to be interviewed, or to be cautious in their conversations with us. The controversial nature of school desegregation issues, the partisan environment within which the courtroom use of applied social science occurs, and the dangers of breaches of confidentiality surely mitigated against free and open discussions. Given this context, we were quite pleased with both the response rate and the level of completeness of the interviewing process.

Interview Format

Given the complex and sensitive nature of the issues we were investigating, and the relatively small sample size, we decided to utilize in-depth interviews with open-ended questions. Closed-ended instruments would have been more amenable to quantitative data analysis, and would have provided more standardization. However, the potential for sophisticated quantitative analysis was limited by our sample size. Moreover, the richness and depth of information we could obtain from in-depth interviews seemed to justify any loss in standardization.

The interviews with social scientists dealt with eight major substantive areas:

1. Decision to testify: How did informants get involved in testifying and what did they consider in deciding whether to testify? For whom did they testify and how often?

2. Preparation for testimony: How did informants prepare themselves, and how were they prepared by their lawyers for testifying? Had they testified before?
3. Testifying experience: What tensions did experts experience while testifying? Did they find cross-examination particularly difficult or stressful? What other forms of testimony might be useful?
4. Role conflict: Did informants experience conflict between the roles of scholar and witness?
5. Testimony: What was the content of their testimony? The effects? Did they feel that their testimony helped shape the judge's decision?
6. Applied social science: What did informants feel was the appropriate role of social science in responding to social problems in general?
7. Consequences of testifying: Were there any political, personal, or professional consequences for the scholar?
8. Attitudes about desegregation: How did informants evaluate court-ordered school desegregation in general?

The interviews with attorneys dealt with seven substantive areas:

1. Decision to use social scientific evidence: Why did they decide to use expert witnesses? How did they decide which experts to use?
2. What was at stake in the case: What was the legal theory guiding the attorney's actions? What legal issues were at stake? What remedies were possible?
3. Preparation for trial: How did the attorney prepare himself and expert witnesses? How did he prepare for cross-examination?
4. Testimony: What was the content of social scientists' testimony? Did it appear probative? Was it effective? How else might it have been helpful?
5. Social scientists: What were the scientists like?
6. The judge: What tactics were used to influence the judge? Was the judge open to argument, to evidence?
7. Attitudes about desegregation: How did informants evaluate school desegregation as a national policy? What other ways of settling these kinds of disputes makes sense?

The interviews with the judges dealt with six substantive areas:

1. The issues in the case: What were the issues in violation and remedy in the case?
2. Social scientific evidence: What social science evidence made sense or was useful? Who presented it effectively? How else might it be useful?
3. Testimony: What other testimony was important?
4. External pressures: What role did the community, appeals courts, and the government play in the decision?
5. Was there any use of consultants or monitors in helping to create or implement the order?

6. Attitudes toward desegregation: What is the future of desegregation as a national policy?

The interviews contained a pattern of broad and general questions followed by a set of more specific probes. For example, we asked scholar-experts:

What factors did you consider in deciding to testify?
Did the decision generate any conflict for you?
Did you anticipate any tensions between the role of scholar and that of expert witness? (If yes)
What was the nature of that tension?

Another example comes from the interviews with attorneys:

What was your legal strategy?
What did you need to show or prove?
How did you plan to show this?

The general questions enabled informants to identify and discuss issues that were most salient to them. Once we obtained their definition of the issues, we gradually introduced other issues we felt were important. If informants anticipated and responded to a particular problem in their reply to the general questions, that probe was not asked. If they brought up an interesting issue not included in our questions, interviewers temporarily departed from the interview format and pursued the issue. Thus, although we made sure to ask our questions in a relatively systematic and standardized manner, the conversations themselves were anything but standardized. Different attorneys, judges, and scholars had different perspectives and reactions to share; they also had different personal needs to share information and experience that were sometimes painful and distressing, but also intriguing and provocative.

Interview Process

We conducted pilot interviews in the summer of 1978 with eight scholars and seven attorneys who had been extensively involved in school desegregation litigation. We also held informal preliminary conversations with two judges. The pilots involved conversations about their experiences, and helped us identify and refine issues that were later included in the formal interviews. Some of these pilots were extensive enough to be included in the sample. Other persons were reinterviewed.

The prime interviewing period extended from December 1978 to August 1979. The bulk of the interviews was done by the three of us: a white male socialpsychologist, a white male lawyer-sociologist, and a white female doctoral student in sociology. The remaining interviews were conducted by two female advanced law students, one white and one black. It is possible that some bias was created by the use of different interviewers. However, it is also possible that this procedure generated a richer data set than if one person had done all the interviewing.

Most informants generally appeared to be open and involved in the interviews. There were several indications of their involvement. First, they allowed more time for the interviews than we had originally anticipated. We planned on one-hour interviews, but interview length actually ranged from forty-five minutes to four hours. The average length was between an hour and a half to two hours. Second, only ten informants refused to have their interviews taped. Third, several remarked that they had enjoyed the interview and were pleased to have had an opportunity to talk about issues that they had previously not found a forum to discuss. This served an educational and cathartic function for some informants, allowing them to examine a set of conflicts that they had not publicly discussed before. Some informants explicitly stated that the interview had provided new insights into their courtroom experience. Finally, many remarked that they were pleased that these issues were being systematically investigated, and most expressed interest in seeing the results of the study.

These interview data are subject to all the potential biases of any set of questions which pertain, at least in part, to retrospective reports from informants. Lapses in memory, conscious or unconscious distortion of prior beliefs or experiences, and even relatively minor "shaping" in the communication of values and events have occurred. Moreover, given the controversial and moral or normative tone to many of the issues focused on in the interviews, there may be cases in which informants' reports and interpretations of events were self-serving in nature, helping to make the individual look and/or feel more "whole," wise, or effective. As we coded and analyzed the data, we took care to double check reports for their internal accuracy, and in this book we draw the reader's attention to situations in which these potential problems may be especially relevant or important.

In addition to interviews, we collected several other kinds of data. For each case, we read some depositions and transcripts of experts' testimony in court. For instance, the courtroom dialogues reported in chapter 8 are culled from some 2,500 pages of cross-examination in these cases. We also read some attorneys' briefs and appellate arguments, and many published judicial opinions. In addition, we read the articles and books that many scholars used to back up their arguments or as other forms of their own professional and political work. The unique database of the study, of course, remains the interviews. Given the immense amount of material generated in these kinds of cases, we read only selectively from these other materials. Perhaps a more extensive content analysis of these transcripts and other materials is warranted; it would take a great deal more time and money even to gather the materials, let alone analyze them.

Data Analysis

From the outset of the study, we were interested in describing and analyzing all actors' experiences as well as in using both qualitative and quantitative forms of data and data analysis. On some issues we proceeded in a somewhat deductive manner, having identified ahead of time not only variables but also ways of targeting these variables in the data set and the analysis. On some issues, we proceeded much more inductively, discovering themes and issues in the data that began a search to identify actors' experiences and the meanings they attributed to these experiences.

Therefore, some chapters evidence a style of data analysis and presentation that uses microcoding of the interviews and that generally resulted in quantitative analyses of the differences between lawyers and scholars, or between various subcategories of lawyers and scholars (plaintiff attorneys vs. defense attorneys, one-time testifiers vs. repeat players, scholars selecting scientific norms vs. those selecting legal norms). Other chapters reflect the identification of a major conceptual issue or argument, and benefit from a systematic search through the interview materials for evidence illuminating one or another position. The analysis of patterns of influence on judges, or of reasons for and against the panel mechanism for the use of expert testimony, reflects this approach. So does the chapter on attorneys' decision to use scientific evidence. In other chapters, and on other issues, we primarily set out to describe an issue or a problem in the language and meaning sets identified for us by the actors interviewed. Our encounter with these perceptions and reactions was, of course, also conceptualized in ways that seem to us to sort and categorize actors' experiences. The chapters on characteristics of the good witness, scholarly preparation for witnessing, and cross-examination most clearly reflect this approach.

As an example of the use of a qualitative mode of analysis, consider the kinds of data reported in chapter 5, the characteristics of a good witness. Our interviews with attorneys, scholars, and judges convinced us that each of these actors made some distinctions between good and bad witnesses; indeed, certain key scholars were identified as outstanding witnesses by many people. We were curious as to the specific meaning of this concept; what is it that a good witness looks like, or has, or does? We proceeded to read through all the interviews with all the actors, to underline and select out examples of things that were said about witness characteristics. Thus, the chapter is liberally sprinkled with quoted material that we think gives the flavor of the issue, as identified by our informants. Obviously, part of the issue was appearance, or illusion. With this understanding in mind, we were prepared to test the extent and distribution of the problem as we now understood it. The more we looked, the more it began to be clear that there was not an infinite number of characteristics; on the other hand, the issue did not simply come down to personality. Rather, there were a number of things that people were able to agree on as being general characteristics. On this basis, we were able to categorize the unique statements about witness characteristics into a limited set of categories, noted in the tables in chapter 5. This was essentially a coding scheme, and comments could be fit into that scheme. Although the tables actually pulled this material together at the end of this process, we present them at the beginning of the chapter (rather than at the end) for the reader's convenience.

Another analytic approach required the identification of a problem and an analytic frame ahead of time. Then, the coding and analysis were based on a long process of reading the complete transcripts of experts' interviews. For instance, the general reading of scholars' transcripts was inevitably guided by the anticipation that experts would experience conflict between the supposedly neutral role of scholar and the supposedly partisan role of expert witness. However, we made a concerted attempt to remain open to other sources of conflict for scholar-experts that might be more salient than the experience of role conflict, as well as to the possibility that some experts may not have experienced conflict in the courtroom.

An instance in which the data required reorganization of our preliminary ideas occurred in the analysis of lawyers' responses to the idea of a panel. Initially, we thought all the attorneys would be opposed to this idea, because it violated the basic adversary norms of the courtroom. However, a number of attorneys favored the panel, under certain conditions; the conditions themselves were more illuminating than general agreement/disagreement. As chapter 10 indicates, a revised inquiry format led to the discovery of themes of negotiation in a community controversy, power and control of the courtroom, and perceptions of social science bias as relevant issues.

Some data were analyzed in order to clarify *within-group* differences. For instance, within the group of scholars, we examined differences in how plaintiff witnesses and defense witnesses responded to various issues, or how they selected from among competing roles and normative standards (scientific vs. legal-adversary). Other data were analyzed in order to clarify *between-group* differences. For instance, we compared how lawyers and scholars experienced or evaluated certain testimony or styles of witnessing. And finally, some data were analyzed in order to *triangulate any and all groups'* perceptions of key issues. For instance, in trying to understand the criteria for being a good witness, or the relevance of a panel as a mechanism for providing scholarly testimony, we brought all groups' perceptions to bear on the problem.

We always carefully checked the qualitative categorization of interview excerpts, to ensure that we agreed on the informants' meaning of a phrase or idea. It was therefore unwise and dangerous to rip statements out of context, and we tried to ensure the use of statements (or quoted excerpts) that were rooted in a context of similar meaning. On most occasions, moreover, we check-coded our quantitative materials, to ensure that more than one observer agreed on the placement of an actor within a given category. For instance, twenty-five interviews were coded by a second coder (not associated with the study) for the normative stance experts reported adopting in the courtroom. There was perfect agreement about the reported normative stance of twenty-four out of the twenty-five experts. Another reliability check was done on the coding of experts' actual normative stance as reflected in the court transcripts of their testimony. Six court transcripts were analyzed by two coders and there was perfect intercoder agreement on the actual stance of five of the six experts.

Other details about the analytic methods we used are presented in the chapters where they are most relevant. In all chapters the names and identifying characteristics of all actors we interviewed have been omitted. In some cases, that has required us to make minor modifications in the interview transcriptions, or in the materials taken from depositions or court transcripts. This step was taken to preserve the anonymity and confidentiality of the data, and the privileged conversations we had with informants. Sometimes, when informants discussed another scholar, a second or third party, we have included such identification where it seemed to us to be both appropriate and a useful specification of an issue or concern. Moreover, when an actor's remarks have appeared in print (in a published article or opinion, for instance), we have not hestitated to identify the person and the source as such. We have, however, chosen to maintain anonymity with respect to trial transcript material. Although this material is officially a matter of public record, it is also true, as Wolf (1981) notes, that "the expert testimony given during a trial is virtually a secret as far as the 'scientific forum' is concerned" (274). We can see no purpose to be served by identifying the individuals who testified.

Although we have used a variety of data analysis techniques, in no case have we found that these different approaches to the data led us to competing or mutually exclusive conclusions. Our own experience is that it has been useful to explore and experiment with these different styles of analysis, and that the product (this manuscript as well as other materials) will have been enriched considerably by the use of more than one framework. We do not claim that this particular version of our findings represents a true integration of various analytic modes, but it does present several different ways of approaching a common data set.

Appendix B
Interview Formats and Post-Interview Questionnaire

Interviews with Social and Educational Scientists

1. How did you happen to testify in the _____ case? (Or, in these cases?)
2. What factors did you consider in deciding to testify?
   a. Did the decision generate any conflict for you?
   b. Did you anticipate any tensions between your (usual) role as a social (educational) scientist and as an expert witness? (Or, between your role in the academy and the courtroom?)
      What was the nature of this tension?
   c. Did the decision seem consistent with other things you do as a social (educational) scientist . . . or was it something of a departure?
   d. Did the decision seem distinct from earlier decisions to do research on issues relevant to desegregation?
3. How did you prepare to give testimony?
   a. What type of legal briefing did you receive?
   b. Was there a consensus between you and the lawyers you were working with regarding the nature of your testimony? Were there any discrepancies?
   c. How did you decide on how you would present yourself . . . your style and dress and manner of presentation?
   d. Did you talk ahead of time with other social scientists who had testified in similar cases?
      Did you seek advice from anyone else?

As we indicated in Appendix A, these formats were used as guides to conversations with informants. The questions were not all asked in precisely the same manner, or order, in all interviews.

4. What kinds of issues did you face while testifying?
   a. Did you ever wonder whether the judge understood what you were saying?
   b. Were you cross-examined? Was that stressful?
   b.¹ What major areas of your testimony did the opposing attorney challenge?
   b.² Were your integrity or credentials ever challenged?
   b.³ Was opposing social science evidence ever presented in rebuttal to your testimony?
   How did you evaluate that evidence?
5. When testifying, did you in fact experience tension between your roles as a scholar and as a witness?
   Was this anything like what you had anticipated ahead of time?
   a. Did you experience any conflicts in loyalty between your commitments to professional standards and commitments to the clients in the case?
   b. Some people have argued that expert testimony can be most effective when presented as part of a consultant panel to a judge, personally, rather than as open testimony in a courtroom. That would do away with the opportunity for cross-examination, etc. What would you think of this approach?
   c. If you had been asked to testify for the opposing party in the case, would you have?
   Under what circumstances? (Could your data have been used in other ways?)
   d. Have you ever been asked to present data that were inconsistent with your own values and beliefs?
   What did (would) you do?
6. We've been talking about the conflicts associated with the role of expert witness. What about some of the positives? What did you enjoy about testifying? Why do you do it?
   a. Do you get paid to testify? If so, how much?
7. What legal issues did you address?
   a. Were they primarily matters of merit or of remedy?
   b. What kinds of things did you actually say?
   c. Did you ever say anything you weren't absolutely sure of?
   c.¹ Did you ever testify to anything you would be uncomfortable arguing in front of a group of academic colleagues?
   d. Have you ever seen (or heard directly of) other scientists who have presented testimony in court they couldn't back up scientifically?
   What do you think of that? Is that OK? Really bad?
8. Do you have any sense or impression of the role your testimony played in shaping the judge's ruling?
9. What do you see as the appropriate roles of social science (education) in responding to social problems in general?
   What mix of scholarship and application, of research and action, seems most useful and appropriate?

a. Are there some other social problem areas, besides desegregation, where you have played an active role? Such as . . .

b. Have you played an active role other than as an expert witness? Where and when?

10. How have you managed to integrate your role as an expert witness in this case (these cases) with your role as a scholar?

a. Did testifying alter your concept of your scholarly role?

a.[1] Or of your role as witness?

b. Are the roles of scholar or expert witness very different from that of an informed citizen?

c. Have you had disagreements with, or criticism from, other social scientists about the propriety or wisdom of testifying?

d. Have there been any professional consequences of testifying, either positive or negative?

e. Do you think there are any problems raised for the discipline as a whole by the numbers of social scientists who are testifying in these cases?

e.[1] For instance, does it negatively or positively affect the credibility or autonomy of the social sciences?

11. What is your evaluation of court-ordered desegregation as a national policy?

12. There certainly are plenty of controversies in the social sciences. What do you think accounts for the special heat generated by these issues related to desegregation . . . minority achievement, existence of racism, white flight, etc.?

13. What seem to be some of the major unanswered research questions relevant to school desegregation?

a. In what areas of desegregation policy making can social scientists (educators) be most helpful?
Where can we not be helpful?

Interviews with Attorneys

1. How (and/or why) did you get involved in the _____ case? (Or, in these cases?)

a. Have you been involved in other school desegregation cases?

b. Who was your client, exactly?

2. What was your legal theory or strategy in the case?

a. What legal issues were at stake?

b. What evidentiary issues?
What did you have to show?
How did you plan to show it?

3. Did you use any social scientific evidence or witnesses on your side of the case?

IF YES:

a. What were you trying to show with them?

b. Who were they?

c. How did you get hold of them?
   Where did you hear about them?
d. What kinds of information did they present?
   IF NO:
a. What about the opposition, whom did they bring in?
b. What were their names?
c. What were they trying to show?

4. Did you prepare your witnesses in any way ahead of time (if used)?
   a. Did you meet with them ahead of time?
   b. What did you tell them about the case?
   c. About the courtroom process?
      About cross-examination?

5. Did you prepare yourself in any way for the opposition's witnesses?
   a. What were they like?
      Fair and impartial?   Advocates?
      What did you try to do in cross-examination?
      How did it go?

6. What makes a witness good or effective in court, in general?
   a. Who was a good witness, for example?
      Why was she/he good?
   b. Who was not so good?
      Why?

7. Do you think the social science evidence had any impact on the judge and
   on his decision?
   a. Which witnesses made the most sense to him, do you think?
   b. Was he pretty open, or had he already made up his mind?
   c. Did you plan ahead of time how to influence him?
      On what basis?

8. In some cases, a number of people have begun talking about an alternative
   procedure for using expert witnesses, a panel of experts appointed by the
   judge and accountable to him.
   Have you heard about this?
   If NO: Explain a bit more about the Los Angeles example.
   a. What do you think of such a procedure?

9. What is the legal status of the _____ case now?

10. What do you think the future of these cases is going to be?
    a. How do you deal with incremental segregative effect issues?
    b. What are some reasonable remedies, as you see it?
       Metro?
    c. Do cases ever end?

11. What do you think of school desegregation, and how it's working across the
    country?
    a. How about in this community?
    b. What about the quality of education in general?

Interviews with Judges

1. What were the important legal issues in the _____ case?

   a. How did any of the social science evidence touch on these issues?
2. Do you remember who the expert witnesses were?
   a. What kinds of evidence did they offer?
   b. Did they have any impact on you and your decision?
   c. What did you think of their testimony?
3. What makes an expert witness credible as far as you are concerned?
   a. Who were some especially credible witnesses?
   b. Who wasn't?
4. Are there ways in which social science evidence is any different from other kinds of evidence?
   a. What about when there is conflicting social science evidence? How can you resolve it?
   b. Were there other witnesses, not necessarily social scientists, who were impressive in this case?
   c. Are there any suggestions you have for procedures which might make it easier to use scientific information?
5. In some cases, people are talking about using a scientific panel, a court-appointed body of experts that would report directly to the judge. Have you heard of or used such a panel in any cases?
   a. What do you think of it? Does it have any advantages over the party witness procedure?
6. How did you decide your findings in the case?
   a. What helped make up your mind?
   b. How did you construct a remedy?
   c. Did you use any social science evidence?
   d. Did you set up a monitoring procedure? Do you think the community and school people will cooperate pretty well, or not?
7. Sometimes it appears that these cases never end, what with appeals, changing conditions, and so on. What do you think will happen in this case?
   a. What are the implications of some other recent Supreme Court findings for the future of school desegregation? (name recent cases, such as Dayton and Columbus).
8. How have people in the community reacted to you, as a result of this case?
   a. Do you think judges in other cases have been put into some tight binds as a result of their roles and decisions?

Questionnaire for Social Scientists Testifying in School Desegregation Cases

1. Please list the cases in which you have testified, and check the column(s) which describes the nature of your testimony in each case. (If you have testified in more than 5 cases, list just 5 illustrative ones and give the total number of appearances.)

Case	Appearance in Courtroom	Deposition	Affidavit
1.			
2.			
3.			
4.			
5.			

2. Do you expect to continue to testify in desegregation cases? If not, why not?

3. Have you served in other roles in the area of desegregation that utilized or applied social science knowledge (e.g., master or monitor, consultant to a party or agency)? What kinds of things did you do? (If your involvement was linked to a specific case/city, please specify.)

4. Is there any written work available describing or reflecting on your role(s) in these cases? If yes, please attach a copy or include a reference.

5. Are there desegregation cases in which you were asked to participate in some way (testify, consult, monitor) and you declined? If yes, what influenced your decision?

6. Do you know of any other social scientists who were asked to testify and declined? Who? Do you know why he/she declined?

7. Different scientists have presented different kinds of "evidence" in court. Would you please check the following chart to indicate the types of evidence you have presented . . . ever?

Please check
if presented

A. Data you collected ....

Data collected by another social scientist....................

(If checked, who collected it?)

Data collected by a local school system......................

Data collected in the geographic area covered in litigation ....

Data collected specifically for court presentation ....

B. Survey data ....

Experimental data..

Ethnographic data..

Case study data...

C. Conclusions about the meaning of data you collected ....

Conclusions about the meaning of data collected by others ....

D. Conclusions or speculations not specifically tied to a data set ....

8. Has anyone ever presented data you collected as part of their testimony? If yes, how did you feel about the uses made of it?

9. Please specify the names of your 3 closest professional colleagues and check any columns which describe the work they do.

Name	In the Area of Deseg.	Policy Relevant Work	Have Influenced Your Decision To Testify
1.			
2.			
3.			

10. Do you consider yourself a "social scientist" or is there another term you feel fits better? (What other term?)

Thank you.

Table of Cases

Bibliography

Ackerman, B. 1984. *Reconstructing American law*. Cambridge: Harvard University Press.

Adam, B.D. 1978. Inferiorization and "self-esteem". *Social Psychology* 41:47–53.

Aiken, M., and N. Demerath 1967. The politics of tokenism in Mississippi's Delta. *Trans-Action* 4:26–34.

Allport, G. 1954. *The nature of prejudice*. Garden City, N.Y.: Doubleday Anchor Books.

Amir, Y. 1976. The role of intergroup contact in change of prejudice and ethnic relations. In *Toward the elimination of racism*, ed. P. Katz, 245–308. New York: Pergamon Press.

Anderson, M. 1966. *Children of the South*. New York: Farrar, Straus and Giroux.

Anonymous. 1983. Politics dominate research programs at NIE. *Footnotes* (American Sociological Association) 11 (March): 1, 10–11.

Aranow, G. 1980. The special master in school desegregation cases. *Hastings Constitutional Law Quarterly* 7:739–775.

Armor, D. 1972. The evidence on busing. *Public Interest* 28:90–124.

Armor, D. 1973. The double double standard: A reply. *Public Interest* 30:119–131.

Armor, D. 1980. White flight and the future of school desegregation. In *School desegregation: Past, present and future*, ed. W.G. Stephan and J.R. Feagin, 25–50. New York: Plenum Press.

Armor, D., and W. Genova. 1970. METCO student attitudes and aspirations: A three year evaluation. Manuscript.

Aronson, E. 1978. *The jigsaw classroom*. Beverly Hills, Calif.: Sage.

Aronson, E., N. Blaney, J. Sikes, C. Stephan, and M. Snapp. 1975. Busing and racial tension: The jigsaw route to learning and liking. *Psychology Today* 8:43–50.

Asher, S.R., and V.L. Allen. 1969. Racial preference and social comparison processes. *Journal of Social Issues* 25:157–166.

Bailey, F.L., and H.B. Rothblatt. 1971. *Successful techniques for criminal trials*. Rochester, N.Y.: The Lawyers Cooperative Publishing Co.

Banks, W.C. 1976. White preference in blacks: A paradigm in search of a phenomenon. *Psychological Bulletin* 83:1179–86.

Bell, D. 1976. Serving two masters: Integration ideals and client interests in school desegregation litigation. *Yale Law Journal* 85:470–516.

Bell, D., ed. 1980a. *Shades of Brown: New perspectives on school desegregation.* New York: Columbia University, Teachers College Press.

Bell, D. 1980b. Brown v. Board of Education and the interest-convergence dilemma. *Harvard Law Review* 93:518–533.

Berger, J. and M. Zelditch, eds. 1985. *Status, rewards, and influence: How expectations organize behavior.* San Francisco: Jossey-Bass.

Berman, P., and M. McLaughlin. 1980. Factors affecting the process of change. In *Schools, conflict and change,* ed. M. Milstein, 57–71. New York: Columbia University, Teachers College Press.

Black, C. 1960. The lawfulness of the segregation decisions. *Yale Law Journal* 69:421–430.

Bland, R. 1973. *Private pressure on public law.* Port Washington, N.Y.: Kennikut Press.

Blaustein, A., and C. Ferguson. 1962. *Desegregation and the law.* New York: Vintage.

Boas, F. 1911. *The mind of primitive man.* New York: Macmillan.

Bohannan, P. 1965. The differing realms of the law. In *American Anthropologist, special publication: The ethnography of law,* ed. L. Nader, 67(6), pt. 2:33–42.

Bolner, J., and R. Shanley. 1974. *Busing: The political and judicial process.* New York: Praeger Publishers.

Brickman, P., R. Folger, E. Goode, and Y. Schul. 1980. Macro and micro justice. In *The justice motive in social behavior,* ed. M.J. Lerner, 173–202. New York: Plenum.

Buckhout, R. 1986. Personal values and expert testimony. *Law and Human Behavior* 10:127–144.

Bullock, C.S. 1980. The Office for Civil Rights and implementation of desegregation programs in the public schools. *Policy Studies Journal* 8(4):597–616.

Bullock, C.S. 1984. Equal educational opportunity. In *Implementation of civil rights policy,* ed. C.S. Bullock and C.M. Lamb, 55–92. Monterey, Calif.: Brooks/Cole.

Bullock, C.S., and C.M. Lamb, eds. 1984. *Implementation of civil rights policy.* Monterey, Calif.: Brooks/Cole.

Burges, W. 1978. *Good things can happen: Your community organization and school desegregation?* Cleveland: Federation for Community Planning.

Burstein, P. 1985. *Discrimination, jobs, and politics: The struggle for equal employment opportunity in the United States since the New Deal.* Chicago: University of Chicago Press.

Cahn, E. 1955. A dangerous myth in the school segregation cases. *New York University Law Review* 30:150–169.

Cahn, E. 1956. Jurisprudence. *New York University Law Review* 31:182–195.

Campbell, D.T. 1977. *William James Lectures.* Cambridge: Harvard University

Press. Cited in *Social psychology in court* (1978), ed. M.J. Saks and Reid Hastie, 206. New York: Van Nostrand Reinhold Co.

Caplan, N. 1979. The two-communities theory and knowledge utilization. *American Behavioral Scientist* 22(3):459–470.

Carmichael, S., and W. James. 1957. *The Louisville story*. New York: Simon and Schuster.

Carter, R.L. 1965. De facto school segregation: An examination of the legal and constitutional questions presented. In *De facto segregation and civil rights*, ed. O. Schroeder, Jr., and D.T. Smith, 28–57. Buffalo, N.Y.: William S. Hein & Co.

Carter, R.L. 1968. The Warren Court and desegregation. *Michigan Law Review* 67:237–248.

Cavanaugh, R., and A. Sarat. 1980. Thinking about courts: Toward and beyond a jurisprudence of judicial competence. *Law and Society Review* 14:371–420.

Chayes, A. 1976. The role of the judge in public law litigation. *Harvard Law Review* 89:1281–1316.

Chesler, M. 1971. Teacher training designs for improving interaction in interracial classrooms. *Journal of Applied Behavioral Science* 7:612–641.

Chesler, M., J. Crowfoot, and B. Bryant. 1978. Institutional changes to support school desegregation. *Law and Contemporary Problems* 42(4):173–213.

Chesler, M., C. Jorgensen, and P. Erenberg. 1970. *Planned educational change: Integrating the desegregated school*. Washington, D.C.: U.S. Department of Health, Education and Welfare.

Chesler, M., J. Sanders, and D. Kalmuss. 1981. *Interactions among scientists, attorneys and judges in school desegregation litigation*. Final Report to the National Institute of Education, Center for Research on Social Organization, Ann Arbor, Michigan.

Clark, K. 1953. The social scientist as an expert witness in civil rights litigation. *Social Problems* 3:211–214.

Clark, K. 1959/60. The segregation cases: Criticism of the social scientists' role. *Villanova Law Review* 5:224–240.

Clark, K. 1977. Social science, constitutional rights, and the courts. In *Education, social science, and the judicial process*, ed. R.C. Rist and R.J. Anson, 1–9. New York: Columbia University, Teachers College Press.

Clark, K. 1979. Preparation of the social scientists' brief. Presentation at the annual meeting of the Society for the Psychological Study of Social Issues, New York, September.

Clark, K., and M. Clark. 1947. Racial identification and preference in Negro children. In *Readings in social psychology* (1st ed.), ed. T. Newcomb and E. Hartley, 169–178. New York: Holt.

Clune, W. 1984. Courts and legislatures as arbitrators of social change. *Yale Law Journal* 93:763–779.

Cohen, D., and J. Weiss. 1977. Social science and social policy: Schools and race. In *Education, social science and the judicial process*, ed. R.C. Rist and R.J. Anson, 72–96. New York: Columbia University, Teachers College Press.

Cohen, E. 1973. Modifying the effects of social structure. *American Behavioral Scientist* 16:861–879.

Cohen, E. 1975. The effects of desegregation on race relations. *Law and Contemporary Problems* 39(2):271–300.

Cohen, E. 1980. Building effective multi-ethnic schools: Evolving models and paradigms. In *School desegregation: Past, present and future*, ed. W.G. Stephan and J.R. Feagin, 251–80. New York: Plenum.

Cohen, E., M. Lockheed, and M. Lohman. 1976. The center for interracial cooperation: A field experiment. *Sociology of Education*. 49:47–58.

Coleman, J. 1972. *Policy research in the social sciences*. Morristown, N.J.: General Learning Press.

Coleman, J. 1974. *Power and the structure of society*. New York: Norton.

Coleman, J. 1976. Response to professors Pettigrew and Green. *Harvard Educational Review*. 46(2):217–24.

Coleman, J. 1979. Presentation to Massachusetts legislature—March 30, 1976. In *New perspectives on school integration*, ed. M. Friedman, R. Meltzer, and C. Miller, 111–123. Philadelphia: Fortress Press.

Coleman, J., E. Campbell, C. Hobson, J. McPartland, A. Mood, F. Weinfeld, and R. York. 1966. *Equality of educational opportunity*. Washington, D.C.: U.S. Government Printing Office.

Coleman, J., S. Kelly, and J. Moore. 1975. *Trends in school segregation 1968–1975*. Washington, D.C.: Urban Institute.

Columbus Social Science Brief. 1979. School segregation and residential segregation: A social science statement. Appendix to Plaintiffs brief in *Penick v. Columbus, Ohio Board of Education*. Reprinted in *School desegregation: Past, present and future*, ed. W.G. Stephan and J.R. Feagin, 231–249. New York: Plenum Press, 1980.

Comment. 1967. The courts, HEW, and southern school desegregation. *Yale Law Journal* 77:321–365.

Cook, S. 1984. The 1954 social science statement and school desegregation: A reply to Gerard. *American Psychologist* 39:819–832.

Cooley, C.H. 1902. *Human nature and the social order*. New York: Charles Scribner's Sons.

Crain, R. 1968. *The politics of school desegregation*. Chicago: Aldine.

Crain, R. 1976. Why academic research fails to be useful. In *School desegregation: Shadow and substance*, ed. F.H. Levinshon and B.D. Wright, 31–45. Chicago: University of Chicago Press.

Crain, R., and K. Carsrud. 1985. The role of the social sciences in school desegregation policy. In *Social science and social policy*, ed. R.L. Shotland and M.M. Mark, 219–236. Beverly Hills, Calif.: Sage.

Crain, R., and R. Mahard. 1978. Desegregation and black achievement. *Law and Contemporary Problems* 42:17–56.

Crain, R., R. Mahard, and R. Narot. 1982. *Making desegregation work: How schools create social climates*. Cambridge, Mass.: Ballinger.

Craven, J. 1975. Further judicial commentary: The impact of social science evidence on the judge: A personal comment. *Law and Contemporary Problems* 39:150–156.

Crowfoot, J. and M. Chesler. 1981. Implementing "attractive" ideas: Problems and prospects. In *Effective school desegregation: Equity, quality and feasibility*, ed. W.D. Hawley, 265–96. Beverly Hills, Calif.: Sage.

Dahl, R. 1961. *Who governs?* New Haven: Yale University Press.

Dentler, R. 1978. Desegregation planning and implementation in Boston. *Theory Into Practice* 17(1):72–77.

Dentler, R.A. and M.B. Scott. 1981. *Schools on trial: An inside account of the Boston desegregation case.* Cambridge, Mass.: Abt Books.

Desegregation without turmoil: The role of the multiracial community coalition in preparing for smooth transition. 1976. New York: Community Relations Service and National Center for Quality Integrated Education.

Dimond, P. 1985. *Beyond busing: Inside the challenge to urban segregation.* Ann Arbor: University of Michigan Press.

Diver, C. 1979. The judge as political pawnbroker. *Virginia Law Review* 65:42–106.

Dollard, J. 1937. *Caste and class in a southern town.* New Haven: Yale University Press.

Doyle, W. 1977. Can social science data be used in judicial decisionmaking? In *Education, social science and the judicial process*, ed. R. Rist and R. Anson, 10–19. New York: Columbia University, Teachers College Press.

Drury, D.W. 1980. Black self-esteem and desegregated schools. *Sociology of Education* 53:88–103.

Dunn, J.R. 1967. Title VI, the guidelines and school desegregation in the South. *Virginia Law Review* 53:42-88.

Dworkin, R. 1977. Social science and constitutional rights—the consequences of uncertainty. In *Education, social science and the judicial process*, ed. R. Rist and R. Anson, 20–31. New York: Columbia University, Teachers College Press.

Edmonds, R. 1974. Advocating inequality: A critique of the civil rights attorney in class action desegregation suits. *Black Law Journal* 176.

Eisenger, P.K. 1973. The conditions of protest behaviour in American cities. *American Political Science Review* 67:11–28.

Entin, J.L. 1986. Sweatt v. Painter: The end of segregation, and the transformation of education law. *The Review of Litigation* 5:3–71.

Epps, E. 1975. The impact of school desegregation on aspirations, self-concepts and other aspects of personality. *Law and Contemporary Problems* 39(2):300–313.

Epps, E. 1978. The impact of school desegregation on the self-evaluation and achievement orientation of minority children. *Law and Contemporary Problems* 42:56–76.

Etzioni, A. 1971. Policy research. *American Sociologist* 6(Supplement):8–12.

Evans, S.S. and J.E. Scott. 1983. Social scientists as expert witnesses: Their use, misuse, and sometimes abuse. *Law and Policy Quarterly* 5:181–214.

Farley, R. 1975a. Racial integration in the public schools, 1967–1972; Assessing the effects of governmental policies. *Sociological Focus* 8:3–26.

Farley, R. 1975b. Residential segregation and its implications for school litigation. *Law and Contemporary Problems* 39(1):164–193.

Farley, R. 1975c. School integration and white flight. Paper presented at the Symposium on School Desegregation and White Flight, Brookings Institute, Washington, D.C.

Farley, R. 1984. *Blacks and whites: Narrowing the gap?* Cambridge: Harvard University Press.

Farley, R., H. Schuman, S. Bianchi, D. Colasanto, and S. Hatchett. 1978. Chocolate city, vanilla suburbs: Will the trend toward racially separate communities continue? *Social Science Research* 7:319–344.

Feagin, J.R. 1980. School desegregation: A political economic perspective. In *School desegregation: Past, present and future*, ed. W.G. Stephan and J.R. Feagin, 25–50. New York: Plenum Press.

Fiss, O. 1965. Racial imbalance in the public schools: The Constitutional concepts. *Harvard Law Review* 78:564–617.

Fiss, O. 1971. The Charlotte-Mecklenberg Case. *University of Chicago Law Review* 38:697–709.

Fiss, O. 1976. Groups and the Equal Protection Clause. *Philosophy and Public Affairs* 5:107–177.

Fiss, O. 1979. The Supreme Court 1978 Term forward: The forms of justice, *Harvard Law Review* 93:1–58.

Fiss, O. 1983. The bureaucratization of the judiciary. *Yale Law Journal* 92:1442–1468.

Forehand, G., and M. Ragosta. 1976. *A handbook for integrated schooling.* Washington, D.C.: U.S. Office of Education.

Forehand, G., M. Ragosta, and D. Rock. 1976. *Conditions and processes of effective school desegregation.* Princeton, N.J.: Educational Testing Service.

Foster, G. 1973. Desegregating urban schools: a review of techniques. *Harvard Educational Review* 43(1):5–36

Frankel, C. 1976. *Controversies and decisions: The social sciences and public policy.* New York: Sage.

Freeman, J. 1983. A model for analyzing the strategic options of social movement organizations. In *Social movements of the sixties and seventies*, ed. J. Freeman, 193–210. New York: Longman.

Fritz, H. 1963. *The movement for Indian assimilation 1860–1890.* Philadelphia: University of Pennsylvania Press.

Fuller, L. 1971. The adversary system. In *Talks on American law*, ed. H. Berman, New York: Vintage Books.

Fuller, L. 1978. The forms and limits of adjudication. *Harvard Law Review* 92:353–409.

Galanter, M. 1974. Why the haves come out ahead: Speculation on the limits of legal change. *Law and Society Review* 9:95–160.

Gardiner, J., ed. 1977. *Public law and public policy.* New York: Praeger Publishers.

Gardner, W. 1979. Expert witnesses in employment discrimination cases. *Litigation* 5(2):18–26.

Gerard, H. 1983. School desegregation: The social science role. *American Psychologist* 38:869-877.

Gerard, R. and N. Miller. 1975. *School desegregation: A long-range study.* New York: Plenum Press.

Gerhardt, U. 1973. Interpretative processes in role conflict situations. *Sociology* 7(2):225–250.

Gewirtz, P. 1986. Choice in the transition: School desegregation and the corrective ideal. *Columbia Law Review* 86:728–798.

Glaser B. and A. Strauss. 1967. *The discovery of grounded theory.* Chicago: Aldine.

Glazer, N. 1972. Is busing necessary? *Commentary* 53(3):39–52.

Glazer, N. 1975. *Affirmative discrimination: Ethnic inequality and public policy.* New York: Basic Books.

Goering, J.M. 1972. Changing perceptions and evaluations of physical characteristics among blacks: 1950–1970. *Phylon* 33:231–241.

Goffman, E. 1967. *Interaction ritual: Essays on face-to-face behavior.* Chicago: Aldine.

Goodman, F. 1972. "De facto school desegregation: A constitutional and empirical analysis. *California Law Review* 60:275–437.

Gouldner, A. 1957. Theoretical requirements of the applied social sciences. *American Sociological Review* 22:52–102.

Gouldner, A. 1962. *Notes on technology and the moral order.* Indianapolis: Bobbs-Merrill.

Graglia, L. 1976. *Disaster by decree.* Ithaca, N.Y.: Cornell University Press.

Granovetter, M. 1986. The micro-structure of school desegregation. In *School desegregation research: New directions in situational analysis*, ed. J. Prager, D. Longshore, and M. Seeman, 81–142. New York: Plenum Press.

Green, R.L., ed. 1985. *Metropolitan desegregation.* New York: Plenum Press.

Greenberg, J. 1973. Litigation for social change: Methods, limits and role in democracy. Cardozo Lecture no. 30, Association of the Bar of the City of New York, Oct. 31.

Greenwald, H.J., and D.B. Oppenheim. 1968. Reported magnitude of self-misidentification among Negro children: Artifact? *Journal of Personality and Social Psychology* 8:49–52.

Gregor, J. 1963. The law, social science and school segregation. *Western Reserve Law Review* 14:621–636.

Griffiths, J. 1984. The division of labor in social control. In *Toward a general theory of social control. Volume 1, Fundamentals*, ed. D. Black, 37–70. Orlando, Fla.: Academic Press.

Guskin, A., and M. Chesler. 1973. Partisan diagnosis of social problems. In *Processes and phenomena of social change*, ed. G. Zaltman, 353–376. New York: Wiley.

Haddad, F. 1979. Cross-examination of the medical expert. *American Journal of Trial Advocacy* 3:238–247.

Hahn, J. 1973. The NAACP Legal Defense and Education Fund: Its judicial strategy and tactics. In *American government and politics*, ed. S.L. Wasby, 387–400. New York: Charles Scribner's Sons.

Hain E. 1978. Sealing off the city. In *Limits of justice: The courts' role in school desegregation*, ed. H.I. Kalodner and J.J. Fishman, 223–308. Cambridge, Mass.: Ballinger.

Hamilton, C. 1968. Race and education: A search for legitimacy. *Harvard Educational Review* 38:669–684.

Handler, J.F. 1978. *Social movements and the legal system: A theory of law reform and social change*. New York: Academic Press.

Hawley, W. 1981. Equity and quality in education: Characteristics of effective desegregated schools. In *Effective school desegregation*, ed. W.D. Hawley, 297–307. Beverly Hills, Calif.: Sage.

Heiss, J., and S. Owens. 1972. Self evaluations of blacks and whites. *American Journal of Sociology* 78:360–370.

Horowitz, D.L. 1977. *The courts and social policy*. Washington, D.C.: The Brookings Institution.

House, E. 1974. *The Politics of educational innovation*. Berkeley, Calif.: McCutchen.

Hughes, L.W., W. Gordon, and L. Hillman. 1980. *Desegregating America's schools*. New York: Longman.

Imwinkelried, E.J. 1982. *The methods of attacking scientific evidence*. Charlottesville, Va.: The Michie Company.

Jeans, J. 1975. *Trial advocacy*. St. Paul: West Publishing Co.

Johnson, D., and R. Johnson. 1975. *Learning together and alone: Cooperation, competition and individualization*. Englewood Cliffs, N.J.: Prentice-Hall.

Jones, J.A. 1955. Problems, opportunities and recommendations. *Ethnohistory* 2(4):347–356.

Kalmuss, D. 1980. *Scholars in the courtroom: Normative discrepancies and role conflict*. Ph.D. diss., University of Michigan, Ann Arbor.

Kalmuss, D. 1981. Scholars in the courtroom: Two models of applied social science. *American Sociologist* 16:212–223.

Kalmuss, D.S., M. Chesler, and J. Sanders. 1982. The impact of the school desegregation cases on the relation between scientific evidence and legal theory. In *New directions for testing and measurement: Volume 14, Impact of desegregation*, ed. D.J. Monti, 21–38. San Francisco: Jossey-Bass.

Kalodner, H.I., and J.J. Fishman, eds. 1978. *Limits of justice: The courts' role in school desegregation*. Cambridge, Mass.: Ballinger.

Kantrowitz, A. 1977. The science court experiment. *Trial* 13:48–49, 54.

Katz, P. 1976. The acquisition of racial attitudes in children. In *Towards the elimination of racism*, ed. P. Katz, 125–54. New York: Pergamon Press.

Keeton, R. 1973. *Trial tactics and methods*. 2d ed. Boston: Little, Brown.

Kelly, A. 1965. Clio and the court: An illicit love affair. In *The Supreme Court review*, ed. P. Kurland, 119–158. Chicago: University of Chicago Press.

Killian, L., and C. Grigg. 1964. *Racial crisis in America*. Englewood Cliffs, N.J.: Prentice-Hall.

Kirp, D., and G. Babcock. 1981. Judge and company: Court appointed masters, school desegregation and institutional reform. *Alabama Law Review* 32:313–397.

Kirp, D.L. 1981. Legalism and politics in school desegregation. *Wisconsin Law Review* 1981:924–969.

Kirp, D.L. 1982. *Just schools: The idea of racial equality in American education.* Berkeley: University of California Press.

Klineberg, O. 1934. Cultural factors in intelligence test performance. *Journal of Negro Education* 3:478–483.

Kluger, R. 1975. *Simple justice: The history of Brown v. Board of Education and black America's struggle for equality.* New York: Alfred A. Knopf.

Kornblum, G. 1974. The expert as witness and consultant. *The Practical Lawyer* 20(3):13–31.

Ladd, E., and S. Lipset. 1975. *The divided academy: Professions and politics.* New York: Norton.

Laue, J., and D. Monti. 1980. Intervening in school desegregation conflicts: The role of the monitor. In *Research in social movements, conflict and change. Vol. 3,* ed. L. Kriesberg, 187–218. New York: JAI Press.

Lee, M.A. 1978. *Sociology for whom?* New York: Oxford University Press.

Lempert, R., and J. Sanders. 1986. *An invitation to law and social science: Desert, disputes and distribution.* New York: Longman.

Lerner, D., and H. Laswell. 1951. *The policy sciences.* Stanford, Calif.: Stanford University Press.

Levin, B. 1978. School desegregation remedies and the role of social science research. *Law and Contemporary Problems* 42(3):1–8.

Levin, B., and W.D. Hawley, eds. 1978. *The courts, social science and school desegregation.* New Brunswick, N.J.: Transaction Books.

Levin, B., and P. Moise. 1975. School desegregation litigation in the seventies and the use of social science evidence: An annotated guide. *Law and Contemporary Problems* 39(1):50–133.

Levin, H. 1975. Education, life chances, and the courts: the role of social science evidence. *Law and Contemporary Problems* 39(2):217–240.

Lewin, K. 1946. Action research and minority problems. *Journal of Social Issues* 2:34–64.

Lively, D. 1986. Separate but equal: The low road reconsidered. *Hastings Constitutional Law Quarterly* 14:43–76.

Loewen, J.W. 1982. *Social science in the courtrom.* Lexington, Mass.: Lexington Books.

Lofgren, C. 1987. *The Plessy case: A legal historical interpretation.* New York: Oxford University Press.

Loftus, E. 1983a. Silence is not golden. *American Sociologist* 38:564–572.

Loftus, E. 1983b. Whose shadow is crooked? *American Sociologist* 38:576–577.

Loftus, E. 1986. Ten years in the life of an expert witness. *Law and Human Behavior* 10:241–263.

Loh, W.D. 1984. *Social research in the judicial process: Cases, readings and text.* New York: Russell Sage Foundation.

Longshore, D. 1982. Social psychological research on school desegregation: Toward a new agenda. In *New directions for testing and measurement. Volume 14, Impact of desegregation*, ed. D.J. Monti, 39–52. San Francisco: Jossey-Bass.

Macaulay, S. 1963. Non-contractual relations in business: A preliminary study. *American Sociological Review* 28:55–67.

Mack, R., ed. 1968. *Our children's burden: Studies in desegregation in nine American communities*. New York: Vintage Books.

Manners, R. 1956. The land claim cases: Anthropologists in conflict. *Ethnohistory* 3(1):72–81.

Martin, J.A. 1977. The proposed science court. *Michigan Law Review* 75:1058–1091.

McAdam, D. 1983. The decline of the civil rights movement. In *Social movements of the sixties and seventies*, ed. J. Freeman, 298–319. New York: Longman.

McCarthy, J.D., and Yancey, W.L. 1971. Reply to Washington. *American Journal of Sociology* 77:590–591.

McCarthy, J.D., and M.N. Zald. 1973. *The trend of social movements in America: Professionalization and resource mobilization*. Morristown, N.J.: General Learning Press.

McCarthy, J.D., and M.N. Zald. 1977. Resource mobilization and social movements: A partial theory. *American Journal of Sociology* 82:1212–1239.

McCloskey, M., and Egeth, H. 1983a. Eyewitness identification: What can a psychologist tell a jury. *American Psychologist* 38:550–563.

McCloskey, M., and H. Egeth. 1983b. A time to speak, or a time to keep silence? *American Psychologist* 38:573–575.

McCloskey, M., H. Egeth, and J. McKenna, eds. 1986. The ethics of expert testimony. *Law and Human Behavior* 10, nos. 1 and 2.

McCormick on evidence. 1984. 3d ed., ed. E.W. Cleary. St. Paul: West Publishing Co.

McDougall, W. 1909. *Introduction to social psychology*. Boston: J.W. Luce.

McElhaney, J. 1974. *Effective litigation—trials, problems and materials*. St. Paul: West Publishing Co.

McGurk, F. 1959/60. The law, social science and academic freedom—a psychologist's view. *Villanova Law Review* 5:247–254.

McMillan, J.B. 1977. Social science and the district court: The observations of a journeyman trial judge. In *The courts, social science, and school desegregation*, ed. B. Levin and W.D. Hawley, 157–163. New Brunswick, N.J.: Transaction Books.

McNeil, G.R. 1983. *Groundwork: Charles Hamilton Houston and the struggle for civil rights*. Philadelphia: University of Pennsylvania Press.

Mead, G.H. 1934. *Mind, self and society*. Chicago: University of Chicago Press.

Meier, A., and E. Rudwick, eds. N.d. *Papers of the NAACP. Part 3, The campaign for educational equality: Legal department records, 1919–1950*. Frederick, Md.: University Publications of America. Microfilm.

Menkel-Meadow, C. 1984. Toward another view of legal negotiation: The structure of problem solving. *UCLA Law Review* 31:754–842.

Merritt, G. 1983. Owen Fiss on paradise lost: The judicial bureaucracy in the administrative state. *Yale Law Journal* 92:1469–1486.

Merton, R. 1938. Science and the social order. *Philosophy of Science* 5:321–327.

Merton, R. 1957. Role of the intellectual in public bureaucracy. In *Social theory and social structure*, ed. R. Merton, 261–278. New York: Free Press.

Metz, M.H. 1978. *Classrooms and corridors: The crisis of authority in desegregated secondary schools*. University of California Press.

Milstein, M., ed. 1980. *Schools, conflict and change*. New York: Columbia University, Teachers College Press.

Mnookin, R., and L. Kornhauser. 1979. Bargaining in the shadow of the law: The case of divorce. *Yale Law Journal* 88:950–997.

Monahan, J., and Walker, L. 1986. Social authority: Obtaining, evaluating and establishing social science in law. *University of Pennsylvania Law Review* 134:477–517.

Monti, D. 1980. Administrative foxes in educational chicken coop: An examination of the critique of judicial activism in school desegregation cases. *Law and Policy Quarterly* 2:233–256.

Monti, D.J. 1985. *A semblance of justice: St. Louis school desegregation and order in urban America*. Columbia, Mo.: University of Missouri Press.

Moreland, K. 1963. *Token desegregation and beyond*. Atlanta and New York: Southern Regional Council and Anti-Defamation League.

Mosteller, F., and D. Moynihan. 1972. *On equality of educational opportunity*. New York: Random House.

Myrdal, G. 1944. *An American dilemma*. New York: Harper.

Nakamura, R., and F. Smallwood. 1980. *The politics of policy implementation*. New York: St. Martins Press.

National Institute of Education. 1977. *School desegregation in metropolitan areas: Choices and prospects*. Washington, D.C.: NIE, DHEW.

National Opinion Research Center. 1973. *Southern schools: An evaluation of the effects of the emergency school assistance program and of school desegregation*. Chicago: National Opinion Research Center.

Newby, I.A. 1969. *Challenge to the Court: Social scientists and the defense of segregation*. Rev. ed. Baton Rouge: Louisiana State University Press.

Noar, G. 1966. *The teacher and integration*. Washington, D.C.: NEA.

Noblit, G.W., and B. Johnston, eds. 1982. *The school principal and school desegregation*. Springfield, Ill.: Charles C. Thomas.

Noll, E., and P. Rossi. 1966. General social and economic attitudes of college and university faculty members. National Opinion Research Center, University of Chicago. Cited in *The divided academy: Professions and politics*, ed. E. Ladd and S. Lipsett, 26, 141. New York: Norton, 1975.

Note. 1976. Reading the mind of the school board: Segregative intent and the de facto–de jure distinction. *Yale Law Journal* 86:317–355.

Nyhart, J. 1981. *Science technology and judicial decision-making*. Cambridge: MIT, Sloan School of Management.

Nystrand, R., and W. Staub. 1978. The courts as educational policy makers. In

The courts and education—the 77th yearbook of the National Society for the Study of Education, ed. C. Hooker, 27–53. Chicago: University of Chicago Press.

O'Barr, W. 1982. *Linguistic evidence: Language, power and strategy in the courtroom.* New York: Academic Press.

Oberschall, A. 1973. *Social conflict and social movements.* Englewood Cliffs, N.J.: Prentice-Hall.

Orfield, G. 1975. How to make desegregation work: The adaptation of schools to their newly-integrated student bodies. *Law and Contemporary Problems* 39(2):314–341.

Orfield, G. 1978a. *Must we bus? Segregated schools and national policy.* Washington, D.C.: The Brookings Institute.

Orfield, G. 1978b. Research, politics and the anti-busing debate. *Law and Contemporary Problems.* 42(4):141–173.

Orfield, G. 1980. School segregation and residential segregation: Prefatory statement. In *School desegregation: Past, present and future*, ed. W.G. Stephan and J.W. Feagin, 227–229. New York: Plenum Press.

Orfield, G. 1983. *Public school desegregation in the United States, 1968–1980.* Washington, D.C.: Joint Center for Political Studies.

Orfield, G. 1987. Personal communication.

Pearce, D. 1985. Beyond busing: New evidence on the impact of metropolitan school desegregation and housing segregation. In *Metropolitan desegregation*, ed. R.L. Green, 97–122. New York: Plenum Press.

Pearce, D.M., R.L. Crain, and R. Farley. N.d. *Lessons not lost: The effect of school desegregation on the rate of residential desegregation in large central cities.* Manuscript.

Pearson, J., and J. Pearson. 1978. Keyes v. School District No. 1. In *Limits of justice: The courts' role in school desegregation*, ed. H. Kalodner and J. Fishman, 167–222. Cambridge, Mass.: Ballinger.

Peltason, J. 1974. *Fifty-eight lonely men: Southern federal judges and school desegregation.* Urbana: University of Illinois Press.

Perry, M. 1977. Disproportionate impact theory of racial segregation—a presumption of uncertainty. *University of Pennsylvania Law Review* 125:540–589.

Peterson, G.T. 1935. The present status of the Negro separate school as defined by court decisions. *Journal of Negro Education* 4:351–374.

Pettigrew, T. 1971. Sociological consulting in race relations. *American Sociologist* 6 (Supplement):44–47.

Pettigrew, T. 1979. Tensions between the law and social science: An expert witness view. In *Desegregation, Vol. 1 of Schools and the courts*, eds. J. Greenberg, T. Pettigrew, S. Greenblatt, W. McCann, and D. Bennett, Eugene, Oreg.: University of Oregon, ERIC Clearinghouse on Educational Management.

Pettigrew, T., and R. Green. 1976. School desegregation in large cities: A critique of the Coleman white flight thesis. *Harvard Educational Review* 46(1):1–53.

Pettigrew, T., E. Useem, C. Normand, and M. Smith. 1973. Busing: A review of "the evidence." *Public Interest* 30:88–118.

Philo, H., and L. Atkinson. 1978. Products liability: The expert witness. *Trial* 14(11):37–41.

Porter, J.R. 1971. *Black child, white child: The development of racial attitudes.* Cambridge: Harvard University Press.

Porter, J.R., and R.E. Washington. 1979. Black identity and self-esteem: A review of studies of black self-concept. *Annual Review of Sociology* 5:53–74.

Poythress, N. 1980. Coping on the witness stand: Learned responses to "learned treatises." *Professional Psychology* 11:139–49.

Prager, J., D. Longshore, and M. Seeman, eds. 1986. *School desegregation research: New directions in situational analysis.* New York: Plenum Press.

Pride, R.A., and J.D. Woodard. 1985. *The burden of busing: The politics of desegregation in Nashville, Tennessee.* Knoxville: University of Tennessee Press.

Radin, B.A. 1977. *Implementation, change and the federal bureaucracy: School desegregation policy in H.E.W., 1964–1968.* New York: Columbia University, Teachers College Press.

Raffel, J.A. 1980. *The politics of school desegregation: The metropolitan remedy in Delaware.* Philadelphia: Temple University Press.

Raffia, H. 1982. *The art and science of negotiation.* Cambridge: Harvard University Press.

Ravitch, D. 1978. The white flight controversy. *Public Interest* 51:135–149.

Rebell, M.A., and A.R. Block. 1982. *Educational policy making and the courts: An empirical study of judicial activism.* Chicago: University of Chicago Press.

Recent cases. 1967. Equal protection of the laws: The HEW guidelines are minimum standards for a free choice school desegregation program. *Harvard Law Review* 81:474–488.

Rein, M., and S. White. 1977. Can policy research help? *Public Interest* 49:119–136.

Resnick, J. 1983. Managerial judges. *Harvard Law Review* 96:374–448.

Richardson, R., and K. Vines. 1970. *The politics of federal courts.* Boston: Little, Brown.

Rist, R.C. 1976. *The invisible children: School integration in American society.* Cambridge: Harvard University Press.

Rist, R.C. 1978. On the making of educational social policy in the judicial area. Paper presented at the 1978 American Sociological Association meetings, San Franciso.

Rist, R.C., ed. 1979. *Desegregated schools: Appraisals of an American experiment.* New York: Academic Press.

Rodgers, H., and C. Bullock. 1972. *Law and social change: Civil rights laws and their consequences.* New York: McGraw-Hill.

Roof, W.C., ed. 1979. Race and residence in American cities. *Annals of the American Academy of Poltical and Social Science,* vol. 441.

Rose, A. 1956. The social scientist as expert witness. *Minnesota Law Review* 40:205–218.

Rosenberg, M. 1986. Self-esteem research: A phenomenological corrective. In

School desegregation research: New directions in situational analysis, ed. J. Prager, D. Longshore, and M. Seeman, 175–204. New York: Plenum Press.

Rossell, C. 1975/76. School desegregation and white flight. *Political Science Quarterly* 90:675–695.

Rossell, C. 1978. School desegregation and community social change. *Law and Contemporary Problems* 42(3):133–183.

Rossell, C. 1985. Estimating net benefit of school desegregation reassignments. *Educational Evaluation and Policy Analysis* 7:217–227.

Rothenberg, J., and M. Chesler. 1980. Authorities' responses to community challenge during desegregation. Paper presented to meetings of SSSP, New York.

Sabatier, P., and D. Mazmanian. 1979. The conditions of effective implementation. *Policy Analysis* 5(4):481–504.

Sagarin, E. 1980. Taboo subjects and taboo viewpoints in criminology. In *Taboos in criminology*, ed. E. Sagarin, 7–22. Beverly Hills, Calif.: Sage.

Saks, M.J., and R. Hastie. 1978. *Social psychology in court*. New York: Van Nostrand Reinhold.

Saks, M., and R. Van Duizend. 1983. *The use of scientific evidence in litigation*. Williamsburg, Va.: National Center for State Courts.

Saltzberg, S. 1978. The unnecessarily expanding role of the American trial judge. *Virginia Law Review* 64:1–84.

Sanders, J., 1980. Two models of the school desegregation cases. Working Paper no. 216. Ann Arbor: University of Michigan, Center for Research on Social Organization.

Sanders, J., B. Rankin-Widgeon, D. Kalmuss, and M. Chesler. 1981/82. The relevance of "irrelevant" testimony: Why lawyers use social science experts in school desegregation cases. *Law and Society Review* 16:403–428.

Schelling, T.D. 1978. *Micromotives and macrobehavior*. New York: Norton.

Schmuck, R., and M. Miles, eds. 1971. *Organizational development in schools*. Palo Alto, Calif.: National Press Books.

Schofield, J., and A. Sager. 1979. The social context of learning in an interracial school. In *Desegregated schools: Appraisals of an American experiment*, ed. R.C. Rist, 155–200. New York: Academic Press.

Schofield, J. 1978. School desegregation and intergroup relations. In *Social psychology of education: Theory and research*, ed. D. Bar-Tal and L. Saxe, Washington, D.C.: Hemisphere Publishing Co.

Schroeder, O., and D.T. Smith, eds. 1965. *De facto segregation and civil rights*. Buffalo, N.Y.: William S. Hein & Co.

Schubert, G.A., ed. 1964. *Judicial behavior: A reader in theory and research*. Chicago: Rand-McNally.

Schur, E. 1968. *Law and society* New York: Random House.

Schwartz, A. 1978. Social science potential for judicial formulation of educational policy. *Educational Research Quarterly* 3(2):3–11.

Schwartz, B. 1986. *Swann's Way: The school busing case and the Supreme Court*. New York: Oxford University Press.

Shils, E. 1956. *Torment of secrecy: The background and consequences of American security problems*. New York: Free Press.

Shubow, L., and C. Bergstresser. 1977. Handling the psychiatric witness. *Trial* 13(7):32–35.

Sieber, S. 1974. Toward a theory of role accumulation. *American Sociological Review* 39: 567–578.

Slavin, R. 1977. How student learning teams can integrate the desegregated classroom. *Integrated Education* 15(6):56–58.

Slavin, R. 1978. Student teams and comparison among equals: Effects on academic performance and student attitudes. *Journal of Educational Psychology* 70:532–538.

Slavin, R. 1980. Cooperative learning. *Review of Educational Research* 50:315–342.

Slavin, R. 1983. *Cooperative Learning*, New York: Longman.

Smylie, M. 1984. *Covering school desegregation: A deskbook for education writers*. The Educational Equity Project, Institute for Public Policy Studies. Nashville, Tenn.: Vanderbilt University.

Sparshott, F. 1972. *Looking for philosophy*. London: McGill-Queens University.

Sperlich, P.W. 1980. Social science evidence and the courts: Reaching beyond the adversary process. *Judicature* 63:280–289.

Sperlich, P.W. 1985. The evidence on evidence: Science and law in conflict and cooperation. In *The psychology of evidence and trial procedure*, ed. S.M. Kassin and L. Wrightsman, 325–361. Beverly Hills, Calif.: Sage

St. John, N. 1975. *School desegregation: Outcomes for children*. New York: Wiley.

Steel, L.M. 1968. Nine men in black that think white. *New York Times Magazine*, 13 October.

Stephan, W.G. 1978. School desegregation: An evaluation of predictions made in Brown v. Board of Education. *Psychological Bulletin* 85:217–238.

Sternhell, C. 1986. Life in the mainstream: What happens when feminists turn up on both sides of the courtroom? *Ms.*, July 1987, 48.

Stinchcombe, A., and D. Taylor. 1980. On democracy and school integration. In *School desegregation: Past, present and future*, ed. W.G. Stephan and J.W. Feagin, 157–186. New York: Plenum Press.

Stoper, E. 1983. The Student Nonviolent Coordinating Committee: Rise and fall of a redemptive organization. In *Social movements of the sixties and seventies*, ed. J. Freeman, 320–334. New York: Longman.

Street, D., and E. Weinstein. 1975. Problems and prospects of applied sociology. *American Sociologist* 10:65–72.

Strong, J. 1970. Questions affecting the admissability of scientific evidence. *University of Illinois Law Forum* 70:1–22.

Struening, E., and M. Guttentag, eds. 1975a. *Handbook of evaluation research*, vol. 1. Beverly Hills, Calif.: Sage.

Struening, E., and M. Guttentag, eds. 1975b. *Handbook of evaluation research*, vol. 2. Beverly Hills, Calif.: Sage.

Stryker, S., and A. Macke. 1978. Status inconsistency and role conflict. *Annual Review of Sociology* 4:57–90.

Sumner, W.G. 1906. *Folkways*. Boston: Ginn.

Suttles, G. 1986. School desegregation and the "national community." In *School desegregation research: New directions in situational analysis*, ed. J. Prager, D. Longshore, and M. Seeman, 47–80. New York: Plenum Press.

Taeuber, K. 1975. Demographic perspectives on housing and school desegregation. *Wayne Law Review* 21:833–850.

Taeuber, K. 1979. Sociological practice in the courts. *Wisconsin Sociologist* 16:112–122.

Taeuber, K., and Taeuber, A. 1965. *Negroes in cities*. New York: Atheneum.

Taylor, D.G. 1986. *Public opinion and collective action: The Boston school desegregation conflict*. Chicago: University of Chicago Press.

Taylor, M.C., and E.J. Walsh. 1979. Explanations of black self-esteem: Some empirical tests. *Social Psychology Quarterly* 42:242–253.

Taylor, W.L. 1978. The Supreme Court and recent desegregation cases: The role of social science in a period of judicial retrenchment. *Law and Contemporary Problems* 42(3):37–56.

Taylor, W.L. 1986. Litigation as a tool of empowerment. *Citizen Participation* (Winter):1–9.

Terez, D.G. 1986/87. Protecting the remedy of unitary schools. *Case Western Reserve Law Review* 37:41–71.

Tompkins, R. 1976. Techniques of desegregation. *Citizens guide to desegregation*. Cleveland: Citizens Council for Ohio Schools.

Topeka Social Science Brief. 1953. The effects of segregation and the consequences of desegregation: a social science statement. Appendix to Appellants Brief in the School Segregation Cases, U.S. Supreme Court, 1952. *Minnesota Law Review* 37:427–439.

Tushnet, M.V. 1987. *The NAACP's legal strategy against segregated education, 1925–1950*. Chapel Hill: University of North Carolina Press.

Tyack, D. and A. Benavot. 1985. Courts and public schools: Educational litigation in historical perspective. *Law and Society Review* 19:339–380.

United States Commission on Civil Rights. 1967. *Racial isolation in the public schools* Washington, D.C.: U.S. Commission on Civil Rights.

United States Commission on Civil Rights. 1973. *School desegregation in ten communities*. Washington, D.C.: U.S. Commission on Civil Rights.

United States Commission on Civil Rights. 1974. *Milliken v. Bradley: The implications for metropolitan desegregation*. Washington, D.C.: U.S. Commission on Civil Rights.

United States Commission on Civil Rights. 1975. *The federal civil rights enforcement effort—1974. Volume 3, To ensure equal educational opportunity*. Washington, D.C.: U.S. Commission on Civil Rights.

United States Commission on Civil Rights. 1976. *Fulfilling the letter and spirit of the law*. 1976. Washington, D.C.: U.S. Commission on Civil Rights.

Van den Haag, E. 1960. Social science testimony in the desegregation cases: A reply to Professor Kenneth Clark. *Villanova Law Review* 6:69–79.

Van Horn, C., and D. Van Meter. 1977. The implementation of intergovernmental policy. *Policy Studies Annual Review* 1:97–120.

Vidmar, N., and N.M. Laird. 1983. Adversary social roles: Their effects on witnesses' communication of evidence and the assessment of adjudicators. *Journal of Personality and Social Psychology* 44:888–898.

Von Euler, M. 1977. Meeting the courts' new research needs. *Education and Urban Society* 9(3):277–302.

Vose, C.E. 1959. *Caucasians only: The Supreme Court, the NAACP and the restrictive covenant cases.* Berkeley: University of California Press.

Wald, P. 1983. Bureaucracy and the courts. *Yale Law Journal* 92:1478–1486.

Wasby, S.L. 1984. How planned is "planned litigation"? *American Bar Foundation Research Journal* 1984:83–138.

Wasby, S.L. 1986. The Multi-Faceted Elephant: Litigator Perspectives on Planned Litigation for Social Change. *Capital University Law Review* 15:143–189.

Wasby, S.L., A. D'Amato, and R. Metrallier. 1977. *Desegregation: From Brown to Alexander.* Carbondale, Ill.: Southern Illinois University Press.

Weber, M. 1946. Science as a vocation. In *Max Weber: Essays in sociology,* ed. and trans. H.H. Gerth and C.W. Mills, 129–156. New York: Oxford University Press.

Weick, K.C. 1976. Educational organizations as loosely-coupled systems. *Administrative Science Quarterly* 21:1–19.

Weinberg, M. 1970. *Desegregation research: An appraisal.* Bloomington, Ind.: Phi Delta Kappa.

Weinberg, M. 1975. The relationship between school desegregation and academic achievement: A review of the research. *Law and Contemporary Problems* 39:240–270.

Weinberg, M. 1977. *Minority students: A research appraisal.* Washington, D.C.: National Institute of Education.

Weinberg, M. 1983. *The search for quality integrated education: Policy and research on minority students in school and college.* Westport, Conn.: Greenwood Press.

Weinberg, P. 1978. Science court controversy: Are our courts and agencies adequate to resolve new and complex scientific issues? *Record* 33:8.

Weiss, C., ed. 1972. *Evaluating action programs.* Boston: Allyn & Bacon.

Weiss, C. 1976. Policy research in the university: Practical aid or academic exercise? *Policy Studies Journal* 4(3):224–228.

Weiss, J. 1976. Using social science for social policy. *Policy Studies Journal* 4(3):234–238.

Weschsler, H. 1959. Toward neutral principles of constitutional law. *Harvard Law Review* 73:1–35.

Wilkinson, J.H. 1979. *From Brown to Baake: The Supreme Court and school integration: 1954–1978.* New York: Oxford University Press.

Williams, J.E., and J.K. Morland. 1976. *Race, color and the young child.* Chapel Hill, N.C.: University of North Carolina Press.

Williams, P. 1957. The practitioner speaks: Witness performance as viewed by the United States attorney general. *Journal of Social Issues* 13(2):34–36.

Willie, C.V. 1984. *School desegregation plans that work*. Westport, Conn.: Greenwood Press.

Willie, C.V., and S.L. Greenblatt, eds. 1981. *Community politics and educational change: Ten school systems under court order*. New York: Longman.

Wirth, L. 1931. Clinical sociology. *American Journal of Sociology* 37:49–66.

Wisdom, J. 1975. Random remarks on the role of the social sciences in the judicial decision-making processes in school desegregation cases. *Law and Contemporary Problems* 39:134–149.

Wise, M., comp. and ed. 1977. *Desegregation in education: A directory of reported federal decisions*. Notre Dame, Ind.: University of Notre Dame, Center for Civil Rights.

Wolf, E.P. 1976. Social science and the courts: The Detroit schools case. *Public Interest* 43:102–120.

Wolf, E.P. 1977a. Courtrooms and classrooms. *Educational Forum* 41(4):431–453.

Wolf, E.P. 1977b. Northern school desegregation and residential choice. In *The Supreme Court review*, ed. P. Kurland, 63–86. Chicago: University of Chicago Press.

Wolf, E.P. 1981. *Trial and error: The Detroit school segregation case*. Detroit: Wayne State University Press.

Wolfgang, M. 1974. The social scientist in court. *Journal of Criminal Law and Criminology* 63(2):239–247.

Wolters, R. 1984. *The burden of Brown: Thirty years of school desegregation*. Knoxville: University of Tennessee Press.

Woodward, C. 1957. *The strange career of Jim Crow*. New York: Oxford University Press.

Wright, S. 1965. Public school desegregation: Legal remedies for de facto segregation. *New York University Law Review* 40:285–309.

Yellin, J. 1981. High technology and the courts: Nuclear power and the need for institutional reform. *Harvard Law Review* 94:489–560.

Yinger, M. 1986. The research agenda: New directions for desegregation studies. In *School desegregation research: New directions in situational analysis*, ed. J. Prager, D. Longshore, and M. Seeman, 232–251. New York: Plenum Press.

Yudof, M. 1978. School desegregation: Legal realism, reasoned elaboration and social science research in the Supreme Court. *Law and Contemporary Problems* 42(4):57–111.

Zald, M.N., and J.D. McCarthy, eds. 1979. *The dynamics of social movements*. Cambridge, Mass.: Winthrop Publishers.

Zangrado, R.L. 1980. *The NAACP crusade against lynching, 1909–1950*. Philadelphia: Temple University Press.

Zeigler, H., and M. Boss. 1974. Racial problems and policy in the American public schools. *Sociology of Education* 47:319–336.

Zemans, F.K. 1983. Legal mobilization: The neglected role of the law in the political system. *American Political Science Review* 77:690–703.

Index